RADICAL IN<TER>VENTIONS

❖

SUNY SERIES, IDENTITIES IN THE CLASSROOM

DEBORAH P. BRITZMAN AND JANET L. MILLER, EDITORS

RADICAL IN<TER>VENTIONS

IDENTITY, POLITICS, AND DIFFERENCE/S IN EDUCATIONAL PRAXIS

❖

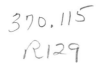

EDITED BY
SUZANNE DE CASTELL AND MARY BRYSON

FOREWORD BY MAXINE GREENE

STATE UNIVERSITY OF NEW YORK PRESS

Cover: Photograph of Francisco Ibanez taken by Philip Barden. © 1993 Philip Barden. Reprinted with permission.

Translation: "It is hard to give birth to colors when all they want from you is black and white."

Indexing by Mary Bryson

Published by
State University of New York Press, Albany

For information, address State University of New York Press,
State University Plaza, Albany, N.Y. 12246

Production by M. R. Mulholland
Marketing by Dana E. Yanulavich

Library of Congress Cataloging-in-Publication Data

Radical in(ter)ventions : identity, politics, and difference/s in
   educational praxis / edited by Suzanne de Castell and Mary Bryson.
       p.   cm. — (SUNY series, identities in the classroom)
    Includes bibliographical references and index.
    ISBN 0-7914-3561-X (hc : alk. paper). — ISBN 0-7914-3562-8 (pbk.
: alk. paper)
       1. Critical pedagogy. 2. Education, Higher—Political aspects.
    3. Postmodernism and education. 4. Feminism and education.
    5. Homosexuality and education. I. De Castell, Suzanne.
    II. Bryson, Mary, 1959–   . III. Series.
    LC196.R33 1997
    370.11'5—dc21   97-4953
                                                                          CIP

10 9 8 7 6 5 4 3 2 1

CONTENTS

Part III. Life in Classrooms:
Teaching and Learning against the Grain

ACKNOWLEDGMENTS

We express our appreciation for permission to reprint the following:

Britzman, D. (1995). "What is this thing called love?" *Taboo: The Journal of Culture and Education*, 1 Spring, 65–93.

Bryson, M., and de Castell, S. (1993). En/Gendering equity. *Educational Theory*, 43(4), 341–355.

Bryson, M., and de Castell, S. (1993). Queer Pedagogy: Praxis makes im/perfect. *Canadian Journal of Education*, 18(3), 285–305.

Eyre, L. (1993). Compulsory heterosexuality in a university classroom. *Canadian Journal of Education*, 18(3), 273–284.

Henry, A. (1993). "Missing!": Black self-representation in Canadian education research. *Canadian Journal of Education*, 18(3), 206–222.

Hoodfar, H. (1993). Feminist anthropology and critical pedagogy: The anthropology of classrooms' excluded voices. *Canadian Journal of Education*, 17(3), 303–320.

Ng, R. (993). "A woman out of control": Racism, sexism, and the "inclusive" university. *Canadian Journal of Education*, 18(3), 189–205.

This volume represents a collaboration across differences by educators working both in and out of the academy from locations where struggles for agency and legitimacy are usually waged at a high cost. We are grateful to series editor Deborah Britzman, whose invitation provided an ideal context for bringing these diverse papers into a collection and sending them back out into the world. Above all, thanks to the contributors, who have persisted in working with this project in spite of its seemingly interminable timeline. We dedicate this book to all those who have fought/are fighting to create "difference"/s at the heart of educational and cultural work.

VINCENTA CLOTILDA NICOLA SUKAINA XU-HU
ANCHORA OLYMPIA DELPHINA LUCRETIA
ROLAINDA VIOLA BERNARDA PHUONG PLANCINE
CLORINDA BAO-SI PULCHERIA AUGUSTA

—Monique Wittig, *Les Guerilleres*

FOREWORD

MAXINE GREENE

In one of the essays collected in her *Sister Outsider*, Audre Lorde wrote:

> Institutionalized rejection of difference is an absolute necessity in a profit economy which needs outsiders as surplus people. As members of such an economy, we have *all* been programmed to respond to the human differences between us with fear and loathing and to handle that difference in three ways: ignore it, and, if that is not possible, copy it if we think it is dominant, or destroy it if we think it is subordinate. But we have no patterns for relating across our human differences as equals. As a result, those differences have been misnamed and misused in the service of separation and confusion.

> Certainly there are very real differences between us of race, age, and sex. But it is not those differences between us which are separating us. It is rather our refusal to recognize those differences, and to examine the distortions which result from our misnaming them and their effects upon human behavior and expectation. (1984, 115)

Lorde, who called herself a "Black lesbian socialist feminist mother of two," was a poet as well as a teacher and activist; and she was personally and marvelously sensitive to what it signifies to look from the margins and see things normally concealed. Suzanne de Castell and Mary Bryson's present book does much to keep Lorde's hopeful, outraged, and eloquent presence alive. They have done so not only through their own remarkable writing but by bringing together a community of writers, each one looking through their own vantage point at the culture, the classroom, the play of power—and, in so many cases, enabling us to see what we have never seen.

Together, these scholars move beyond Lorde and her contemporaries, certainly, when they hold the concept of gender up to question, when they deconstruct such notions as liberal pluralism, when they problematize what is thought of as emancipatory education and what it is intended to bring about in college and high school classrooms. Over and over in essay after essay, the members of what may be an emergent community of explorers shock us into new awareness, arouse from taken-for-grantedness with regard to what is viewed as "normal," "liberal," "inclusive," and "right."

It would be absurd for anyone attempting to write a foreword to this book to take up a position at the "center" or to try to induct readers into it from a neutral, disengaged, or disembodied point of view. As someone who became (at least to some degree) intellectually alive just before and during World War II, at a time when what was "democratic" was antifascist, humane, and altogether good, the notions linked to identity politics, to difference, and (certainly) to marginalization remain earthshaking. This particular writer was (she only now realizes) acquainted with marginalization as a Jew, and as someone thought to be hopelessly "radical." Yes, she wanted to be a free woman, to have a career, to bypass the make-up counters, the sororities, the charge cards, the marriage showers. But that meant becoming more like her father, for all his disapproval of the prospect. Equality of opportunity: that was the goal, in a social domain governed by the same norms, the same rules that had long defined the male-dominated heterosexual world. In the great community we had in mind (we radical liberals), differences would be obliterated in time; we would be caught up in an ideal *persona* described as the "American Adam" or the "imperial self," sometimes the Hemingway hero, sometimes Jay Gatsby, an image of male becoming to which a young person in quest was expected to conform.

This book throws someone like this foreword-writer back upon her own history, her middle-class illusions, her particular benevolence, her suspicion of the view from the margins—even when that view was her own. What Haraway calls the need for a "powerful infidel heteroglossia" was never acknowledged; this writer, like so many others, believes she achieved whatever she did achieve in academe by assuming the existence of a common language, which she would learn to speak despite all, and which would give her the means of articulating what she would learn to say. Only now, looking back, can some of us realize how much we had to repress in our shame at being marginal, how much we pretended, how much we masked.

The essays in this book challenge us to rewrite and to revise. And, perhaps strangely, they lurch us from some of our liberal complacencies, which could only (if we really looked and listened to which surrounds us all) break our hearts in time. It may be that, as these writers tell us, we will be impelled to devise a strategy of social and moral transformation by what this book reveals. To recognize the influence of heterosexual hegemony, to realize the disguises forced on us by talk of multiculturalism, for example, or talk of pluralism, to come to terms with the projections involved in our talk of classroom emancipation or even conscientization: all of this is to feel ourselves moved to open new perspectives, to engage with strangers and to learn from strangers, to dare to enter narratives that expose us to worlds too long denied.

Perhaps that suggests the most crucial point of all with regard to de Castell's and Bryson's book. We have imposed our own stories far too long—our stories about gender equity and inclusion and emancipation; and the time has come to rewrite our own narratives as well as those we ascribe to the "others." It is time, also, to acknowledge the fearful power of fixed standards, paradigms, models. The more the intoxication of the so-called free market increases, the more a communication marked by sound-bytes replaces deliberative communication and reflective conversation, the more invisible will be the workings of hegemony. A book like this pulls the curtains aside; it provokes us to reconceive what freedom means and equity and human rights. Here is Lorde again, ending the above-mentioned essay with a poem:

> if we win
> there is no telling
> we seek beyond history
> for a new and more possible meeting (123)

This book may herald just such a meeting.

Teacher's College, Columbia University

Reference

Lorde, A. (1984). *Sister outsider: Essays and speeches*. Freedom: CA: The Crossing Press.

Introduction:
Identity, Authority, Narrativity

Suzanne de Castell and Mary Bryson

The Con/Text

This volume brings together participants from a diverse range of positionings all in some way at odds with the mainstream and sequestered at the margins of academic discourses and practices in the institutional sites where "education" is realized. Each of the volume's contributors writes from a radical conception of educational intervention *as invention,* and out of a deeply felt commitment to creating alternative and potentially subversive forms of praxis in relation to "difference/s." These essays address (a) the complex and often contradictory implications of theoretical debates concerning identity politics/essentialism juxtaposed with the embodied actualities of producing, negotiating, performing, and troubling difference/s in educational contexts; (b) difficulties, contradictions, and risks produced by institutional "equity" policies and related practices of "inclusion"; (c) the difference "difference/s" make to curriculum and pedagogy in the classroom; and (d) specific implications of conducting educational research from an explicitly "partisan" standpoint.

Educational research and writing has largely constructed "otherness"—often referred to in contemporary discourses as "alterity"—as, at best, the *object* of study. One of our main purposes in the present collection is to consider the inversions effected when "others" and otherness occupy a *subject* position in educational accounts and accounting practices. What might educational research and scholarship colonized by so-called marginalized subjects look like? What key concepts would change, and how? What practices become im/possible? What questions would disappear, and what new ones appear in their place?

In this volume, then, "minority" scholars, crafting radical praxis within what are often *profoundly* hostile contexts of daily work, describe concretely and interrogate theoretically the lived actualities of radical in<ter>vention in education. These questions have centrally to do with survival, with pedagogy, with the *practices* of research and theory, and they have to do, perhaps most important of all, with the fact of speaking from particular positions/locations, which make it essential to grapple in an urgent and serious way with institutionally sanctioned assumptions about what can and should be done by students and teachers in relation to demands for "equity," "inclusion," and "respect for differences."

Disciplinary practices denying the significance of identity for speaking subjects in educational theory and research secure, thereby, the centrality of hegemonic voices in the academic world. This is a subject positioning which becomes visible only as it is challenged by Others researching and writing *as* Others, and not *about* them. But, in classrooms it is no longer enough (if it ever was) to "make room" for the participation of education's traditional Others. The difference which makes a difference here is between "diversity management"—a deceptively simple "inclusion" of marginal subjects (e.g., "Add women and stir!")—and radical inversion, which is construed here as a destabilization of "the normal" and as the invention and proliferation of multiple new centers and agentive subjectivities.

The privileging of individual, purportedly authentic "voices" of teachers and students has led to a valorization of polyphony in the classroom—a plurality/multiplicity of voices—engaged in a pedagogic carnival of dialogically accomplished empowerment. But, as in all carnivals, there is a sinister side to things: who is *really* the speaking subject here and at whose expense the discursive revelry? As Bakhtin (1981) asks us to consider, "Who is doing the talking" in these "institutionally bound" discursive genres?

Behind the dizzying plurality of postmodern voices may be discerned the fundamental eeriness of postmodern theories of "the self," a self—or, rather, a pseudo-self constructed in and out of performativity, which has proven difficult to endorse for subjectivities on the margins; subjects for whom, to paraphrase Braidotti (1987), a "death announcement" may be premature when proclaimed before the subject now in question has had the opportunity to speak, act, and be recognized *as* a subject. As has frequently been observed, postmodernism seems to require of us an abandonment of identities and projects (e.g., "women" and "feminism") just as it seems such identities and projects might at last be in sight of their goals. In *educational* terms, our problem now is that postmodern pedagogies of "possibility" seem precisely to replicate this dilemma.

How do we respond, as people of whom "difference/s" are inescapably predicated, to the claim that, through a pedagogic practice that privileges emancipatory dialogical discourses, voices from the margins, voices that have so long been refused any hearing, any significant space in public discourses, stories perennially excluded from the narratives that most readily circulate within the classroom, are now to be free, or, more accurately, compelled to speak freely, or, more accurately still, obliged to confess an othered subjectivity? The chapters in this collection testify to a pervasive and prevalent discursive violence in so-called dialogical interactions, explaining how and why Bakhtinian "heteroglossia" in the classroom is not now and cannot under foreseeable conditions become a safe space for speakers of the multitude of languages of difference.

These chapters, although written from very diverse subject positions, are all concerned with fundamentally similar questions of identity, voice, agency, and the difference that alterity makes in everyday work, as this offers alternative perspectives on progressive educational praxis. Our specific focus is on how one goes about "doing" educational work *from a position* of difference and *in relation to students* "of difference." Our principal concern here is, therefore, with explicitly situated practice (Lave and Wenger 1991), with attempts to work pedagogically from positions "out of bounds." These are accounts which do not subordinate their experiences in classrooms to the good news of critical and postcritical pedagogical theory, which scarcely ever describes what its work actually looks like on the ground, beyond its inspiring textual articulations. This set of essays seeks to describe and to critically interrogate what it is to work "against the grain" of everyday institutional practices, to work against the grain of lived actuality, not textuality (without of course denying the constitutive power of what Smith (1993) calls the "active text" as a mediator of lived actuality). Its purpose is to speak, not just about things that are difficult, or challenging, but about things which are impossible. The authors of these accounts insist on the importance of acknowledging what is not supposed to exist in schools, tell forbidden tales—stories that may not be told, voices that may not be heard—about dangers lived out daily, about what is not permitted to be seen or, if seen, may not be acknowledged—or, if acknowledged, about the cost of that speaking.

Each of the contributors to this volume is engaged in a perilous activity of telling tales "out of school" (Bryson and de Castell 1994)—unpopular tales about what is not working and why and, in some cases, about the enormity of the obstacles to be faced in daily practice, and about why there is little ground for optimism. Speaking "out" about our everyday practices—it is important to be very clear—means knowingly placing oneself in jeopardy. This is quite the opposite of what eventuates from the Sheherezade-like seductions of accepted educational narratives, which bring to their teller not just continued survival, but indeed kudos, admiration, reputation, and, not least, material gain. So let us be quite clear that we who have worked on this volume have in fact no reason to expect anything but trouble to follow from our tellings of these unpopular tales.

So in this collection it has been a priority for us to find work which gives clearer answers to these very basic questions about practice/s and which speaks explicitly and self-consciously about that practice from specified institutional positions, whether as teachers, as students, as researchers, as activists and popular educators, as policy makers, as beginning lecturers without tenure, or as professors emeriti speaking from the standpoint of long years of struggle both in and beyond the academy. At the same time, however, we have wanted to present work by educators having no programmatic commitment to the currently popular confessional practice of "telling our stories"; these accounts are not, then, to be read as "teacher-narratives," those peculiarly venerated vehicles for sense making. In particular, we have eschewed "narratives of redemption" as their apotheosis in too much contemporary educational writing.

We have tried, collectively, to define and to demarcate questions of a different kind about new terrain and the very conceptualization of "identity" and "difference." But we have wanted, at the same time, to pay careful attention to the institutional contexts within which difference is experienced, codified, and normalized, and inclusion attempted, and we have sought to explore how attempts at inclusion backfire, all too often transforming purportedly progressive institutional initiatives into just another species of backlash for teachers and students living "out of bounds" of institutionally sanctioned identity borders.

Education today remains a field of discourse governed by the obligation to "be positive," and in which, increasingly, no one dares to speak of obstacles, impediments, difficulties without in the same breath expounding on "solutions"; the categorical imperative to remain positive at all costs reigns here, even at the cost of willful blindness, misrepresentation, a kind of *studied* ignorance which cannot be other than intentional, where full-grown "men of good will" speak unashamedly of the "wonderful world of education," utterly disregarding reminders to us that there are certain things in this wonderful world about which we cannot any longer be permitted *not* to know, things which we may no longer claim not to have seen, not to have understood, and that there must be an end to demands for "further evidence."

It is surely by means of these deceits, after all, that we have come to this point in educational institutions and no less in educational discourses/practices, when cries of "Fag!" ring through virtually every school corridor, students are assaulted and sometimes killed in their schoolyards, where racism flourishes as productively in staffrooms and professional journals, in faculty lounges and board offices, as in the classroom and in the curriculum. And as female students and teachers who dare to contest male privilege are greeted with catcalls of "man-hating dyke" or, only slightly less awful, "feminist"—a label not so long ago invoked in Montreal as a warrant for fourteen murders but since celebrated and parodied in university skits. Amidst all of this, it is obligatory to intone liberal and postcritical mantras about pedagogic possibilities to be located in "contestation and resistance," about the pursuit of empowerment and excellence. This "wonderful world of education" is one, let us just this once not refuse to see, where students are instructed to plan the "perfect rape" as a learning strategy, where school cops patrol the halls in order to protect classrooms in which, after all, the very same patterns of privilege and deprivation, of educational success and failure, continue unabatedly to reproduce what Porter (1965) so long ago referred to as a "vertical mosaic"—a sociopolitical design—another richly evocative term—in which racial and class-based differences are played out as disadvantage notwithstanding purportedly multicultural public policies of "inclusion." In these sites of discursive and physical violence, of persisting inequality, of aggressively policed strategies enforcing normalization at all costs, including as acceptable losses, the educational project itself, let us just this once actually *look* at what nowadays passes for knowledge and competence in so many of the schools we visit, where, paradoxically, nothing but the good news may enjoy any hope of being heard, let alone listened to.

Where institutional commitments to equity and empowerment are nowadays increasingly being forged (and we use the term advisedly here), fully intending its conceptual echoes of fabrication, artifice, fraudulence to be heard—what actualities greet those educators, researchers, theorists, who take up the challenges and who seek in their actual daily practice to redeem the promises of these policies and institutional commitments? This book offers one set of educators' accounts of what greeted them as they embarked on their different voyages into liberatory, empowering, and equitable educational engagements. Their stories are not pretty, not positive, not redemptive. Of critical importance in reading them is an appreciation of positionality. These are accounts by educators who do not, who, as a matter of identity politics, *may* not speak and act from positions of dominance, even if they would, and who tell of the enormous difference difference/s can make to the plausibility and viability in practice of the kinds of progressive pedagogies with which, we are told, empowerment becomes possible, alterity is celebrated, borders are crossed, equity is realized. There are no promises of consensus, here; surely this is after all a premature hope. Our hope, for now, is simply that we can learn from these kinds of stories from the front lines, particularly when they are told, not naively, as transparently literal narratives of personal experience, but from a commitment to, a profound respect for, theoretical inquiry as an indispensable basis for ethical praxis.

A no less important intent in these tellings has been to destabilize popular narratives about doing work with education's favorite Others—the "at risk" child—here meaning, of course, the minority child—poor, of color, female, and the like. Resituating questions about educational interventions firmly within a politics of identity contests dominant narratives about educational progress, and by this means we hope to, as Dorothy Smith (1993) puts it, "surprise discourse" in these really very ordinary tellings of the resistances, obstacles, and impossibilities of the everyday as it is experienced from very particular and specific identities, positions, locations within educational institutions. We seek thereby to resist the kind of "papering over" which educational narratives of redemption would have us tell. Our hope is that, in these tellings, the obligatory redemptive educational discourse of progress, emancipation, diversity—of the pursuit of liberal dreams of pluralism and inclusion—will be sufficiently "surprised" that it might be forced to "re-write itself, to learn, to [come to] know other than it has done thus far" (Smith 1993, 189).

The Essays

The first section, "Out of Bounds: Institutional Policies and the Politics of Inclusion," maps out basic conceptual terrain—postmodern theories of difference/s, radical notions of pedagogy and curriculum, and discourses of identity politics—and embarks from that standpoint to a critical discussion of the significance of institutional location, engaging with and forcefully challenging institutional policies and practices (such as "gender equity" or "antidiscrimination" policies) created in order to deal programatically with the perceived challenges of pluralism. In chapter 1, Maria de la Luz Reyes' study of Chicana academics at a major crossroads in their professional careers (mid-career and tenure reviews) examines the often contradictory demands of community and academy as these exert a push-pull effect on cultural identity and academic practice. Reyes analyzes the ways in which walking a tightrope between the two presents Chicana academics with an almost insurmountable challenge as they must negotiate a perilous balancing act burdened with the added weight of membership in a systemically racist workplace that relegates them to the fringes of academia.

In chapter 2, Roxana Ng uses a particular teaching experience as a starting point for examining the tensions, contradictions, and possibilities of learning and teaching oppression and liberation in the purportedly "inclusive" university. Ng explores how we may begin to rupture sexism, racism, and other forms of marginalization, not just as ideas, but as constitutive practices in organizational settings in which we all participate.

In chapter 3, Kathleen Martindale asks: "If institutionalization is the answer for gay and lesbian studies, what is the question?" Offering a symptomatic reading of pedagogical disaster stories by radical teachers, queer, lesbian, and gay, who, in attempting to teach "un/popular cultures" have been caught in the stranglehold of identity politics in their classrooms, Martindale suggests that it is to pedagogy, rather than to the institutionalization of disciplinary "difference/s" that we must look if we truly hope to progress beyond homophobia 101.

In chapter 4 Mary Bryson and Suzanne de Castell narrate the activities of a Ministry of Education committee whose undertaking was to design an educational "gender equity" policy and reveal the highly contradictory forces at work in what is often construed as a moment of transformative possibility. The ultimately undermining impacts of both the process of policy formation and its outcomes as implemented in curriculum and pedagogy are described, and the painful question of how such work can ever be more than reactionary in effect is confronted.

In the second section, "Discovery as In<ter>vention: Identity, Authority, and Responsibility in Educational Research," the essays elucidate methodological implications of research practices explicitly informed both by specific locations and by the effects of marginality/marginalization on the human subjects in/of research. In these research practices, discovery and invention are seen to be necessarily reconfigured once identity is at stake. More general ethical and epistemological implications of this shift in our understanding of the project of educational research are identified and discussed. In chapter 5, Francisco Ibanez takes us into the "translations" made by gay males of AIDS-prevention educational discourses and is centrally concerned with the difference effected in practices of ethnographic interviewing and participant observation, when the researcher and the research subject/s occupy a common subject position. This chapter, accordingly, discusses issues of representation, authority and identity, research ethics, and epistemology and educational possibilities, concluding that "studying ourselves" can effect a productive transformation of the processes and outcomes of interviewing, from "confession" to "dialogue."

In chapter 6, Annette Henry explicates fundamental epistemological issues underpinning research from a Black feminist perspective, and describes theoretical and practical alternatives to the liberal multicultural initiatives that are most meaningful for children of African descent. Henry takes up the notion of "diaspora literacy" (King, 1992) and critiques the kind of education that children receive in "inclusive" school settings. To "see blackness with a new eye," Henry further argues, necessitates the invention of alternative praxis.

The central argument of Sheila Te Hennepe is that respect is crucial both to the way research questions about First Nations people are raised and to the way such research is conducted and reported. In chapter 7, native students speak to Te Hennepe about their experiences in anthropology classes. Te Hennepe is a white teacher-educator with whom they have collaborated on this research project. The enormous impediments to respectful research involving First Nations subjects that arise when the researcher is nonnative are described, and Te Hennepe invokes a series of unconventional, diverse, and continuously disrupted forms and styles of reporting, in order to capture, however fleetingly, and to preserve, however incompletely, the voices of the students and the purpose for which they have shared their often profoundly painful experiences.

In chapter 8, Deborah Britzman considers what we have learned— and what we have not—from existing research traditions concerned with identity in education. She explores the ways in which schooling can be shown to produce not just knowledge and particular relations to it, but more centrally, how school knowledge produces and organizes the racial, cultural, gendered, and sexualized identities of students. In dealing with this question, Britzman explores what the field of Lesbian and Gay Studies offers to "the education of education," and describes a radical discursive terrain from which educators may effect a re-vision both of their students and of themselves.

The essays in the third section, "Life in Classrooms: Teaching and Learning against the Grain," position analytical discussions of identity politics and critical/postmodern pedagogies within concrete contexts of radical classroom practice. This juxtaposition enables a clearer understanding of the ways in which progressive educational discourses are readily mastered by students who, notwithstanding, refuse (or are unable) to act on them, and the ways in which transformative educational practices are, paradoxically, unworkable for marginalized subjects. From this standpoint, critical pedagogy can be seen as itself an exclusionary discourse.

In chapter 9, Homa Hoodfar argues that debates within critical pedagogy should include voices from those outside dominant social groups and ethnicities. She demonstrates this perspective "at work" by reviewing some of her teaching experiences as a woman of color, and shows the ways in which not all teachers share the same relationship to critical pedagogy: indeed, somewhat paradoxically, only members of dominant groups, and not Others, Hoodfar argues, can successfully participate in this "progressive" praxis.

In chapter 10, Linda Eyre takes the reader into her classroom as she describes her attempts to integrate a critique of heterosexism and heterosexual privilege into an undergraduate teacher education course. Eyre questions the possibility of liberatory pedagogy in teacher education and ultimately in schooling, at a time when prospective teachers are establishing their own sexual identities and are greatly concerned with issues of public accountability and job security.

Recounting experiences of backlash resulting from action by students of color to engage with a white professor in a graduate English literature course, Charmaine Perkins addresses popular articulations of racism as these percolate into the everyday intellectual politics of student life. Perkins' analysis challenges university teachers to reconsider what they do in the name of purportedly "inclusive" curricular revision and testifies to the untenable position student activists occupy and the intolerable costs they must incur in order to speak out about what might be wrong with what they are required to endure in the name of "education."

In the final chapter, Mary Bryson and Suzanne de Castell address the issue of problematized sexual identities and liberatory pedagogy from within the specific context of an undergraduate Lesbian Studies course that they cotaught. They describe the goals, organizing principles, content, and outcomes of this engagement in the production of "queer pedagogy," which the authors describe as a radical form of educative in<ter>vention implemented deliberately to interfere with the production of normalcy in school/ed subjects. Argued for here is an explicit "ethics of consumption" in relation to curricular inclusions of marginalized subjects and subjugated knowledges.

And so, as against irrepressibly enthusiastic exhortations about the "possibilities" of feminist, critical, and postcritical pedagogies, vigorous proclamations about "meeting new challenges" to "accommodate differences," this volume is concerned with impediments, obstacles, insufficiencies, unkept promises, work not done—and this in the face of institutional imperatives to demonstrate progress and productivity in the attainment of educational equity and despite insistent demands for reassurance, for solutions. These essays, then, tell tales of quite a different kind—tales of the difficulty and danger of educational work against the grain of the institutional culture and politics of schooling. This is the critical question posed by these accounts: "What is the difference between a progressive theory of inclusion which can be worked in practice only by those already included, and no theory of inclusion at all?" Homa Hoodfar (this volume) puts the point succinctly when she argues that the risks of practicing critical pedagogy are clearly not the same for everyone. Nor, equally clearly, are its benefits.

These essays testify, then, to the extent to which emancipatory and/or progressive educational theories and practices are themselves built upon, and ongoingly shaped by, fundamentally exclusionary assumptions, the "capillary forms" in terms of which power is filtered throughout institutional contexts of educational work, such that the possibilities of critical/progressive policy/pedagogy/curriculum are fully available only to those of whom "difference" is never predicated. As such, they pose questions that are not supposed to be asked, questions that induce discomfort, embarrassment, perhaps even shame, the kinds of questions that are forbidden, those dangerous kinds of questions, for the asking of which, the questioner places herself at risk—the kinds of questions, in short, in which much besides a disinterested pursuit of knowledge is at stake.

References

Bakhtin, M. (1981). *The dialogic imagination*. Austin: University of Texas Press.

Braidotti, R. (1987). Envy: or With my brains and your looks. In A. Jardine & P. Smith (Eds.), *Men in feminism* (233–241). New York: Routledge.

Bryson, M., and de Castell, S. (1994). Telling tales out of school. *Journal of Educational Computing Research, 10,* 199–221.

King, J. (1992). Diaspora literacy and consciousness in the struggle against miseducation in the Black community. *Journal of Negro Education, 61,* 317–341.

Lave, J. and Wenger, E. (1991). *Situated learning: Legitimate peripheral participation.* New York: Cambridge University Press.

Porter, J. (1965). *The vertical mosaic.* Toronto: University of Toronto Press.

Smith, D. (1993). High noon in textland. *Sociological Quarterly, 34,* 183–192.

PART I

OUT OF BOUNDS: INSTITUTIONAL POLICIES AND THE POLITICS OF INCLUSION

❖

1

CHICANAS IN ACADEME: AN ENDANGERED SPECIES

MARÍA DE LA LUZ REYES

The more I talk to Chicanas, and other women of color in the academy, the more I come to the conclusion that academic success and upward mobility in the academy requires an allegiance, a tacit oath which, if written, would go something like this:

> I pledge allegiance
> to a white academy,
> and to the scholarship which it reveres,
> one paradigm, under white males,
> monolithic, homophobic, and Eurocentric—for *all*.

This pledge embodies the conflict and contradictions Chicanas must endure in the academy. It demands that we disassociate ourselves from our cultural identities, punishes and demeans us for having research interests with links to our own lives and our community, attempts to make us forget that we can make a difference, and demands a heavy price for full admission, one that many Chicanas are refusing to pay (Reyes 1992).

Introduction

This chapter focuses on three case studies. They are part of a larger study on Chicana academics which took place at Major University (pseudonym) between 1992 and 1994. Major University is the flagship university in a state where Chicanos (Americans of Mexican decent) make up nearly a quarter of the population. The university was founded over 125 years ago. It currently boasts a student enrollment of 25,000 and approximately 1,100 tenure-track faculty. Although it is located only thirty-five miles from the largest Chicano enclave in the state, at the time of the study, there were fewer than 1,000 Chicano *and* Latino students and a total of 24 Chicano faculty (male and female). Of these 24, only *one* Chicana was *tenured*, at the associate professor rank. There were no Chicana professors.

The irony was that despite this small number of Chicano professors, Major University still had eleven women faculty members—among the largest critical mass of Chicanas in any major *research* university in the Southwest. These Chicanas represented earned Ph.D.s from elite institutions such as Berkeley, UCLA, Yale, UT-Austin, Stanford. In this chapter I attempt to illustrate how, despite the impressive credentials and accomplishments of these Chicanas, their resistance to being molded into traditional Eurocentric scholars and their deeply engrained commitment to the social transformation of the Chicano community mitigate against their success in academe and contribute to their "endangered" status.

Cultural and Political Forces Affecting Chicanas in Academe

Though highly educated and independent, the majority of Chicana academics still struggle to balance their own cultural identity and the political struggle of their community with the Eurocentric, patriarchical, and hierarchical requirements for success set by a majority white, male academy. The importance of *familia*, the traditional extended family, remains at the heart of Chicano values (Baca-Zinn 1980). This centrality of *familia* affects them in two ways. First, Chicanas—regardless of their educational level or their own personal preferences—continue to feel the pressure from the larger community outside academe to accept the traditional role of mother and wife still predominant in Chicano culture. Young Chicanas pursuing graduate studies, for example, are often confronted with, "Yes, but do you have any prospects for marriage?" Married Chicana academics with children face additional pressures of maintaining the role of wife and mother as well as that of scholar. The lifestyle of an academic which requires much solitary work—long hours of research and writing—is often incompatible with maintaining a traditional family life. It is not coincidental that many of the most successful Chicana academics are either single, divorced, or lesbian. Second, for the Chicana the value of *familia* translates into a concern for the common good of that community. Imbedded in Chicana consciousness is a responsibility to "give back" to the community who throughout the history of Chicanos has collectively nourished its members and fought against their oppression. This responsibility is critical and at times weighs heavily on Chicanas in the academy.

The demands of the academy as well as their own desire to give back to the Chicano community exert a unique "push-pull effect" between their professional career and their cultural identity. On the one hand, the academy applies strong pressure to conform to Eurocentric definitions of scholarship. It attempts to remold Chicanas into what they do *not* want to be: brown copies of white scholars. On the other hand, Chicanas are more interested in utilizing their academic knowledge for the social transformation of their community. As one of my Chicana colleagues put it, "We get our Ph.D. for different reasons. . . . [We] are here [in the academy] for a different purpose." Yet the warnings from the academy are clear: avoid "brown on brown" research (Reyes and Halcón 1988), steer clear of issues affecting your own ethnic community. Walking a tightrope between these two forces creates a major challenge as Chicanas must do this within a hegemonic system buttressed by both racist and sexist structures.

Chicana academics, for example, are expected to achieve success in spite of their "triple oppression" (de la Torre & Pesquera 1993): discrimination on the basis of ethnicity, which they share with Chicanos; gender discrimination, which they share with white women; and discrimination as *women of color*, members of *two oppressed groups*. Like other women of color, they are victims both of racism and of sexism. When it comes to special opportunities or key positions, Chicanas frequently feel passed over: first, for white males; second, for white females; and third, for ethnic males (Reyes 1992).

Alienation and invisibility in the academy are common experiences for Chicanas. This alienation from their white colleagues is exacerbated by the fact that Chicanas also feel excluded both from the dominant Chicano discourse that has typically focused on ethnic and class domination without addressing gender differences, and from white feminist theory that ignores white privilege and the marginal location of women of color within the academy. This exclusion by white women is primarily, but not always, from heterosexual women. Neither of these groups with whom they share common experiences has championed their cause in any significant manner.

Chicanas with a strong cultural identity feel tremendous conflict in having to choose between their commitment to community and academic success. Sacrifices in their personal and professional lives required for success in the academy (i.e., achieve tenure) are often too high. Thus, a number of them are leaving academia before facing the pressures of the tenure process, or shedding their cultural identity to succeed in the academy. For those who remain in higher education, a good number remain frozen at the lower ranks. Many others transfer out of Ph.D.-granting institutions, further reducing their potential to influence the nature of the academy and reducing the number of Chicanas in academe.

Endangered Status

The majority of Chicanas in faculty positions in major research universities are first-generation academics and can be divided into three significant waves of Chicanas completing Ph.D.s. The first wave completed their degrees in the late sixties and midseventies and have been teaching an average of twenty years; a majority of the tenured full professors are from this wave. The second wave graduated in the midseventies to mideighties. And the third wave (which comprises most of the women in my study) completed their doctorates in the mideighties to the early nineties.

My assertion is that Chicanas in academe are an "endangered species." By the best of estimates, Chicana *full* professors at major research universities across the country *in all disciplines* except law and medicine total about fifty. I arrived at this estimate by contacting individual members of the small network of prominent Chicanas in research institutions around the country and cross-referencing that information with estimates from Centers for Chicano Research at Stanford, Arizona State University, San Antonio, Houston, the Tomás Rivera Center, and the Postsecondary Education Commissions in California and in Texas.

As a Chicana with eleven years in academe, what I have learned about other Chicanas in research universities is that they generally fall into three categories: I know them, I know *of* them, or I know someone who knows them. Because the network is so small, this is also what other Chicana and Chicano colleagues have told me about this network of women. Thus, in the absence of accurate data sources—most of which group all Latinos together (Mexican American, Puerto Rican, Cuban, South Americans, etc.), I surveyed key Chicanas, well known in their fields, to generate lists from their own personal knowledge of other Chicana academics across the country. The fortunate thing was that the network is small enough to make a good estimate possible; the unfortunate reality is that the numbers are minuscule.

Definition of Terms

My claim that Chicanas in academe are an endangered species is based on my definition of the word *academe* as Ph.D.-granting institutions focused primarily on research. My rationale is that these universities are considered the bastions of intelligentsia, where degrees are conferred to those destined to occupy positions of leadership in America.

It is at research institutions like these where the majority of published scholarship is generated—books, articles, and reports that influence the direction of policies affecting the wide spectrum of life in America—where future leaders are prepared, where the "baton of leadership" is passed on to the next generation of doctoral students who will take their place. Faculty at research institutions serve on most editorial boards, national professional boards, and commissions and hold office in professional organizations that determine the direction of their fields and comprise the pool of nationally known "experts" in every field imaginable.

My premise, as I have discussed elsewhere, is that the *center of power* lies within the ranks of the tenured full professor. Tenured full professors control the most powerful committees in academe: governance, curriculum, budget, promotion, review, and tenure. I believe that without voice at this level, Chicanas will have little access to knowledge-generating positions that will influence learning for *all* college graduates (Reyes and Halcón 1988; Reyes and Halcón 1991).

Limiting the definition of academe in this manner in no way implies my endorsement of this academic pecking order nor minimizes the many important contributions made by Chicanas in non-research universities; it merely acknowledges the dominant construction of the term *academe*.

I use the term *minority* in its standard sociological sense, rather than in a numerical sense; it refers to people relatively powerless in the hierarchy of power and authority.

The word *Chicana* refers to a U.S.-born woman of Mexican descent. It is a term that more specifically identifies and clarifies her minority status vis-à-vis the dominant group and positions her in a unique historical, social, and political context. It is different from the generic term *Latina* which may refer to other women from Spanish-language backgrounds or Spanish-speaking countries. Additionally, the terms *Chicano* and *Chicana* (in contrast to Mexican American) connotes self-affirmation as well as a strong political, cultural, ethnic, and/or linguistic identity. Although Chicana feminists have constructed new ideological and political formations that make more rigid distinctions between the terms *Chicano* and *Chicana* to highlight "privileged male forms of identity" (Chabram Dernersesian 1993, 39), my use of these terms refers respectively to men and women in the Chicano (a more inclusive term for males and females) community.

Theoretical Framework

My work is largely informed by the work of Paulo Freire (1970). Education for emancipation and the concept of 'conscientizaçao', (critical consciousness) resonates well with the experiences of oppressed groups. For Chicanas with strong cultural identity who value commitment to the social transformation of their community, there is a strong connection between the essence of Freire's critical theory and their own sense of struggle for emancipation both from racial and from sexual domination. The writings of women of color, particularly Chicana scholars and poets (Anzaldua 1983; Castillo 1994; Chabram Dernersesian 1993; Cervantes 1992; Cisneros 1991; de la Torre and Pesquera 1993; Facio 1993; Nieto-Gómez 1975, Pérez 1993; Ruíz 1993; Sánchez 1990; Segura 1993) and African American and other women scholars (Collins 1991; hooks 1994; hooks and West 1991; Lorde 1983; Morrison 1990; Ng 1991; 1993; Rains 1995; Williams 1991) influence my perspective as well as my analysis. Bolstered by the perspectives of these women scholars of color, I make the assumption that Chicanas, like other women of color, understand the sources of their triple oppression and yet are able to develop a strong self-identity while appearing to conform to the pressures of the academy. They continue to resist and to find solace and friendship with others who sustain them in their struggle. However, this resistance does not necessarily mean that they remain in academe.

My Role as a Chicana Researcher

My own position is that of "womanist" (see Henry, this volume) rather than strictly feminist—a woman concerned with empowerment of the *entire* oppressed community of color—*males and females*. As a womanist—who is Chicana—my interests are in advancing the concerns of my community, improving the literacy and graduation rates among our youth, and improving its economic and political status. I believe that Chicanas cannot be "liberated" when our people—both males and females—continue to be subjugated by the dominant, racist power structures.

The kinds of experiences I observed closely, as well as those revealed to me by the women in this study, are experiences that I, as a Chicana, and other women faculty of color, encounter on a regular basis. They relate to issues that touch me deeply, some specifically or similarly, others merely by virtue of membership or association with this group. They force me to grapple with the contradictions of my multiple locations—my continued identification with my poor, working-class upbringing *within a Chicano family* and that of my current middle-class status with membership in both a privileged and elite academy where I play the role of a researcher and academic, yet as a brown woman—marginal in the overall system of authority and privilege. I recognize that I cannot help but speak from an insider's perspective for that is who and where I am. In Alan Peshkin's words, however, "I have looked for myself where, knowingly or not, I think we all are—and unavoidably belong: in the subjective underbrush of our own research experience" (Peshkin 1990, 20). What I mean is that I reject the notion that I as the knower/writer or researcher can be "objective," or that *any* writer can occupy a position which transcends all viewpoints (Ng 1991).

In the following section, I will provide a brief biography of each of these women, highlighting their educational experiences as minorities in schools, then discuss common themes that emerged from my interviews with them. Finally, I analyze these themes in light of these women's struggles in balancing their identity as Chicanas with the demands of the academy which contribute to their endangered status. The names I use here are pseudonyms. I have also purposely camaflouged specific details in broad, generic terms to protect the identity of these women who are part of a very small network of Chicana academics.

Case Studies

Data collection included a survey questionnaire (part of the larger study) which asked about the working climate, job satisfaction, support for research, and other aspects of academic life. In addition, three in-depth interviews were conducted with each woman to explore their life histories; the details of their experiences as academics in their respective fields; and their reflections on the intellectual, cultural, and emotional connections between their work and their lives.

These interviews averaged over two hours each and approximately eight hours per participant. Data also included field notes from participant observation in their public presentations, observations of their interactions with students in class, on campus, and/or in social settings related to University activities; a review of their vitas; and readings of their scholarly publications and stories in campus newspapers.

In the year prior to this aspect of the study, I was a participant observer in, and a member of a group known as the Chicana Faculty

Network (CFN) made up of the eleven Chicana faculty at the University
of Colorado where I also taught. During that year, we met informally
once a month for purposes of getting acquainted, networking, and sup-
porting each other in our professional endeavors on and off the campus.
Our gatherings were usually around breakfast or dinner at local restau-
rants or at each others' homes. Throughout this first year of monthly
gatherings with these women, I kept some notes and conducted some
unstructured, informal interviews. Data from these field notes and my
interactions with these women serve as a larger social and political backdrop for my analyses and discussion of these three case studies.

Elvira

Elvira is a graduate of one of the top-ranked campuses in the
western section of the country where she earned her Ph.D. in the area
of social science. She is a petite woman in her mid thirties with dark,
olive skin—readily identifiable as a Chicana.

Elvira was born in a migrant labor camp. Her parents and
extended family made a living by working in the fields picking cher-
ries, apples, and other crops. Unlike the other children who worked
alongside their parents, Elvira felt "spoiled and privileged" because
she had the luxury of being allowed to play and run freely in the fields.
"I was spoiled," she recalled. "I didn't work when I was 3 to 4 years
old. I was treated like a little queen—the Little Princess of the Labor
Camp. Yes, that's what I was: a princecita" (Interview, November 2,
1993). She attributed her "privilege" to the fact that she was the first
grandchild in a large extended family.

Both her mother and her grandfather pushed her to get a good
education so she could get out of the migrant stream. In fact, her parents befriended a woman, "Mamá Lupe" (no family relation), who took
little Elvira into her home until she was about 10, so she could attend
school without the seasonal interruptions required of migrant workers
to follow the crops. Elvira loved school and made good grades throughout elementary and junior high school. In the fifth grade she and her
Chicano friends discovered the "secret to school success," an inevitable
reality discovered by all minority students. Elvira recalls, "The teachers
didn't want us to act Mexican. The more white we acted, the better they
treated us." Elvira's mother understood this reality and reinforced it by
telling her daughter, "Don't speak Spanish in school, and always be
clean—you know what they think of us!"

In spite of Elvira's good command of English and her excellent
grades, she and her Chicano friends never received well-deserved
recognition; instead, they were assigned to sit in the back of the class

and were reprimanded for speaking Spanish. She recalls, "We weren't rewarded like the white kids although we were just as good, got good grades, [but] they were given the certificates; they were class monitors. We were *never* class monitors!"

Elvira's high school years were rocky as they were for many adolescents in the seventies. "I noticed," she said, "that [the girls] in my community were all getting pregnant." There were other problems. "Why is everyone running away? I'd ask. Why is everyone doing drugs? I saw juvenile delinquency everywhere, and I started thinking about social change," she said. Many of her friends were dropping out of high school. Recognizing the tragedy of those statistics, she emphasizes, "I happened to be one of the fortunate ones." Notwithstanding all the problems around her, Elvira graduated from high school with honors and went on to a major university where she got involved in the Chicano movement, joined the farm workers' picket lines, and became a strong community activist.

Angela

Angela has a Ph.D. from a top-ranked university in the eastern United States where she majored in a math-related, nontraditional field for women, especially minority women. She is a tall, slender, attractive woman with long, dark hair. Although her good looks are the envy of many women, she believes they have been a source of frequent sexist comments and unwelcome sexual advances. She often is asked if she is Italian, a question she resents because she recognizes it for what it is, a rejection of her Mexicanness. Angela was raised in a small ranch town in the Southwest where she grew up with her extended family: her parents, siblings, grandparents, and a great aunt. Her mother returned to work, leaving Angela, at five, a great deal of time with her Spanish-speaking grandparents and aunt who filled her life with rich cultural stories and Mexican traditions. "I attribute my school success partly to my position in the family, and that I was a curious child," she said. Her grandfather encouraged this curiosity and spend a great deal of time with Angela. She recalled, "He sat me down with *Hit* and *Super Hit*, two baseball magazines in Spanish, so that's how I learned to read in Spanish." Although there were no kindergarten classes in public schools, she was sent to the home of an Anglo woman who taught a group of about twelve children a readiness curriculum. "I was the only Mexican in the group," she recalls.

She attended a Mexican/Chicano elementary school of about five hundred students and junior and high schools of about one hundred each.

The school was 80 percent Mexican and 20 percent Anglo, but they tracked—even in first grade they tracked you in A or B track. B class was always Mexican and A class was Anglo, occasionally some Mexicans—depending on whose parents went and fought for their kids. [But] ordinarily, your last name assigned you to your track. My mother went and fought. She said, my kids are all going to be in A track 'cause they've got veterans' benefits to go on to college . . . cause my dad had died. He was a major [in the army], so that was one of the things we knew we all had so we all went A track from the beginning. We all knew we had to do very well in school because it was our responsibility to go on to college. . . . That we were going to be the generation to go to college . . . it was what our father wanted. . . . My grandfather used to tell me when I was six, "You're going to be the lawyer in the family."

Throughout her school years she was always in trouble. She recalls, "I was very bright and got very good grades, but I was too curious and I was always reprimanded for being too talkative, asking too many questions, raising my hand, wanting to engage the teacher in stuff beyond what was supposed to be taught, and that caused me to get Fs in deportment."

Like most Chicanos, Angela had her taste of racism in grade school. In fifth grade, she recalled:

This white boy from another ranch pulled my hair and called me a "dirty Mexican," he said, "Yeah, we all know about you dirty Mexicans." I just lost it; I got on top of my desk, turned around waving my arms, and yelled, "I'm not dirty. I take a bath every day. I take a shower just as often as you do, Jimmy. And I wouldn't want to be white and pale like you!" The teacher was scandalized. She punished me [because] the appropriate behavior would have been for me to ignore it; so *I* had to stay after school. Nothing happened to Jimmy.

Math always played a prominent role in Angela's life. Even as young as six, it was Angela's responsibility to help translate for her aunt, help her in the exchange of any money over ten dollars (*in dollars and pesos*) and figure the bus route across the border to Mexico and back. "My grandfather," she said, "treated me like a male with respect to the role of Mexican family." In high school, he counseled all her other female cousins to take typing and bookkeeping, but he told

Angela "not to bother" with these, arguing that she should take trigonometry and calculus.

In high school, Angela excelled in math and sports. She finished high school in three years and earned a basketball scholarship to an elite university in the Southwest. From there Angela transferred to a university in the East and went on to earn her Ph.D. in a field requiring advanced knowledge of mathematics, and not coincidentally into a predominantly male-dominated field.

Cynthia

Cynthia earned her doctorate in social science in a major university in the Southwest. She comes from mixed heritage parents; her mother is white, and her father is Chicano. This explains, in part, her blondish brown hair, light skin, and why most people do not easily identify her as Chicana. Throughout her life this has shielded her from overt racism, but it has also prevented her from getting close to other Chicanos who have not readily accepted her or who have resented her for being able to pass for white.

Cynthia was raised in a border town in the Southwest where her father was a public school administrator in the same district where she attended school. She loved school and made excellent grades, but her father also fueled her competitive spirit: "When I took a report card with 6 A+s and one A, he'd say, 'How come this one's not an A+?' . . . He used to tell us that education was very important. 'Get that degree 'cause no one can take that away from you,' he'd say."

Unlike most Chicanos, Cynthia grew up in a middle-class environment, but the schools she attended were predominantly Mexican American. In fact, many of her elementary and junior high teachers were Mexican American. Of her teachers, she said, "I had great teachers, really *good* teachers. . . . I remember being challenged by my teachers." Her father was also a role model for her. He had a master's degree, and her mother was in graduate school while Cynthia was still in elementary school.

When she was in junior high school, her parents divorced, forcing Cynthia to take on the major responsibilities of running a household. She recalled, "I was coping with the pressure of doing all the cooking, cleaning, ironing and menu planning for my dad and [two] brothers, . . . so I was not happy from junior high to high school." These responsibilities made her social life in high school difficult.

After high school she went on to college and graduate school in a major institution in the Southwest. She found laboratory research exciting, and she published 3 articles in premier journals in her field *before earning her Ph.D.* Then she accepted a postdoctorate at a prestigious university in England where she worked as an intern under a renowned scholar in her field.

Common Experiences in Academe

These women, as well as the majority in the larger study, shared many painful experiences in academe, many of them stemming from overt racism and sexism. In this chapter, I focus only on three themes: alienation from their colleagues and sometimes even students, lack of an on-going support system to sustain them through difficult times, and lack of deference, power and authority in their positions as faculty. Although it was not planned, the interviews of the three women in these case studies occurred within the backdrop of their third-year review.

Alienation. A common theme among these women was that of alienation and isolation in their work environment. This was due, in part, to the fact that each was the only Chicana in her department. None had any real friends in their primary unit. With some exceptions, Cynthia found some professional acceptance from at least one or two colleagues who would take the time (during work hours) to read her manuscripts or sit and listen to her ideas. However, she recognized that they were not always aware of her ethnicity, "They know I'm *Lopez,* but they don't see me as Chicana. . . . My skin and hair color prevents me from being viewed as Chicana." Outside the campus, she rarely socialized with them.

Angela and Elvira found it more difficult to feel connected, to have colleagues within their own departments who understood, appreciated, or even respected them or their work. In fact, they felt a high level of resentment from members of their departments who frequently assumed that they were affirmative action hires and thus not likely to be fully qualified for the positions they occupied. Angela reported, "People remind me overtly and covertly, 'you're a double protected class hire. We have a special budget for you'" (Interview, February 12, 1994).

This feeling was fairly consistent among the majority of Chicanas on campus. One woman said of her own hiring, "I've had people say to me, 'You got the job only 'cause you're Mexican.' . . . Forget that I have a Ph.D., never mind that I'm qualified for the job—there's a suspicion, a stigma attached before I even walk in the door!" (Interview, November 28, 1993).

As mentioned above, at the time of the study, Elvira, Angela, and Cynthia were all going through their third-year review. Their general feeling of isolation from colleagues and lack of professional support was exacerbated during this period. The three described their reviews as needless and especially stressful. They were provided little information, or *vague* explanations about the process, the preparation of their dossiers, or their research statements. Angela likened her mid-career review to "psychological hazing." She viewed it as nothing more than a display of power by white males. "My colleagues' behavior and responses were 'let's keep her scared [and] jumping.'" The three reported an attitude of "See if you can figure it out for yourselves," or "See if you can guess what we want" (Interview, February 12, 1994).

In the case of Elvira and Angela, their department chairs had informed them they had plenty of time to prepare their files and then sprung on them a deadline nearly a month earlier. Neither one was mentored through the process. Little or no clerical assistance was provided for preparation of their materials. Instead, they felt taunted as they passed through what seemed a gauntlet. Cynthia, who had six publications in premier journals in her field—a major accomplishment for three years in academe—was told by her committee chair, "You're on the edge" (Interview, April 12, 1994).

Angela and Elvira were told: "You don't have enough publications,"

"You're publishing in the *wrong* journals," "You have too much service to community." Of her four referred journal articles and published book, Elvira, whose research was on Chicanos, was told: "Well, this work is *okay* for *now*, but your next book better be from an academic press or you won't get tenure," and "Listen, *for your own good*, you need to stop writing about minority issues" (Interview, November 4, 1994).

Even after the three women had received a majority vote for renewal of their contracts, they were constantly reminded of their "tenuous track positions" (Reyes and Halcón 1991) and demeaned or ridiculed. Instead of congratulations, their white colleagues said things like: "Just because you got a unanimous vote, *don't think you've made it*" and "Being a minority woman didn't hurt you" (Interview, February 12, 1994). Even a Chicano colleague offered Elvira little comfort. He told her: "You're just a midcareer review case, you're not that important; they're just fattening you up for the kill" (Interview 11-6-94).

The verbal harassment they experienced during the review process took a physical toll on all three women. Even with an impressive publication record, Cynthia suffered stomach problems. Elvira, who experienced the most overt kind of racism from her supervisors and white colleagues, lost ten pounds and suffered blackouts caused by intense anxiety. Angela also lost ten pounds and developed a severe muscle spasm in her neck that made it impossible for her to turn her neck for a nearly a month. Both women were already quite thin at the beginning of this review process.

Their third-year review was further complicated by the fact that other Chicanos on campus went public in demanding to be transferred out of their department. In a united voice, they accused their department chair of overt racism and publicly cited examples of what they alleged was a hostile working climate. To make matters worse for all three women, this incident coincided with a student hunger strike aimed at pressuring the university for an ethnic studies department and major, as well as for tangible commitment to the principles of cultural diversity in the curriculum. Although the student group included a cross-section of all students on campus—whites, African Americans, Asians, Native Americans and Chicanos—it was perceived as a "Chicano rebellion." These incidents in tandem created a climate of suspicion of all Chicanos, both male and female, across the campus.

Lack of support system. In addition to their professional isolation, the three women also felt keenly their lack of a sustained personal support system. Friendships with other Chicanas on campus, and the social outings with them, albeit limited, were of tremendous support, but inadequate for the intense pressures and barrage of racist and sexist comments they experienced almost daily. Elvira was even admonished for seeking other minorities and told it would be a liability for her: "Stay away from the ethnic studies center if you want to get a good review" (Interview, November 4, 1993). Angry and eyes filled with tears, she uttered: "How dare they tell me to stay away! That's my *only* safety net. What else do I have? Who's there to support me? . . . . I realize everything is so petty, [like review] and tenure. If they don't give it to me, it's their loss. I would be devastated, but I'm not gonna live and die for this stuff" (Interview, November 4, 1993). Yet she sobbed as she described her hurt and her feelings of exasperation that her white colleagues would deny her need for support from other people of color in whom she could confide.

Lack of deference, power, and authority. Elvira's and Angela's relationships and interactions with white students were generally strained. They felt a lack of access to deference, power, and authority as ethnic female professors. This was true for most of the Chicanas on campus, except for Cynthia, whose looks *and* work resembled closely the Eurocentric model.

Elvira and Angela felt their authority constantly challenged. Elvira described an example of this:

> I teach of class of over 200 undergraduates, mostly white males; a core course. The students are confrontational, questioning; they want [to know] my credentials. They want me to justify every-thing—justify why I chose the questions I chose for an exam, for example! They can't stand that I'm down there on the platform, the classroom auditorium—as the professor. They *resent* that a brown woman is telling them their business. . . . When I talk about racism and sexism they say, "That's a bunch of crap; that really doesn't happen!" (Interview, November 6, 1993)

Students in her classes complained that there were too many class readings by too many people of color, by too many Marxists, too many women. "They tell me I am offensive because of the types of issues I talk about. They look at me like, "how dare I have the audac-ity, the audacity of some brown woman to prance her brown ass in front of the class as if she were in charge!" Elvira added, "First and foremost [students] react to my color; we don't look like their other professors. We're short, we're dark . . . [and] we also dress nicer than they do!" (Interview, November 6, 1993)

Moving into positions previously reserved for white males was more likely to result in a higher incidence of hostile, cruel, and demeaning comments in their teaching evaluations. The tenor of the comments was generally personal and sexist. For example, in response to the question "How would you improve this course?" a student wrote about Angela's class: "Assassinate the bitch!" (Field notes, March 1992).

For these Chicanas, student evaluations left a bitter, long-lasting sting. Often, student evaluations included comments such as, "In spite of the fact that she's Hispanic, she can still get the material across [to the class]." Elvira and Angela reported that the normal chain of com-mand was often violated when it came to their dealings with students. For example, it was not unusual for students to go straight to male department chairs rather than directly to them with their complaints. They felt that this action underscored the students' lack of respect for them as minorities and especially as women, particularly in those instances when the male department chair did nothing to support or to validate their authority. Angela regarded this power struggle between herself and white students as the ultimate symbol of resis-tance to her position of authority as faculty. In some instances, their students did not even offer the kind of professional acknowledgment and courtesy greetings offered to other faculty.

In describing her tenuous relationship with white students and how they responded to her as an African American law professor, Patricia Williams (1991) provides a good example of how women of color and these Chicanas walk a thin line with students. She writes,

> I am expected to woo students even as I try to fend them off; I am supposed to control them even as I am supposed to manipulate them into loving me. Still I am aware of the *paradox of my power* over these students. I am aware of my role, my place in an institution that is larger than myself, *whose power I wield even as I am powerless, whose shield of respectability shelters me even as I am disrespected.* (Williams 1991, 95–96, emphasis mine)

Another theme among Chicanas was that, in an ironic fashion, and in spite of the fact that service did not count for tenure or promotion, the university expected them to provide service to minority students and minority communities. Cynthia reported that during her job interview an administrator asked her, "Are you gonna be a good role model?" She responded, "If you're looking for a role model, don't hire me because I don't fit in either group!" (Interview, April 12, 1994).

None of the women objected to working with students or community, but they resented the fact that their respective colleagues *expected them to bear the responsibility for all minorities* whether they were Chicanos or foreign students and that their superiors often reprimanded them for doing so. They both felt resentful that their white colleagues would not work with minority students. When Elvira specifically informed her colleagues that she could not take on any white students because she had *all* the minorities in the department and this was five to seven more students than the average number of advisees per faculty member in her department, she was accused of "reverse racism."

Discussion

The dominant theme in the study of Chicanas was the conflict between their cultural identity and the demands of academic scholarship as measured by Eurocentric standards, a variation on the notion of having to act white to succeed. In ivory tower terms, this translates into tremendous pressure to assimilate and emulate Eurocentric models of scholarship in order to be successful. It implies that expertise in minority-related topics is inherently nonintellectual. The myth of a pure, objective scholarship generated by the so-called cognitive elite and defined by white Eurocentric America plays a major role in legitimizing inequality in higher education. This view forces a large number of minorities who are unsuccessful in attaining tenure to accept the unequal features of the larger society.

It ignores the fact that identification, classification, or category is specifically located and historically placed. Academic knowledge is tied to who we are, how we think (Ng 1991). Expertise in our field is filtered through who we really are outside our academic shell, outside the ivory tower. Our identity, our academic knowledge is situated in the social relations in which we engage. The myth of pure scholarship ignores the fact that an individual may be a woman of color, the only Chicana in a department, the only minority, the only Spanish speaker, the only woman in a predominantly male field, or the only ethnographer in a quantitative field—and it attempts to define scholarship and evaluation methods as either good or bad.

Being Chicana has everything to do with how we construct our identity as scholars and as women. But the academy tries to separate our cultural, sexual, and linguistic identity from our professional identity. It would have us believe that mixing the two dilutes the rigor of scholarship. This creates a continual conflict for us. Scholarship without purpose, meaning, and relevance goes counter to our very nature, against who we are as Chicanas, against why we are in higher education in the first place. One of the participants in the study expressed it well, "I have a *lifetime* of research because *my community is my research.* There's so much to do. It's not just a job; it's my life!" This is true for many Chicanas. We view our education as a means of our own liberation and that of our community.

The findings from this study and other writings that attest to these experiences of Chicanas in academe imply that if universities are to retain these women, they must affirm genuine diversity, even the kind that challenges the dominant paradigm. They must legitimate and respect ethnic identity and its expression in their work. They must recognize the negative effects of racism, sexism, and white privilege on women of color and create safe places for public discussion of these issues in the academy.

The extinction of Chicana academics must be fought at two fronts: among Chicanas and in the academy. As Chicana academics we can slow the tide of our own extinction in the academy by recognizing that in order to change the system we must learn to live within it, acknowledging the contradictions of our identity. This means that so long as we work in those environments, we must understand that our presence will continue to challenge the status quo and as a result, our treatment might not be equitable, but we must resist, remain firm in our resolve. What we can hope is that if we endure *without* sacrificing our integrity and identity, we will be in a position to effect change through our actions and our writing. This is what other Chicana scholars before us have done.

It is difficult to recognize the progress that has taken place in academia when we find ourselves facing the same issues as previous generations of scholars. When I studied for my bachelor's degree in the late sixties, for example, I did not read a single book written by a Chicano or Chicana scholar, writer, or poet. Today, my students and the students of other Chicana faculty are exposed to, and even required to read, a new version of reality—scholarship generated by Chicanos and Chicanas. This is progress, yet not the kind that provides comfort in the face of overt racist and sexist acts which Chicanas still face. I am by no means suggesting that if we put up with abuse we will succeed. On the contrary, we must hold our ground at every turn.

Universities which hold real power have a major responsibility to slow down the tide of Chicanas leaving academe by taking such concrete steps as hiring more than one Chicana per department, providing incentives for department to do this or disincentives for those that do not, hiring at the middle and upper levels of the professoriate *with tenure*, developing effective mentorship designed by Chicanas, providing diversity training for majority faculty, establishing oversight committees with real power and authority to monitor the treatment of Chicanas, providing antiracism and antisexism training, embarking on exploration of new models of scholarship, and other such things.

However, the reality of it all is that universities are inherently "non-inclusive" (Bryson 1995). They are likely to remain so for the next several generations. Most have a long history of systemic bias and take pride in being *ex*clusive. Universities will also have to appoint more women of color to personnel and tenure committees so that minority women will have a better chance of being evaluated within the context of their scholarship and their positions within their departments. Without this, it will be more difficult for universities to retain these women, few will move up the ranks, and many will remain endangered.

Postscript and Acknowledgment

Of the eleven women, and barely a year after the completion of this study, only six Chicanas remain on the faculty at Major University.

Two are on a leave of absence and are not likely to return to the same university. Two others have left academe all together. (One, anticipating an imminent denial of tenure, left for the private sector; the other refused to continue with so many constraints on her work.) Another woman moved to a university where both she and her academic husband could secure jobs.

Conducting the interviews was a gut-wrenching experience for me. These Chicanas were not "subjects to be studied"—they were my friends, my colleagues, *mis hermanas* (my sisters). Because they put their trust in me and shared so many intimate details of their experiences, I felt honored, close to them. They were willing to share their pain so that other Chicanas might learn from their experiences, so that their situations might be improved. I felt humbled by their trust, in awe of their incredible inner strength, their talents, their intelligence. Getting to know them better was a gift to me. I gained the deepest respect for each of them. In all but one case, each of the women cried, and I cried *with* them; yet I forged ahead with the interviews in hopes that the information would alleviate the struggles of *other* Chicanas. There were nights when I went to bed with a heavy heart, unable to sleep because of the sheer nakedness of their pain. In many cases, I was aware of bits and pieces of the incidents they related to me because of my membership in that tiny network of Chicanas on campus, but I felt the full weight of their struggle when each woman put all the pieces together for me.

A page from the personal journal which I kept during this period provides an example of what I felt throughout this study.

October 4, 1993.

My own heart ached with pain at listening to her. My very throat tightened as she continued telling how she felt and how she feels she's conformed to *everything* else in the academy, but that she won't let them strip her of the only thing that she has left: her identity as a Chicana.

I also began to cry silently as I listened to her talk, describing her pain; as I watched her cry, literally sob in pain. I wanted to stop the interview, to go over and hug her and let her know I knew that pain, too. But in my academic response, I let the recorder continue taking in all her pain so that I could capture the power of her feelings . . . and I felt so guilty doing it.

I struggled with my dilemma to respond to her personal pain, or let the recorder capture it for sake of later informing the larger academic community—via an article—about the reality of the Chicana struggle. During those moments when she cried—and they seemed forever—I hated myself for not throwing the recorder against the wall and responding to her as a human being rather than a subject of my study. For what seemed to be an eternity, I listened to her. Eventually, I couldn't take it any longer; it was too painful. I stopped the tape, and got up and put my arm around her shoulder. She turned and sobbed in my arms.

I was so proud of her strength; so impressed at her courage to stand alone against a system that doesn't understand her or people like her. I was so impressed at how smart and strong she is [she looks so frail] and how I didn't realize the extent of her resilience. She is standing up to her supervisors, she is recognizing how she is getting differential treatment. And, yet she's still standing, almost daring them: "Hit me again. 'Cause now I've got your number." Now she's taken the higher ground and I think she will rattle their conscience—if they have one. She's put them on notice that she won't stand for it any longer—even if she gets fired. My chest ached with pain—literally; and for the rest of the night I felt such a heavy weight. Will the system spare no one?

Prologue

The greatest hope for Chicanas and other minorities, I believe, lies in the development of new institutions designed to be truly universal. Such a one has emerged in the current creation of the University of California-Monterey Bay. Its vision statement reads as follows:

California State University-Monterey Bay is a state university being designed to meet the developing needs of California's diverse student population into the next century. Its evolving mission embodies a commitment to education of the highest quality; to an environment of gender equity and cultural diversity; to the integration of such cross-disciplinary models as those which have emerged from ethnic, women's colonial, and disability studies; to the achievement of an academically effective merger of liberal learning with preparation for the professions; to the integration of learning, working, and residential living within a multicultural and interdisciplinary organization structure; to the use of technology for the enhancement of student learning;

and to sustained support for an intellectual climate that values and promotes public service. (CSUMB Mission Statement 1994)

In January 1995, I left my academic position at Major University to become one of CSUMB's thirteen founding faculty, made up of seven women and six men. Of the total, seven are ethnic minorities and six are of EuroAmerican ancestry. Each of us was granted tenure at full professorship rank. Participating in the development of this university is a dream come true for a Chicana such as myself who has lived on the margins of the academy where my research on Chicanas had little value; here it is promoted. As one of my female colleagues has so aptly expressed it, it is literally a "visceral high" to be in the center of this new experiment in higher education where *pluralism, equity, and service* to community are a given. This is, no doubt, a major reason why we received over five thousand applications from all over the world for twenty-two faculty positions! The stellar qualifications and ethnic diversity of those applicants will forever serve as empirical evidence that there are, indeed, qualified minority academics all over the world who seek inclusive environments and affirmation of their identity and their scholarship.

Our task is an exciting though formidable one, especially in light of the current political climate of California and the general conservatism in the country. All eyes are on us. It will be a major challenge to stay true to our vision. Only time will tell if we succeed.

References

Anzaldua, G. (1983). Speaking in tongues: A letter to 3rd world women writers. In C. Moraga & G. Anzaldua (Eds.), *This bridge called my back: Writings by radical women of color* (pp. 165–173). New York: Kitchen Table Women of Color Press.

Baca-Zinn, M. (1980). Gender and ethnic identity among Chicanas. *Frontiers*. Vol. 5, No. 2, 18–24.

Bryson, M. (1995). Personal communication.

Castillo, A. (1994). *Massacre of the dreamers: Essays on Xicanisma.* Albuquerque, NM: University of New Mexico Press.

Cervantes, L. D. (1992). Poem for the young white man who asked me how I, an intelligent, well-read person could believe in the war between races. In P. S. Rothenberg, *Race, class, & gender in the United States* (pp. 225–226). New York: St. Martin's Press.

Chabram Dernersesian, A. (1993). And, yes . . . The earth did part: On the splitting of Chicana/o subjectivity. In A. de la Torre & B. M. Pesquera (Eds.), *Building with our hands* (pp. 34–56). Berkeley, CA: University of California Press.

Cisneros, S. (1991). *Woman hollering creek.* New York: Vintage Books.

Collins, P. H. (1991). *Black femist thought.* New York: Routledge.

de la Torre, A., and Pesquera, B. M. (1993). Introduction. *Building with our Hands* (pp. 1–11). Berkeley, CA: University of California Press.

Facio, E. (1993). Gender and the life course: A case study of Chicana elderly. In A. de la Torre & B. M. Pesquera (Eds.), *Building with our hands* (pp. 217–231). Berkeley, CA: University of California Press.

Freire, P. (1970). *Pedagogy of the oppressed.* New York: Continuum Publishing Company.

hooks, b. (1994). *Teaching to transgress.* New York: Routledge.

hooks, b., and West, C. (1991). *Breaking bread: Insurgent black intellectual life.* Boston, MA: South End Press.

Lorde, A. (1983). The master's tools will never dismantle the master's house. In Moraga, C. & Anzaldua, G. (Eds.), *This bridge called my back: Writings by radical women of color* (pp. 98–101). New York: Kitchen Table Women of Color Press.

Morrison, T. (1990). *Playing in the dark.* New York: Vintage Books.

Nieto-Gómez, A. (1975). La Chicana. *Women struggle.*

Ng, R. (1991). Teaching against the grain: Contradictions for the minority teacher. In J. Gaskell & A. McLaren (Eds.), *Women and education* (2nd ed., pp. 99–115). Calgary: Detselig Enterprises.

———. (1993). Racism, sexism, and nation bulding in Canada. In C. McCarthy & W. Crichlow (Eds.), *Race identity and representation in education* (pp. 50–59). New York: Routledge.

Pérez, L. E. (1993). Opposition and the education of Chicana/os. In C. McCarthy & W. Crichlow (Eds.), *Race identity and representation in education* (pp. 268–279). New York: Routledge.

Peshkin, A., and Eisner, E. (Eds.) (1990). *Qualitative inquiry in education: The continuing debate.* NY: Teacher's College Press.

Rains, F. (1995). *Views from within: Women faculty of color in a research university.* Unpublished Dissertation. Bloominton, Indiana: Indiana University.

Reyes, M., de la Luz. (1992). Minority Faculty in Academe: Insiders' Perspective. Unpublished Report, Major University. President's Fund for Scholarship on Women and Minorities.

Reyes, M., de la Luz, and Halcón, J. J. (1988). Racism in academia: The old wolf revisited. *Harvard Educational Review*. Vol. 58 (3), 299–314.

———. (1991). Practices of the academy: Barriers to access for Chicano academics. In G. Altbach & K. Lomotey (Eds.), *The racial crisis in American higher education* (pp. 167–186). Albany, NY: State University of New York Press.

Ruíz, V. L. (1993). "Star struck": Acculturation, adolescence, and the Mexican American woman, 1920–1950. In A. de la Torre & B. M. Pesquera (Eds.), *Building with our hands* (pp. 109–129). Berkeley, CA: University of California Press.

Sánchez, R. (1990). The history of Chicanas: Proposal for a materialist perspective. In A. R. Del Castillo (Ed.), *Between borders: Essays on Mexicana/Chicana history* (pp. 1–30). Encino, CA: Floricanto Press.

Segura, D. A. (1993). Slipping through the cracks: Dilemmas in Chicana education. In A. de la Torre & B. M. Pesquera (Eds.), *Building with our hands* (pp. 199–216). Berkeley, CA: University of California Press.

Williams, P. J. (1991). *The alchemy of race and rights*. Cambridge, MA: Harvard University Press.

2

A WOMAN OUT OF CONTROL:
DECONSTRUCTING SEXISM AND RACISM
IN THE UNIVERSITY[1]

ROXANA NG

At the conclusion of a course I taught on minority groups and race relations, a male student brought a complaint against me, charging that I used the class as a platform for feminism. He claimed that as a "white male" he felt completely marginalized. This incident is not unique. In the first year I taught, a male student circulated a petition complaining to the administration that half the materials in my course on "cross-cultural education" contained references to women and gender relations. I was pleased that I had unwittingly achieved a balanced curriculum, but the student and the administration disagreed that this was desirable, and I was asked to change the contents for the remainder of the course (Ng 1991). On at least two other occasions, complaining (male) students have physically threatened me. Indeed, complaints of this kind about my courses' contents and my pedagogical methods have recurred during my ten years' teaching in the university.

The advice administrators and colleagues have given me concerning these incidents generally revolves around contents and styles: perhaps I can tone down my lectures somewhat; change to less controversial materials; acquire more teaching techniques; prepare better. (With reference to the course on "cross-cultural education," the administration suggested I use videos and let the students draw their own conclusions.) As I continued to analyze how gender, race, and class relations operate dynamically in interactional settings, however, I realized that what I experienced has less to do with my competence as a teacher than with who I am.

I am a feminist and a member of a racial minority. My scholarly work focuses on integrating analyses of gender with those of race and vice versa. My insistence on teaching ethnic and race relations with a feminist perspective, and on challenging Eurocentric assumptions in feminist theorizing, has consistently got me into trouble throughout my university teaching career.

Using a critical incident that occurred in one of the courses I teach, I want to draw attention, in this chapter, to how sexism and racism as *power dynamics* operate in everyday life to disempower feminist and other minority teachers. These dynamics, as we are discovering, affect how our formal authority is perceived and received by students, and, by extension, the degree to which we can be effective teachers, especially if our teaching challenges existing norms and forms of thinking and behavior in the classroom, in the university, and in society. (See, for example, in chronological order: Nielsen 1979; Heald 1989; Ng 1991, Hoodfar this volume.)

In their introduction to a special issue of the *Canadian Journal of Education* on feminist pedagogy, Briskin and Coulter (1992) identified three power axes in the classroom: between teacher and students; between students and teacher, especially women and teachers who are women of color; and among students (257). Here I examine an additional power axis: between the minority teacher and her/his colleague(s) in relation to the handling of student complaints. I show how gender and race relations interact to undermine the authority and credibility of minority[2] faculty members, and I deconstruct the complexity of sexism and racism as interlocking relations operating in a specific situation to maintain the subordination and marginalization of minority teachers. The complex and multifaceted character of the critical incident on which I base my analysis illustrates the pervasiveness of sexism and racism and raises questions about the assumption of neutrality and fairness when university administrators and other staff members are asked to adjudicate complaints.

Although my discussion focuses on the teacher's experience, I suggest that other minority staff and students encounter similar situations, in which their experiences are frequently exacerbated because of their relative powerlessness in the university hierarchy. My discussion therefore raises issues about existing equity measures and about how to make the university more inclusive when people enter and participate in it as *unequal* subjects. In the conclusion, I propose an antisexist, antiracist approach to educational matters.

The Incident

Although I use one incident instead of a variety of examples, I am not treating it as typical or generalizable of similar types of situations.

Following Dorothy Smith's (1987) method of problematizing the everyday world, my purpose here is to explicate the social organization that produced and reinforced my position as a gendered and racialized subject in the university. Here is how Smith puts it:

> If you've located an individual experience in the social relations which determine it, then although that individual experience might be idiosyncratic, the social relations are not idiosyncratic. [All experiences] are generated out of, and are aspects of the social relations of our time, of corporate capitalism. These social relations are discernible, although not fully present or explicable in the experiences of people whose lives, by reason of their membership in a capitalist society, are organized by capitalism. (quoted in Campbell n.d.)

The dynamics that partly shaped the interactions described in the incident involve relations of gender, race, and class. These relations, which I call "sexism" and "racism," are not peculiar to this incident but are rather relations that have developed over time in North America and elsewhere as groups of people have interacted. They have become systemic; that is, they are taken for granted and not ordinarily open to interrogation. In examining the incident, my intention is not to attribute blame or to identify victims, but to explicate the systemic character of sexism and racism as they are manifested in institutionalized interactional settings. I maintain that in so doing, we move away from treating these incidents as idiosyncratic, isolated "wrongdoing" perpetrated by a few individuals with attitudinal problems. Instead, we aim at a fundamental re-examination of the structures and relations of universities, which have marginalized and excluded certain groups of people historically and continue to do so despite equity measures implemented in the last ten years or so.

In this particular incident, a student (who identified himself as a "white,"[3] immigrant male) brought a complaint against me regarding a course I taught on minority groups and race relations, one of my primary teaching subjects in various universities since 1982.[4] In this kind of course, I always include discussions of women as a minority group and of race and gender dynamics. As I develop and refine these courses, I incorporate meditative and physical exercises, in addition to small group discussions, as a way to rupture standard modes of scholarly inquiry, which artificially separate body and soul from mind (Currie 1992). These courses are both stimulating and contentious, and although most students seem to enjoy them, I receive complaints every time I teach them. What I report here, then, is not unusual. It signals and pinpoints how approaches that deviate from the perceived norm of teaching can be threatening to and are resisted by students.

Interestingly, the student complainant attended classes for the first four or five weeks, then was absent until the third-last class. During that class, he became very agitated when, in our discussion on antiracist education, we included women's experiences of discrimination. At one point he became extremely angry, interrupted the discussion, and insisted on talking about something else. I interceded and brought the discussion back on track. I also pointed out that this kind of interruption and the ways male and female students reacted to it illustrated the gender dynamics we had been discussing for the past couple of weeks.[5]

The student did not come to the last two classes and complained to the administration about my teaching[6]—at a meeting I attended. During the meeting, he charged that the meditative and physical exercises I conducted (the reasons for which I had explained clearly) were completely inappropriate in a graduate class and that my course outline did not specify my feminist perspective. He further complained that the reading materials, which he had to pay for, were exclusively on feminism and not on race relations, which was untrue. I refused to enter into a debate about the reading materials and suggested that whether they were exclusively feminist was a matter open to examination. He then charged that I was using the course to advance a particular political agenda. He felt that in intercepting his disruption of the last class he had attended, I had marginalized him as a "white male."

Three times in the meeting he told the administrator I was "a woman out of control." When I pointed out that my perspective was very clearly disclosed during the first two classes (indeed, I encouraged students who did not like my approach to withdraw from the course), he turned to the administrator and said, "But I thought it was a phase she was going through. I didn't think that she would keep on like this when I returned after a five-week absence." He finally threatened to take me and the department to court for "false advertising." He told us that his girlfriend, a lawyer, was waiting outside.

During the entire meeting, the administrator maintained a neutral stance. At the end of the student's complaint, he asked the student what would have constituted an acceptable approach, given that we obviously had different perceptions about the course and how it was handled. The student replied that at a minimum he would have expected me to state my perspective explicitly in the course outline. I interjected at this point that if I was to make my perspective explicit, I would expect all my colleagues to do the same. The student replied, "But I don't have problems with other courses! I only have problems with yours." He added that he would ask "a gay" to make his perspective explicit also.[7]

After the student left, the administrator expressed sympathy but suggested I seriously consider the student's request. Apparently the issue of legality (students are getting more militant about the products we claim to deliver and the products we actually do deliver) had been raised at the senior level of the university administration. I declined consideration of the student's request about my course outline and suggested the matter should be raised formally in a faculty meeting.

Sexism and Racism as Systemic

Much work combatting sexism and racism in the education system has emphasized attitudinal and curricular changes (for instance, prejudice awareness/reduction workshops; measures against sexual and racial harassment; introducing other cultures into the curriculum, especially under the rubric of multicultural education). These changes, important and necessary though they are, are based on what Mohanty (1990) has identified as a "liberal pluralist" conception of diversity. Mohanty points out that "the race industry" and prejudice-reduction workshops in universities reduce historical and institutional inequality to an individualist and psychological level:

> In focusing on "the healing of past wounds" this approach also equates the positions of dominant and subordinate groups, erasing all power inequities and hierarchies. . . . [T]he location of the source of "oppression" and "change" in individuals suggests an elision between ideological and structural understandings of power and domination and individual, psychological understandings of power. (Mohanty 1990, 198)

Whereas the institution of women's studies has brought about a radical rethinking of gender relations in society, especially in Western societies, this cannot be said of curricular reform on race. Frequently, attempts in this area take an additive approach, adding an article (or two) to existing materials. There has been insufficient reconceptualization of how race matters in the structuring of social experiences inside and outside the academy. Even more insidious and stifling is the frequency with which, as Mohanty has pointed out, members of minority groups (both faculty and students) are tokenized when racism is treated as an individualistic and attitudinal property. That means that

> specific "differences" (of personality, posture, behavior, etc.) of one woman of color stand in for the difference of the whole collective, and a collective voice is assumed in place of an individual voice. . . . [T]his results in the reduction or averaging of Third World peoples [for example] in terms of individual personality characteristics . (Mohanty 1990, 194)

This approach overlooks the fact that power dynamics, based on one's race, gender, ability, and other characteristics, operate in mundane, taken-for-granted, and "commonsense" ways. Thus, although attitudinal changes and multicultural education (for example) are necessary points of departure for creating an inclusive university, they do not address the embeddedness of sexism and racism as routine operation in the university.

I want to go beyond treating sexism and racism as if they reside only in certain individuals, to examine their *systemic* properties. I begin with the premise that sexism and racism are two systems of oppression and inequality based on the ideology of the superiority of one race and/or gender over others. Thus, "white" European men, especially those of British and sometimes French descent, will typically see themselves as superior to women and to people with other ethnic and racial origins. Systems of ideas and practices have been developed to justify and support this notion of superiority. In Canada these ideas and practices originate in colonization by the British and the French.[8] Over time, ideas about the superiority and inferiority of different groups become accepted ways of thinking and being. Certain behaviors and modes of operation are eventually taken for granted; they become ways of excluding those who do not belong to the dominant group(s).

This understanding is derived from Gramsci's analysis of ideology and of how certain ideas become hegemonic and "commonsensical" over time. Commonsense thinking is uncritical, episodic, and disjointed, but it is also powerful because it is taken for granted (Gramsci 1971, 321–43). Once an idea becomes common sense, it is no longer questioned. In applying Gramsci's historical discussion to racism in contemporary British society, Stuart Hall observes: "[Ideologies] work most effectively when we are not aware that how we formulate and construct a statement about the world is underpinned by ideological premises; when our formulations seem to be simply descriptive statements about how things are (i.e. must be), or of what we can 'take-for-granted' (Hall, quoted in Lawrence 1982, 46).

Collin Leys[9] suggests that when an ideology becomes completely normalized, it is embedded in language. Some examples of common-sense statements are: "Blacks are good at sports but not at academic subjects"; "Women are nurturing"; "Unemployed people are lazy." Although these ideas may originally have been developed by the dominant group, they have become ways cohorts of individuals are "normally" thought of; they are popularly held beliefs.

These normalized ways of thinking (frequently referred to as "stereotyping") have real and profound consequences for people's lives. In her ethnographic research on how high school students are streamed into vocational programs, Jackson found that Chinese boys were advised to go into vocational-stream accounting courses which effectively curtailed their entrance into university. This advice was based on guidance counselors' perception that these boys were good at math but not so good with language. Similarly, Chinese girls were routinely streamed into secretarial programs (Jackson 1987).

Let me give another example from my own research as illustration. My analysis (Ng 1992) of immigration policy reveals that when a household applies to Canada for landed immigrant status, usually only one member of the household is granted "independent" status; the other members are granted "family class" status. This classification system usually accords the man/husband, seen to be the household head, independent status, and designates the woman/wife and children family class immigrants. This system is based on the Western notion of the "nuclear family" with the man/husband being the head of the household; it ignores the facts that other societies have different family structures and that the wife and adult children make essential contributions to the household economy. Furthermore, since family class immigrants are seen as dependents, they are not eligible for state assistance (such as training subsidies) available to the household head. In an immigrant household, then, often the husband can receive such assistance, while the wife is ineligible by virtue of her classification, rendering her dependent on and subordinate to her husband. This is an instance of how sexism operates objectively and routinely in Canadian institutions and illustrates what I mean by "systemic" sexism.

Sexism and racism are systemic in that, routinized in institutions, they have become ways of thinking about and treating groups of people unequally as if these ideas and treatments are "normal"; they are "common sense" and thus not open to interrogation. These ways of doing things keep certain individuals and groups in dominant and subordinate positions, producing the structural inequality we see both in the education system and in the workplace.

Institutionalized sexism and racism are enacted in "everyday" interactions (Smith 1987). In the example of immigration policy above, when an immigration officer classifies people according to the law, she is implicated in the reinforcement of sexism in relation to the immigrant woman regardless of her "personal" attitude toward the person so classified. The way counselors stream Chinese boys and girls into "terminal" vocational programs is another case in point. Acts of sexism and racism, then, go beyond personal intentions and attitudes precisely because they are embedded in institutions and because individuals have different (and at times multiple and contradictory) locations within institutions. Sexism and racism are *power relations* that have crystallized in organizational actions in which we are implicated by virtue of our membership in institutions. We are not and cannot be exempted from them. To see sexism and racism as systemic, then, is to understand that power dynamics (including forms of inclusion and exclusion) permeate the settings in which we live and work. Knowing how these dynamics work can thus be a first step in eradicating sexism and racism.

In analyzing the specific incident introduced at the outset of this chapter, I want to draw attention to the more general interactional dimension of power relations operating as forms of exclusion and marginalization by recognizing that, in addition to our structural positions as students, faculty, and staff in the academy, we are, at the same time, gendered and racialized subjects. Our race and gender, as well as other socially and ideologically constructed characteristics, shape how we see ourselves and how we are seen. They affect, enable, and disable how we negotiate our ways through the university system.

I use "socially and ideologically constructed" to refer to the identification of biological, sexual, and other characteristics as absolute differences. The term "races," for example, is used to denote the supposed differences, based on skin color, brain size, and physical features, and so on, of conventionally differentiated groups of people. These differences, treated as "natural" and therefore immutable, are then used to justify the domination of one group over another. In fact, the construction of different groups as "races" varies historically and across societies (see Miles 1989; Ng 1989; 1993).

To see members of the university community as gendered and racialized subjects is to understand and to acknowledge that we are not created equal. The social structure of inequality on the basis of class, gender, race, ability, and so on, which leaks into and becomes integral to everyday life in the academy, means that we do not participate in the academy as equals.

Deconstructing the Incident

The incident cited above raises four central issues. First, it raises the issue of neutrality, objectivity, and fairness in adjudicating complaints about teaching that challenges societal norms. When dealing with these and other complaints, university administrators and staff frequently take a "neutral" and "objective" stance in the interest of "fairness." To be neutral is to adopt a disinterested position, to presume that people are equal or the same, and to overlook the inequalities that people embody as a result of their unique biographies and their social locations. This neutral stance is the cornerstone of the Western intellectual tradition, established by men to engender and safeguard their privilege and institutionalized in the academy, it is important to keep in mind, at a time when the university was the exclusive domain of certain classes of men.

Feminist scholarship has challenged the notion of objectivity and demonstrated that so-called objective universal knowledge is constructed by men for men (see Smith 1974; Spender 1980). Adrienne Rich (1976) contends that the "detachment" and "disinterest" that constitute objectivity in scientific inquiry are the terms men apply to their own subjectivity.[10] Mary O'Brien (1981) calls this "malestream" thought. Susan Bordo (1987) reminds us that the exclusive preoccupation with reason in scholarly pursuit is a product of Cartesian thinking, which creates an artificial dualism, separating the mind/intellect and the body/emotion. This idea that "truth" exists independent of the social and physical location of the knower is carried over to the adjudication of disputes in the university. But Martin and Mohanty (1986) point out, "The claim to a lack of identity or positionality is itself based on privilege, on a refusal to accept responsibility for one's implication in actual historical or social relations, on a denial that positionalities exist or that they matter, the denial of one's own personal history and the claim to a total separation from it" (208).

It is interesting and revealing that, in spite of (or because of?) our unequal structural positions, the administrator in the incident I recounted attempted to treat the student's complaint on "equal footing" with my course design and pedagogical methods and that he did not see anything out of the ordinary about a student calling a faculty member "a woman out of control." (If he did think this was peculiar, he chose to ignore it, since he did not mention it either during or after the meeting.) This *pretense* of fairness was immensely disempowering to me as a minority teacher, especially since the student deliberately adopted a tone that denigrated me. As Patricia Williams says, "If faculty do not treat women as colleagues, then students will not treat women as members of the faculty" (1991, 63). This example shows precisely how sexism is normalized in men's, and frequently women's, collective consciousness. The attempt at fairness in this instance reveals how men collude with each other, intentionally or unwittingly, to restore the status quo of male dominance (see also Burstyn 1985).[11]

The second issue the incident raises is that of student resistance. This is a complex issue because students resist for different and contradictory reasons: they resist curriculum that challenges the status quo, especially if they identify with the status quo; they resist because certain materials make them realize and reflect on their own oppression; they resist because both the contents and the teacher represent authority in power structures that marginalize them (consider, for instance, the youths in Willis' [1977] and McClaren's [1989] studies); they resist for other social and psychological reasons (see Lewis 1990) too numerous to list here. Here I draw attention to the challenges we encounter in the classroom because of *who we are* as gendered and racialized subjects. Challenges to male teachers, as a colleague observed when I discussed the above incident in a faculty meeting, are frequently directed at course materials, and disagreements are played out as intellectual debates. In the case of a minority faculty member, both course materials and the teacher become targets. As a member of a racial minority and a woman, I have no authority despite my formal position. But it is not only my authority that is at stake here. The knowledge I embody and transmit is also suspect—I *am* a woman out of control. The sexism and racism in this case are based not only on the student's attitude toward minorities in general; they are also based on his attitude toward minorities in positions of authority whose knowledge and expertise are dubious. In reflecting on her own teaching about women in the third world, Homa Hoodfar (this volume) reports on similar experiences. In one course, for example, Hoodfar reports that her knowledge was finally accepted by the students only when it was corroborated by her white female colleague, who gave a guest lecture on the position of women in Uganda.

Third, this incident raises the issue of language. In his outbursts both in the class and in the meeting with the administrator, the student asserted that I was marginalizing him as a "white male." His language use is instructive: as marginalized groups are included and incorporated into the academy, the mainstream is appropriating and subverting feminist and other liberatory discourses for use against the very groups who developed these discourses in the first place. Statements such as "I don't feel safe [or comfortable]" and "I feel silenced [or marginalized]" are now widely used to describe individuals' experiences. This is another instance of the individualization and trivialization of collective experiences;[12] it erases the inequality among people due to race, gender, class, sexual preference, ability, and so on, and reduces systemic inequality to personal feelings. Liberatory language is thus normalized, so that the "white" male student, feeling threatened because his taken-for-granted way of thinking and acting is challenged, can assert that he is "silenced" or "marginalized."

Finally, as universities are increasingly geared toward a consumer and corporate model (Newson and Buchbinder 1988), they have become marketplaces rather than places for people to interrogate existing knowledges and to create new ones. Although I believe that there must be accountability in teaching, and I recognize that students can be and have been shortchanged, I also know, having taught in universities for the last ten years, that student complaints are launched and threats of legal action are evoked in very specific situations: usually when a student is threatened by knowledges that rupture her commonsense understanding of the world. Threats of legality are intended to restore the status quo.[13] In the specific incident discussed above, the legal threat was a tactically clever move on the part of the student, and it bared his class position and his recognition that what was at issue here was power, which he knew he had as a white male and which he intended to use. Raising the possible legal consequences of my pedagogy captured the administrator's attention and summoned[14] him in his role as an administrator rather than as my colleague. That the student threatened legal action and that he received a neutral, if not sympathetic, hearing resulted from his subject position as a "white," articulate male who could invoke the law on his side.

Against the Grain: Combatting Sexism and Racism in the University

To conclude, I want to explore how we may begin to combat sexism and racism in the university in light of my preceding conceptualization and analysis. I recommend that we try to think and act "against the grain"[15] in handling various kinds of pedagogical situations. To act against the grain requires one first to recognize that—and how—routinized courses of action and interactions within the university are imbued with unequal power distributions which produce and reinforce various forms of marginalization and exclusion. Thus, a commitment to redress these power relations involves interventions and actions that may appear "counter-intuitive."[16] We need to rupture ways university business and interactions are "normally" conducted.

In introducing the notion of working against the grain, obviously I am speaking not to those interested in preserving the status quo, but to the increasing numbers of groups and individuals who wish to make the university more inclusive of previously marginalized and disadvantaged groups (recognizing that they by no means represent a monolithic interest or position).

To work against the grain is to recognize that education is not neutral; it is contested. Mohanty (1990) points out that "education represents both a struggle for meaning and a struggle over power relations. [It is] a central terrain where power and politics operate out of the lived culture of individuals and groups situated in asymmetrical social and political positions" (184). We must develop a critical awareness of the power dynamics operating in institutional relations and of the fact that people participate in institutions as unequal subjects. To this end we must take an antisexist and antiracist approach to understanding and acting upon institutional relations, rather than overlooking the embeddedness of gender, race, class, and other forms of inequality that shape our interactions.

In her exploration of feminist pedagogy, Linda Briskin makes a clear distinction between nonsexist and antisexist education, a distinction which is critical to our understanding here. She asserts that nonsexism is an approach which attempts to neutralize sexual inequality by pretending that gender can be made irrelevant in the classroom (Briskin 1990a; 1990b). Thus, for instance, neither asserting that male and female students should have equal time to speak nor giving them equal time adequately rectifies the endemic problem of sexism in the classroom. One of Briskin's students reported that in her political science tutorials, when a male student spoke, everyone paid attention, but when a female student spoke, the class acted as if no one was speaking (Briskin 1990a, 13). Neutrality conceals the unequal distribution of power.

An antisexist and antiracist approach would acknowledge explicitly that we are all gendered, racialized, and differently constructed subjects who do not interact as equals. This goes beyond formulating sexism and racism in individualist terms and treating them as ("flawed") personal attitudes. Terry Wolverton (1983) discovered the difference between nonracism and antiracism in her consciousness-raising attempt: "I had confused the act of trying to appear not to be racist with actively working to eliminate racism. Trying to appear not racist had made me deny my racism, and therefore exclude the possibility of change" (191). Being antisexist and antiracist means seeing sexism and racism as systemic and interpersonal (rather than individual) and combatting sexism and racism collectively, not just personally (as if somehow a person could cleanse himself of sexism and racism).

The first thing we must do, regardless of whether we belong to minority groups, is to break the conspiracy of silence that has ensured the perpetuation of sexism, racism, and other forms of marginalization and exclusion in the university. Patricia Williams' closing remark in her article "Blockbusting the Canon" (1991) is worth quoting at length here:

> It's great to turn the other cheek in the face of fighting words; it's probably even wise to run. But it's not a great way to maintain authority in the classroom. . . . "[J]ust ignoring" verbal challenges from my law students is a good way to deliver myself into the category of the utterly powerless. If, moreover, my white or male colleagues pursue the same path (student insult, embarrassed pause, the teacher keeps on teaching as though nothing had happened), we have collectively created that peculiar institutional silence that is known as a moral vacuum. (63)

Taking an antisexist and antiracist approach means we cannot be complacent as individual teachers or as members of the different collectivities to which we belong (for instance, on committees and in faculty associations). We must speak out against normalized courses of action that maintain existing inequality, although this may alienate us from those in power as well as those close to us. We must actively support our minority colleagues in their teaching, administrative, and other responsibilities and consciously open up spaces for previously silenced or marginalized voices to be heard. We must create spaces for students to interrogate existing paradigms and to explore alternative ones and support them in other endeavors. We must also constantly interrogate our own taken-for-granted ways of acting, thinking, and being in the world.

To explore what these principles may mean in concrete action, I return to the critical incident. I am not suggesting that administrators and staff handling and adjudicating disputes should categorically take the side of "the minority teacher/student." However, I am suggesting that the assessment of any situation should take account of people's varying subject positions within and outside the university. In this case, although the student's complaint was legitimate in that he felt uncomfortable with the materials and my instructions, his behaviour in class and in the meeting was not. It was explicitly sexist and implicitly racist; it was aimed at undermining my authority and expertise.

Administratively, to resolve such a dispute, the student could be advised to withdraw from courses with which he has problems rather than waiting until the end of the term. An appropriate administrative response could be to arrange for the student to withdraw from the course, even though the official deadline had passed (which was actually what this student wanted and proceeded to do).

Pedagogically, the student's complaint, with its sexist, racist, and homophobic subtext, presents an excellent opportunity for challenging the assumptions in his thinking and for educating him about academic freedom. This kind of situation is a valuable pedagogical moment that can be used to engage students in what we teach in a formal classroom setting. To work against the grain as an educator is to close the perceived gap between the formal and the "hidden" curriculum and to use any opportunity we can to challenge normalized and normalizing forms of behavior and thinking.[17]

The concept of academic freedom could be deployed in this instance to educate the student about the nature of university education and about his consumer-oriented mentality toward university education; university education is intended to expose students to a range of perspectives and experiences, not to confirm and/or reinforce their limited views of the world. Taking Fernando's and his colleagues' (Fernando, Hartley, Nowak, and Swinehart 1990) definition of the role of an intellectual and an academic to be that of a social critic trained to challenge dogma and to express critical views (6), it can be argued that a fundamental aspect of our freedom and responsibility as academics is to expose the political and contested nature of education.[18]

Finally, I want briefly to take up the issue of safety and comfort, because these words have become currency in debates around discourses and practices that challenge existing modes of thinking and working. Understanding oppression and doing antiracist work is by definition unsafe and uncomfortable, because both involve a serious (and frequently threatening) effort to interrogate our privilege as well as our powerlessness.[19] To speak of safety and comfort is to speak from a position of privilege, relative though it may be. For those who have existed too long on the margins, life has never been safe or comfortable. Understanding and eliminating oppression and inequality oblige us to examine our relative privilege, to move out of our internalized positions as victims, to take control over our lives, and to take responsibility for change. Such an undertaking is by definition risky and therefore requires commitment to a different vision of society than that which we now take for granted.

Teaching and learning against the grain is not easy, comfortable, or safe. It is protracted, difficult, uncomfortable, painful, and risky. It involves struggles with our colleagues and our students, as well as within ourselves. It is, in short, a challenge, but it is one we ought no longer to have to take up alone, unsupported by the institutions within which we conduct our professional lives.

Notes

1. This article is based on my presentation on a panel entitled Racism, Sexism and Homophobia: Some Threats to Inclusivity and Academic Freedom in the University, at the OCUFA (Ontario Confederation of University Faculty Associations) Status of Women's Conference on Developing Strategies for the Inclusive University, 5–6 February 1993, in Toronto. The other panel members were Johann St. Lewis and David Rayside. Thanks are due Suzanne de Castell, David Bray, Linda Briskin, Roger Simon, and Rebecca Coulter for comments on earlier drafts of this article. Special thanks to Linda Briskin for the title.

2. I use the term *minority* in the standard sociological sense to refer to people who are relatively powerless in a society. Thus, even though women are numerically the majority, they are a "minority" in terms of power and influence. Similarly, ethnic and racial minorities, especially nonwhites, constitute a minority in this society. To avoid repetition, I use the term *minority* to refer *both* to women and to ethnic/racial minorities.

3. I use the term "white" in quotation marks to emphasize that "white," similar to "colored," is a socially and ideologically constructed term. Its designation changes historically according to the dominant-subordinate relations in a given society. I use "white" to refer to groups who have taken part in Canada's colonization and who are perceived to be or who perceive themselves to be part of the dominant groups. In this case, the student referred to himself as a "white male"; his original language, however, was not English. He also told the class he was an immigrant and had been discriminated against in relation to his legal status; but in the course he did not draw parallels between his own marginality as an immigrant and the experiences of other marginalized groups.

4. I am deliberately vague about details of the course to protect the identity of individuals involved. I want to emphasize that my intent is not to personalize the story, but to highlight the embeddedness of gender and racial dynamics in our experiences.

5. It was clear that this student had upset everyone in the class. Some students became angry. Some, especially the younger female students, immediately took on a nurturing role (see Lewis 1990), attempting to protect him

from other students' anger and to painstakingly explain to him the parallels between women's subordination and the subordination of ethnic and racial minorities. When the only other male student in the class spoke up and confronted him about his sexism, he at last took notice, and, in my view, took on the male student as an equal (as opposed to a bunch of hysterical women trying to overwhelm him). By this time the discussion had become a tennis match between the two men, so, using materials we read in the course, I pointed out the gender dynamics occurring in our midst.

6. In highlighting the focus of this article, I have to omit details that detract from the main theme(s). What brought this student's complaint to the administration was actually more complicated. Briefly, in addition to resenting what had occurred in the last class he had attended, the student was upset that I had asked him to make up, by means of written work, the work the class had done in his absence (e.g., small group discussions, debates, and writing exercises). He felt I was being unjust because his absence was due to medical reasons (which I accepted), but I insisted on his making up the work because of the length of his absence. He felt I was discriminating against him because I asked him to do "extra" work not mentioned in the course outline (which specifically stated that attendance, though ungraded, was required). This was unacceptable to him, hence his request for mediation. In the meeting, however, he completely bypassed the original issue and instead criticized the course.

7. This comment, made spontaneously, illustrates both the normalization of heterosexism and the overlapping character of forms of subordination.

8. This is a cursory and simplistic presentation of the complex history of Canada's colonial past. Space and time prevent a fuller exploration and explication of this topic, except to say that although I recognize the subordination of French-speaking peoples, I want to note the two key colonizers of Canada.

9. Special lecture by Collin Leys organized by Tuula Lindholm for a Gramsci study group on March 21, 1993.

10. For an excellent discussion of objective versus subjective knowledge and the constitution of objectivity, see Currie (1992).

11. The myth of objectivity of school knowledge has also been challenged by those writing about the hidden curriculum. For a useful summary, see Giroux (1981).

12. See also Mohanty (1990, 193–96) who raises an important critique of the use of the term *experience* in liberatory discourses which becomes individualized in the university.

13. I base this claim on my own experience and on informal conversations with minority faculty over the past ten years of my university teaching

career. Given the corporatization and rise of politically correct movements in universities, I think this area is worthy of further investigation.

14. I borrow this term from Susan Heald's analysis of state formation (Heald 1990, 149). To summon is to call forth or to command a particular aspect of our multidimensional and contradictory identity.

15. Various writers have used this term—see Cochran-Smith (1991), Ng (1991), and Simon (1992). Although these authors attach slightly different significance and meaning to the term, it generally denotes educational practices aimed at instilling critical perspectives and consciousness in students in the classroom. I suggest it should be extended to our work in other settings.

16. The term *counter-intuitive* is borrowed from Linda Briskin, who used it in a workshop, Negotiating Power in the Inclusive Classroom, we co-facilitated for the Toronto Board of Education on January 21, 1993. Similar to being "against the grain," to be counter-intuitive is to interrogate what we take for granted as the "natural" ways of doing things.

17. Realistically, of course, we cannot and do not seize *every* moment presented to us; however, critical pedagogical moments arise more often than we "normally" think of in our work, and they can be deployed as consciousness-raising opportunities for ourselves and others.

18. The meaning of academic freedom, like the role of education itself, is a topic of heated debates. I will not elaborate on this subject here except to say that the discussion in Fernando and others (1990), together with the literature on critical pedagogy, can be used to reconceptualize the academic freedom debate and related notions of "objectivity" and "fairness."

19. I thank the students in my advanced seminar Sexism, Racism, and Colonialism: Pedagogical Implications (spring 1993) for helping me clarify my own thinking on this subject.

References

Bordo, S. (1987). *The flight to objectivity: Essays on cartesianism and culture.* Albany: State University of New York Press.

Briskin, L. (1990a). *Feminist pedagogy: Teaching and learning liberation* (Feminist Perspectives, No. 19). Ottawa: Canadian Research Institute for the Advancement of Women.

————. (1990b). Gender in the classroom. *CORE [Newsletter of the Centre for Support of Teaching, York University]*, 1(1), 2–3.

Briskin, L., and Coulter, R. P. (1992). Feminist pedagogy: Challenging the normative. *Canadian Journal of Education, 17*, 247–263.

Burstyn, V. (1985). Masculine dominance and the state. In V. Burstyn & D. E. Smith, *Women, class, family and the state* (pp. 45–89). Toronto: Garamond Press.

Campbell, M. (n. d.). *An experimental research practicum based on the Wollstonecraft Research Group.* Unpublished manuscript, Ontario Institute for Studies in Education, Department of Sociology, Toronto.

Cochran-Smith, M. (1991). Learning to teach against the grain. *Harvard Educational Review, 61,* 279–310.

Currie, D. H. (1992). Subject-ivity in the classroom: Feminism meets academe. *Canadian Journal of Education, 17,* 341–364.

Fernando, L., Hartley, N., Nowak, M., and Swinehart, T. (1990). *Academic freedom 1990: A human rights report.* London: Zed Books, with World University Service, Geneva.

Giroux, H. (1981). Schooling and the myth of objectivity: Stalking the politics of the hidden curriculum. *McGill Journal of Education, 16,* 282–304.

Gramsci, A. (1971). *Selections from the prison notebooks* (Q. Hoare & G. Nowell Smith, Eds. and Trans.). New York: International Publishers.

Heald, S. (1989). The madwoman out of the attic: Feminist teaching in the margin. *Resources for Feminist Research, 18*(4), 22–26.

———. (1990). "Making democracy practical": Voluntarism and hob creation. In R. Ng, G. Walker, & J. Muller (Eds.), *Community organization and the Canadian state* (pp. 147–164). Toronto: Garamond Press.

Jackson, N. (1987). Ethnicity and vocational choice. In J. Young (Ed.), *Breaking the mosaic: Ethnic identities in Canadian schooling* (pp. 165–182). Toronto: Garamond Press.

Lawrence, E. (1982). Just plain common sense: The "roots" of racism. In *The Empire strikes back: Race and racism in 70s Britain* (pp. 42–94). Birmingham: University of Birmingham, Centre for Contemporary Cultural Studies.

Lewis, M. (1990). Interrupting patriarchy: Politics, resistance, and transformation in the feminist classroom. *Harvard Educational Review, 60,* 467–488.

Martin, B., and Mohanty, C. T. (1986). Feminist politics: What's home got to do with it? In T. de Lauretis (Ed.), *Feminist studies/critical studies* (pp. 191–212). Bloomington: Indiana University Press.

McClaren, P. (1989). *Life in schools.* Toronto: Irwin Publishing.

Miles, R. (1989). *Racism.* London: Routledge.

Mohanty, C. T. (1990). On race and voice: Challenges for liberal education in the 1990s. *Cultural Critique, 14,* 179–208.

Newson, J., and Buchbinder, H. (1988). *The university means business: Universities, corporation and academic work.* Toronto: Garamond Press.

Nielsen, L. L. (1979). Sexism and self-healing in the university. *Harvard Educational Review, 49,* 467–476.

Ng, R. (1989). Sexism, racism, and Canadian nationalism. In J. Vorst et al. (Eds.), *Race, class, gender: Bonds and barriers* (pp. 10–25). Toronto: Between the Lines Press, with the Society for Socialist Studies.

———. (1991). Teaching against the grain: Contradictions for the minority teacher. In J. S. Gaskell & A. T. McLaren (Eds.), *Women and education* (2nd ed.) (pp. 99–115). Calgary: Detselig Enterprises.

———. (1992). Managing female immigration: A case of institutional sexism and racism. *Canadian Woman Studies, 12,* 20–23.

———. (1993). Racism, sexism, and nation building in Canada. In C. McCarthy & W. Crichlow (Eds.), *Race, identity, and representation in education* (pp. 50–59). New York: Routledge.

O'Brien, M. (1981). *The politics of reproduction.* London: Routledge and Kegan Paul.

Rich, A. (1976). Women's studies: Renaissance or revolution? *Women's Studies, 3*(2), 35–47.

Simon, R. L. (1992). *Teaching against the grain: Texts for a pedagogy of possibility.* Toronto: Ontario Institute for Studies in Education.

Smith, D. E. (1974). Women's perspective as a radical critique of sociology. *Sociological Inquiry, 44,* 7–13.

———. (1987). *The everyday world as problematic: A feminist sociology.* Toronto: University of Toronto Press.

Spender, D. (1980). *Man made language* (2nd ed.). London: Routledge & Kegan Paul.

Williams, P. J. (1991, September/October). Blockbusting the canon. *Ms., 11*(2), 59–63.

Willis, P. (1977). *Learning to labour: How working class kids get working class jobs.* New York: Columbia University Press.

Wolverton, T. (1983). Unlearning complicity, remembering resistance: White women's anti-racism education. In C. Bunch & S. Pollack (Eds.), *Learning our way: Essays in feminist education* (pp. 187–199). Trumansburg, NY: The Crossing Press.

3

QUE<E>RYING PEDAGOGY:
TEACHING UN/POPULAR CULTURES

KATHLEEN MARTINDALE[1]

We have all the answers, it is the questions we do not know.

—Shoshana Felman and Dori Laub,
Testimony: Crises of Witnessing in
Literature, Psychoanalysis, and History

If institutionalization is the answer for lesbian and gay studies in North American universities, what is the question?

I teach women's studies and lesbian studies courses in the largest women's studies program in what is rumored to be the most politically progressive university in Canada. Faculty at my large urban university front radical magazines, go to all the right—that is, left—demonstrations, and there are so many socialist feminists that they used to have monthly dinners until the group got so large they could not find a restaurant big enough to seat them all. The student body is the most multiethnic in the country, and groups and coalitions of people of color, feminists, gays, lesbians, bisexuals, and other minorities are vocal and visible. Nonetheless, based on my teaching experiences and research about the extent of homophobia in women's studies classes (Martindale 1992), my sense is that my university is as predictably homophobic as other otherwise progressive North American university environments. Until very recently, most of the numerous lesbian and gay faculty have been too scared to come out and there have been no explicitly labelled gay and lesbian studies courses; in the spring of 1994, however, students occupied the president's office and demanded an end to homophobia on campus and the introduction of a gay and lesbian studies program.

I mention these facts of my cultural geography because institutional setting plays a crucial but unattended and surprisingly reductionist role in lesbian and gay studies literature in constructing the horizon of expectations about its pedagogical possibilities. While a reader of the literature may deduce that disciplinary, discursive, and political considerations—for example investments or disinvestments in feminism, antiracism, poststructuralism, and a reform studies model—factor strongly in how the field is being constructed, questions have yet to be asked about what we hope to learn and teach differently (and better) if or when institutionalization comes.

Instead of asking questions about how theoretical developments and controversies such as the one over universalizing or minoritizing approaches might inform and affect pedagogical practices, most contributors to the literature so far are fixating on giving answers about whether or not to institutionalize. The assumption seems to be that if only we had the right institutional configuration, whether it is the more modest notion of adding a course to an established curriculum or the more grandiose dream of free-standing, degree-granting programs, we could get beyond homophobia and the way would be clear to do the interesting theoretical work. This focus on institutionalization postpones and displaces questions about what we want lesbian and gay studies to do and whether the field, if it is a field, should be framed as a discourse about minorities designed to promote tolerance and understanding in the general public or as a discourse that unsettles everyone's assumptions about those very categories and who or what is implicated in them.

If institutionalization is the solution, what is the problem? According to most accounts, on the East and West coasts of the United States, in the elite and therefore best progressive schools, liberal attitudes to sexual minorities prevail, lesbian and gay studies are being institutionalized by the best and the brightest theorists, and everything is jake. Everywhere else, that is, in the cultural hinterlands where most of us live and work, homophobia prevails, and theories and practices are a generation or so out of date. If you are not lucky enough to be at Santa Cruz or Princeton, then opportunities for antihomophobic education seem limited.

This fantasy, a form of California Dreamin', overlooks the work that pedagogy does. It also plays down the possibilities that antihomophobic transformation might occur without benefit of freestanding gay and lesbian studies programs' prestigious centers, and the presence of theoretical superstars who teach to the converted. It overlooks the quietly subversive work that a generation of students and teachers has accomplished by raising impertinent questions in the classroom, by slyly getting texts and essay topics on the syllabus, and by humbly learning from their theoretical and pedagogical disasters how to teach and learn about gay and lesbian issues. The fantasy that looks only toward benign institutional change from the top down and intellectual legitimation by a theoretical vanguard overlooks the cognitive and political shifts that can occur in everyday though highly charged encounters between students and teachers, and in seemingly unlikely institutional settings, such as composition classes taught by straight teaching assistants at Indiana University (Berg et al. 1994).

First things first. Even in progressive institutions and where conditions for "doing queer theory" are somewhat favorable, homophobia rules the classroom and instructors must expect to encounter it. When I talk about gay and lesbian issues in my women's and gender studies classes, I am likely to be met with walkouts, uncomfortable silences, occasional boos and hisses, and questions on the order of the one Sarah Schulman's (1984) lesbian speaker has to field in *The Sophie Horowitz Story*: "Do you do it with animals?" (66). As much as I love animals, I would prefer not to engage with the usual homophobic ignorance and install myself in the pedagogical fantasy I call "Beyond Antihomophobia 101." There, my students ask questions a little bit more like the ones I read in the literature about the disciplining of gay and lesbian studies, like the ones Ed Cohen (1991) poses:

> If we accept the assessment that this genealogical coincidence between "sexuality" and "identity" is the effect of a "modern" Western regime of power which implicates human bodies in and as the sites of its discursive (re)production, then how are we to understand the consequences of a politics that grounds itself in/on a "sexual identity"? Or, in other words, to the extent that "sexuality" and "identity" are both predicated upon a constellation of power relations that naturalize their own historical contingency by making themselves knowable as fixed qualities of somatic differentiation, what limitations do the political articulations of "sexual identity" unwittingly import? (81)

How do I get there from here? In my pedagogical fantasy, there is no name-calling or stoney silences and students do not giggle, cover their eyes, or walk out when I show films about lesbians and gays. They have got a language to talk about sexuality; they are not afraid to display an interest by showing up for the lecture on lesbian love poetry or Jeffrey Weeks in about the same numbers as the ones on other subjects. They do not normalize heterosexuality and pathologize everything else, and the English majors talk about gay and lesbian texts in our small discussion groups in the same detached and critically informed way they consider the other material on the syllabus. Right. Ed Cohen, Michael Warner, and others—will you please tell me, as I await (and even work for) the coming of a fully funded, free-standing gay and lesbian studies program, how to get myself and my students beyond antihomophobia 101?

The routine traumas I experience when I teach gay and lesbian subject matter in my progressive institution make the fantasy very attractive. The uneven developments which obtain between the sophistication of poststructuralist queer theory and the crude, rude, and raw realities of my classrooms make me envious and frustrated. Because I have not been able to teach gay and lesbian studies without "the unleashing of unpopular things" (Britzman 1991), I am compelled to theorize about my own failures and to learn from and speculate about those of others. This chapter attempts to bring questions of theory and practice together by doing a symptomatic reading of scenes of pedagogical failure taken from accounts of teaching gay and lesbian material. My intent is not so much to praise or blame teachers or students as it is to uncover the cognitive work that needs to be done and can be done to get beyond antihomophobia 101 with or without benefit of institutionalization.

Though there are many contenders in this category, Richard Mohr's (1988) rebarbative yet acutely observant and personally unsparing account of his first experience, in 1981, of teaching a gay issues course within the philosophy department at the University of Illinois is the most disturbing one in the literature. Entitled "Gay Studies in the Big Ten: A Survivor's Manual," it is not entirely clear who or what survived this trauma or what, if anything, Mohr learned from the experience or did differently in his many subsequent offerings of gay studies courses.

Mohr's account makes for uncomfortable reading, because it is framed by profoundly cynical attitudes to American postsecondary education, especially to the hope that reform studies might inspire political transformation. If my discussion of his discussion seems scathing, I would stress that Mohr's preferred pedagogical persona is that of the curmudgeon, not a gay Mr. Chips. One of my favorite essays by him begins, "I hate students. They are not the death of spirit, they are its malaria" ("The Ethics of Students and the Teaching of Ethics: A Lecturing" 1988, 293). Unlike most contributors to gay and lesbian studies, Mohr rejects the more optimistic views of students' capacities for learning that are generally favored by feminist and other progressive pedagogies. No Paulo Freire he, both Mohr and his class come off rather badly. Unlike much of the writing in this genre, there is no note of triumph, or self-congratulation, and although in a coda he mentions that as a result of his course, one "uptight suburban" woman set up a support group for gay runaways, he seems quite surprised by this development. There are none of the usual paeans to students who took risks and struggled to unlearn their homophobia.

Based on his own self-presentation, Mohr appears an incompetent and insensitive teacher and his students dim-witted homophobes. He runs a teacher-centered classroom, engages in pseudo-Socratic dialogue with students—a class of people he despises—and he regards the university neither as a knowledge factory nor as a consciousness-raising group, but as a four-year cotillion designed primarily to marry off the white middle class to each other (1988, 300). Mohr's cynical yet unfashionable theoretical and pedagogical beliefs make it easier to read his account against the grain, so that the pedagogical chaos he describes can be instructive and provocative rather than merely sympathized with, as in other accounts of homophobia in the classroom

Mohr's class *could* be read as a guide of what *not* to do, but because he does not explicitly reflect on the theoretical understandings that guide his pedagogical practices, he does not state how he connects his theories about sexual and other identities—they are very fixed—with the process of knowledge production. In a short intersession class composed, according to a rather remarkable system of classification, of one-third white suburban females, one-third black football players, and less than one-third gay students (one was lesbian; none of the gays as racially identified), he seems to have managed to offend and alienate everyone.

In his first class, Mohr showed a documentary film which it seemed he thought would get the work of consciousness raising over with. He opened discussion by asking what in the film had made anyone uncomfortable, thereby guaranteeing not only that homophobic responses would be produced but that they would *frame* this crucial initial discussion, and, in many ways, the entire course. The straight women said it "made them sick." In trying to defend gay rights by making an analogy with the black civil rights struggle, Mohr unleashed a wave of crude homophobic slurs and then nearly incited a race riot. The first day ended, writes Mohr, with "everyone yelling and the class . . . on the verge of out-of-control" (281). In his "most successful class" at the end of the course, he asked insulting questions of an invited lesbian separatist academic, who told him to "fuck off" because he was "too stupid to understand," which led the whole class to break into spontaneous applause (290).

Though much of what characterized this class, such as the teacher's puzzled and disappointed expectation that most of the class would be gay and literate about gay cultures, and the disastrous and almost violent response to the first showing of a film, are routine occurrences in accounts of lesbian and gay studies, Mohr, also typically, was unprepared for what transpired. His account of this historic class from hell ends with a flat and sardonic citation of his "triumph" over his cultural geography: "And so gay studies came to this sleepy Republican university in a little Republican town in the tired Republican state of Illinois" (290).

Sometimes, more by virtue of what did not take place or failed to happen, even an account like Mohr's can suggest how to carry out a theoretical practice that would get beyond the normalizing and pathologizing pedagogies framed by homophobia. These accounts show how teachers, given a forced opportunity to learn from classroom debacles, might rethink their pedagogical practices to make them more consistent not only with general poststructuralist claims about the liberatory possibilities of unfixing identities and increasing identifications, but also, more specifically with persuasive and powerful critiques of the ways heteronormativity constricts *everyone's* capacity to learn.

In the growing genre of writing about the disciplining of gay and lesbian studies, most of the literature consists of experiential narratives about how lesbians and gays survive as teachers and students (Garber 1994). Equally popular are "how to" accounts of setting up activist groups and coalitions, centers, workshops, and courses (Minton 1992). These descriptions and prescriptions are mainly tales of individual and institutional heroism or villainy.

While unhappy stories of education outnumber the happy stories in this only seemingly new outpost of the educational literature (which actually goes back at least as far as Plato's "Apology"), the assumption underlying and impelling this writing is that if only we could get the right institutional setting (it must exist somewhere, probably in California, in or around San Francisco), the right teachers (gay and out) and the right students (ditto), the right curriculum (theoretically and politically correct), then the hopes that gay and lesbian studies evoke, as have all the other older but not nearly so chic reform disciplines, will be realized. It is sometimes hard to believe that Michael Warner's (1992) subtitle— "An Army of Theorists Cannot Fail"—is entirely ironic ("From Queer to Eternity: An Army of Theorists Cannot Fail"). Let us then reread some unhappy stories about teaching gay and lesbian studies. Let us question the logic underlying these too confident assumptions about what might be required to "get it right." And let us suggest that what is routinely ignored in them (along with serious discussion of the political climate in which we teach) is the process by which knowledge is produced, that is to say, pedagogy itself.

Not surprisingly, given an orientation toward the praising or blaming of heroic or villainous individuals and the reliance on embattled but eventually triumphant liberal humanist common sense, what is greatly underrepresented in the literature so far is serious discussion about the pedagogies—the processes by which learners come to know and teachers show how they learn—that inform these practices. By pedagogy, I do not so much mean checklists, "how to's," guidelines, and other narratives about techniques and methodologies, although these can be useful, but analyses of how knowledges are produced and resisted.

While there is already an abundance of literature in gay and lesbian studies about how to run an antihomophobia workshop, how to come out to students, how students can organize for lesbian and gay studies, and how to set up and devise curricula for courses in a variety of disciplines and institutional settings, very little has been written about the philosophies of teaching that presumably inform these activities or about their historical and ideological relationship to other and older pedagogies, such as feminist and critical pedagogies, from which they have arisen as critiques (Obear, n.d.; Garber 1994). Only a few authors have taken up closely related issues, such as the differing theoretical paradigms that have informed gay and lesbian studies (Escoffier 1992); or the question of what lesbian and gay studies might learn from the successes and failures of women's studies and other ethnic studies (Yingling 1991); or the threats that a new theoretical and largely white male elite's drive to institutionalize *gay and* lesbian studies will erase the intellectual and political accomplishments of a generation of women working in feminist and lesbian studies (Zita 1994). This situation is as remarkable, it seems to me, as it is contradictory, occurring as it does at a time of crucial theoretical shifts in understanding about the relationships among sexuality, identity, and knowledge.

While the influential writing of Eve Kosofsky Sedgwick has forced a rethinking in many quarters of the theoretical and political limitations of the so-called "minoritizing" approach to the study of hetero/homosexualities, the consequences for pedagogical practices of the theoretical shift toward universalizing discourses and proliferating sexualities have hardly been seriously addressed (Sedgwick 1990; Britzman 1995). Among the more obvious and more potentially encouraging pedagogical shifts in understanding and practice that readings of Sedgwick's work supports are the realizations that everyone has a stake in gay and lesbian studies and that anyone can and should teach and learn from a perspective that is antihomophobic. Far less obvious and potentially more disturbing insights suggest that commonsense assumptions about the work of education no longer obtain; chief among them, and most cherished perhaps, the "domino effect," that ignorance is a passive lack that can be replaced with knowledge, which will in turn replace hatred with tolerance (Sedgwick learned this from Felman 1982, 1987, who learned it from Lacan; Britzman draws out the implications from all of the above, 1995).

In spite of these theoretical shifts in an understanding of what could constitute gay and lesbian studies, most of the published narratives and how- to accounts treat teaching and learning about gays and lesbians as more or less "special events." This is most apparent and most disturbing in the many accounts of attempts to add or otherwise integrate lesbian material into women's studies classes (Frye 1982; Martindale 1992; Griffin 1992). Furthermore, the social situation in which the teaching and learning occurs does not lend itself to a "universalizing" framework. That is, the occasion is almost always external or at best peripheral to the everyday business of the university or the classroom. Outside agitators, whether students or professors, experts from somewhere else, guinea pigs from the gay and lesbian hotline, or trained facilitators are brought in to do the antihomophobia workshop, the guest lecture, "the" lesbian lecture in a women's studies course, the segment of a gender studies, ethnic studies, or other course devoted to gay and lesbian themes.

The entire course devoted to gay and lesbian studies (whatever that might mean) and named as such in the calendar is still rather uncommon at the undergraduate level. There are probably no more of them in all of North America than one could count on one's fingers and toes (my attempts to tabulate them via various gay and lesbian and women's studies electronic billboards came up with rumours that there was a class or a program somewhere (else) rather than much in the way of hard facts). Though the grapevine and other hype machines suggest otherwise, the institutionalization of gay and lesbian studies is as yet mainly a matter of smoke and mirrors.

For example, the Toronto Centre for Lesbian and Gay Studies, an entity often cited in the literature, and with which I have been involved, has—by design—no university attachments, offers no courses, let alone degree-granting programs, and employs no teachers. The center, at the insistence of its visionary-activist founder, Michael Lynch, decided that it could do the most advanced work by locating itself outside academic institutions. It publishes a newsletter (irregularly), offers lectures on "popular" and accessible topics (occasionally), and awards small prizes in memory of Michael Lynch (pin money). Another high visibility/low budget enterprise run by another visionary-activist, Martin Duberman, is the Center for Lesbian and Gay Studies at the City University of New York (CLAGS). CLAGS puts on regular high-profile conferences and seminars, a newsletter, and is the recipient of a Rockefeller grant which will provide one year's support for new scholars for the next few years. That's it; the center has a tiny budget, can make no appointments of its own, and runs no free-standing academic program.

In terms of attaining secure, permanent institutional sites, with all the academic paraphernalia of secretaries, line budgets, teaching positions, and administrators, gay and lesbian studies is a generation behind women's studies and other ethnic studies and is struggling toward the moment of institutionalization—not without lots of internal dissent—in a time of deep vertical cuts to university budgets and social and political backlash. Those are the realities, and that is why the hopes tied up in institutionalization and theoretical gentrification are key components of the pedagogical fantasy of "Beyond Anti-homophobia 101," and why it is so widespread, so appealing and so unhelpful to most of us who are attempting to teach gay and lesbian texts at the undergraduate level.

For most of us, teachers and students alike, are caught in a theoretical and political bind: we exist in institutions which are covertly if not overtly homophobic, where there are few if any "out" lesbian and gay teachers or students and where it is very difficult to get courses with some gay and lesbian content on the books. When the courses are offered, they are taken by students for all manner of reasons, among them, predictably, "It fit into my timetable." As the literature on teaching about gay and lesbian issues indicates, the vast majority of these students are not themselves gay and out, and therefore, not surprisingly, they are illiterate about if not hostile to gay and lesbian cultures. The poignant and paradoxical fact is that this typical student demographic profile exists at the same time that, for many of us who read, think, and write about the intersection of sexuality/identity/knowledge, the limits of teaching and learning about homosexuality in terms of "homophobia," tolerance, and other minoritizing discourses have never seemed so clear.

This is the social context in which I want to ask questions about the possibilities and limits of gay and lesbian pedagogy. What do you do while you're waiting for gay and lesbian studies to come to your (red) neck of the woods, while women's studies (one sessional lecturer and two part-timers) is struggling for survival and not very eager to make room for lesbian studies, while your university undertakes a study which reveals, like all the others, that gays, lesbians and bisexuals are harassed, victimized, and otherwise endangered in all their encounters with everyday life in your academy, and yet most of the faculty and staff say that they know no gays on campus, that there is no problem, so there's no need for antihomophobia workshops, which would just waste university money, and anyway, the Bible condemns sodomy? (That contradictory refrain appears in many of the responses which were collected and most usefully included in the University of Michigan study From Invisibility to Inclusion: Opening the Doors for Lesbians and Gay Men at the University of Michigan.) Deconstructing heteronormativity is the most urgent question for lesbian and gay, or more accurately, antihomophobic education, and it is a question of and for pedagogy rather than one about whether or not to demand to be "institutionalized." The word's unfortunate double meaning ruefully suggests that this legitimizing "solution" might be double-edged and not quite the panacea that some claim it to be (Chinn 1994, 243). If my memory serves me, avant-gardes that became institutionalized, such as the high modernists, never recovered from the experience.

Leaders of workshops on unlearning homophobia; writers of reports on curricular transformation; and feminist, gay, and lesbian teachers routinely refer to the need to break the silence on gay and lesbian issues in the university classroom (Frye 1982; Martindale 1992; Obear n.d.; Ontario Federation of Students 1991; President's Select Committee 1989). Actually, the notion of "silence" is misleading and ultimately not all that helpful to those who are curious about how to imagine let alone to practice a pedagogy that would not be merely gay and lesbian, but would be antihomophobic, even queer (Sedgwick 1990; Britzman 1995).

Homophobia, heterosexism, and a fascination with gays and lesbians are already screaming their presence in our classrooms, perhaps most oddly but not entirely unexpectedly those devoted to women's studies, gender studies, and gay and lesbian studies. Attending to homophobic discourse, learning how to question and reply to it without getting caught within its limited and destructive focus, is, I would argue, currently the first and the most logical step in que(e)rying pedagogy (Felman 1987). Because it can be done by anyone, teacher or student, gay or straight, without the aegis of institutionalized gay and lesbian studies, it can be employed anywhere, in any discipline. At the same time, because figuring out how to do it requires a cognitive reframing of the heteronormative binary, heterosexual us/homosexual them, that makes sense in the classroom, this approach allows the exciting theoretical breakthroughs of queer theory to be practiced in places where most of the professors, let alone the students, would not likely follow the drift of Ed Cohen's questions. Of course, there is a catch: reframing that binary is very hard work. Even recognizing its presence is far from easy.

One short essay, "Breaking the Silence: Sexual Preference in the Classroom," (Berg et al. 1994) stands out in the literature because of the close attention the authors pay to pedagogy as a process of knowledge production in which it is possible to interrupt homophobic logic and make cognitive shifts away from fixed identities and limited identifications. The authors, Allison Berg, Jean Kowaleski, Caroline Le Guin, Ellen Weinauer, and Eric A. Wolfe, who were at the time teaching assistants, and all of them straight-identified, detail how, with the best of intentions, they were complicit in creating a course from hell that almost rivals Mohr's (108–16). Unlike Mohr, however, they seem to have learned how they inadvertently structured the segment of the course on "sexual preference" as a way of teaching in terms of homophobia that objectified gays and lesbians and normalized heterosexuals.

They analyze how they framed a question about homosexuality in a writing assignment in such a way as to remove themselves and what they assumed was the heterosexual majority from consideration by pathologizing everybody else. They innocently asked the students to

> Describe a conversation with someone either of your own or another sexual preference (lesbian, male homosexual, bisexual, asexual, heterosexual) on the issue of homosexuality. Give as many salient details as you can about this conversation, particularly how attitudes about homosexuality were expressed. (110)

The teachers naturally enough received responses that ranged from "violence to disgust" and made the classroom even less safe for sexual minorities (111). When the lecturer in turn delivered an angry lecture in which he condemned the students' responses as unacceptable expressions of homophobia that amounted to fascism, the students erupted, the class became polarized as everyone blamed everyone else, and hostility, alienation, and betrayal reigned (112). Though the authors use the outdated phrase "sexual preference" and do not

reference the theoretical work of Sedgwick and others who have problematized minoritizing approaches to antihomophobic education,
their analysis of what shifted in their understanding of their pedagogical practice is entirely consistent with those poststructuralist and
queer theoretical insights.

On the premise that failures can be instructive, I believe much
can be learned from careful analysis of failed opportunities, two of
them mine, to question and interrupt homophobic discourse in the
classroom. I use my reading of the student questions I or other teachers deflected to make space for a critique of the two chief but implicit
assumptions structuring most discussions of lesbian and gay studies
pedagogy to date; namely, that the "right" gay and lesbian books will
teach themselves and that the presence of the "right" identities in the
classroom, of "out" gay and lesbian teachers and a sufficient number
of similar students, will undo the trauma of homophobia.

However, calling this state of affairs "homophobia," has itself
become more and more conceptually and practically problematic.[2]
Although still used as the principal term of reference organizing and
framing liberal humanist interventions such as anti-homophobia
workshops and university sponsored studies of living and working
conditions for their gay, lesbian, and bisexual minority members,
homophobia and the strategies commonly used for confronting it are
at best instruments of a new social etiquette and at worst a recupera-
tion of heterosexuality as an implacable norm.

Homophobia not only psychologizes but centers the "malady"
from the point of view of the presumed normal heterosexual. Not surprisingly, it has given rise to its twin, "heterophobia," a repellent but
understandably outraged attempt to wrest back conceptual control to
the status quo, on a parallel with "reverse discrimination." Predictably,
when a normal and unquestioned state of affairs stretching from ignoring to murder becomes the focus of inquiry, thereby implying that
things ought to be different, traumas of various kinds result. Though
making the unspeakable speak creates difficulties for sexual minorities
as well as for the ostensible "general population," the distress of the
latter is the usual focus of concern both in antihomophobia workshops
and in university-sponsored studies.

"Out" gay and lesbian teachers, good intentions, and a more
inclusive curriculum are of course desirable, but they are not sufficient
to do this work. It takes intellectual, political, and emotional courage
to withstand and work through the trauma that predictably results
whenever the smooth operation of the normal/pathological binary is
questioned and interrupted. It is because heterosexism and illiteracy

about gays and lesbians are the norm in university culture, and anti-homophobic educational practice does not yet have the moral authority attached to it that antisexist and antiracist pedagogy do, that teacher accounts, my own included, about teaching a session, a section, or an entire course in gay and lesbian texts, are not happy stories.

However, these accounts, painful though they may be to read, have something instructive to tell us, something that goes beyond the easy ascription of teacher or student heroism, villainy, or incompetence. For what they suggest is that the humanist assumptions underlying all reform pedagogies, chief among them that the provision of knowledge about despised and marginalized groups will simultaneously empower them and decrease the bad conduct of dominants, need to be rethought if not rejected outright. These unhappy stories problematize feminist and other radical pedagogical expectations that classrooms can and ought to be "safe havens" for stigmatized minorities. But, finally, while these sad tales cast doubts on the expectations that classrooms will become liberated zones, my reading of them is not meant to support the cynical dismissal of progressivist hopes for educational change as necessarily utopian.

I want, instead, to use these accounts to encourage teachers and theorists to think about what can be learned and made productive from encountering the limits of (humanist) pedagogy. My reading of these narratives is informed by the startling and even disturbing claim of Shoshana Felman (1987) and Eve Sedgwick (1990) that ignorance, the desire to ignore, is actively produced and maintained rather than a mere absence or a passive state. Ignorance, especially perhaps homophobic ignorance, is thus not only less than amenable to pedagogical replacement with antihomophobic knowledge, but becomes more insistent when gay and lesbian material threatens to be introduced into the classroom. Recognizing the active operations of the desire to ignore and learning to expect its predictable present absence are *absolutely crucial* to understanding what happens or fails to happen when gay and lesbian material is brought into the classroom.

The only reasonably sure way to avoid the trauma that results when unpopular things are unleashed is to take the "emperor's new clothes approach" to the teaching of gay and lesbian texts. This is a tried and true method for defusing tension around homophobia in many women's studies classes. For example, in one group interview with women's studies students, straight, bisexual, and lesbian, I was told many anecdotes which suggest that seemingly more inclusive curricula do not in themselves guarantee that these texts will be taught. More than one student mentioned a course on women writers taught

by a feminist professor, with lesbian material on the syllabus, in which
the discussion allotted to two lesbian novels about lesbians written by
openly lesbian writers took place without their subject matter being
addressed. Forty-five minutes of one fifty-minute class on Jane Rule's
Desert of the Heart was devoted to discussing the difficulties of obtain-
ing divorces, until a lesbian asked when the class was going to discuss
the novel. Her question was met with silence, and the class broke up
(Martindale, 1992).

A most instructive treatment of how to avoid teaching lesbian
textuality may be found in Gail B. Griffin's lyrical account of her development as a women's studies teacher, *Calling: Essays on Teaching in the
Mother Tongue*. Griffin's class in women's literature was so intrigued
by Alice Walker's *The Color Purple* that they insisted on extending the
discussion for several days. In an effort to conclude the discussion,
Griffin asked the class whether the ending satisfied them. It did not,
because the class was baffled and disappointed by Celie's continuing
lack of desire for her transformed husband, Albert.

Griffin's perception that this had been a "wonderful interchange" (179) shifted uneasily in the last few minutes of the last class.
The continuing silence of the class's four lesbian students jarred Griffin into noticing that she and the rest of the class had apparently forgotten to mention that Celie's real love, Shug, is another woman. What
seems like a candid confession about how she allowed heterosexism to
subvert the teaching of a potentially "subversive" text is coyly re-
enacted in her account of the incident, in which Griffin once again
makes lesbians and lesbianism unspeakable and invisible. Still unwilling to write out what she refers to as the "L-word," Griffin displays an
impoverished understanding of lesbian sexuality/textuality:

> Now, *The Color Purple* is a most subversive novel. It makes a
> homosexual relationship so inescapably, irrefutably superior to
> any heterosexual choice, so absolutely healthy, vital, and liberat-
> ing, that only the most rigid of homophobes can possibly resist it.
> Although genitals appear specifically and prominently in its
> pages, it is so little about genital sexuality that the issue is virtu-
> ally moot. For this reason, however, the novel can be dangerous.
> You can, in fact, get away with teaching *The Color Purple* without
> ever mentioning the L-word. I had, I realized, just done so.
> Acceptance had slid into avoidance. (179)

What begins as an ironic self-critique of what she failed to say in
several hours of discussion segues into an extremely puzzling and

unwarranted self-celebration of her success at giving voice to and for her lesbian students. In the four euphemistic sentences Griffin generously doles out in the last minute of the last class, she points out that Celie "chose" another woman to love. Still no "L-word" there either. As in the interview material I discussed above, Griffin teaches lesbian texts by not teaching them. "Silence. And the class ended" (180).

The four L-word students are abjectly grateful that they do not have to take the risk and the consequences of educating the class and their teacher themselves. When the class is over, and it is safe to speak because no one else is listening, they offer thanks: "We were sitting there listening and wondering if anybody was going to say it or would we have to do it, and I was trying to get up the nerve, and you saved us" (180). From what? Apparently from the trauma of discussing lesbianism in a women's studies classroom.

Having failed not just to address her students' and her own heterosexism, Griffin also fails to teach lesbian culture. Leaving them as uneducated about lesbians as they were when they entered her class, Griffin blithely concludes her account of how she gave voice to her lesbian students, by appropriating for herself Adrienne Rich's paean to teachers who "made a difference." While on the evidence of her own narrative Griffin egregiously failed, even refused, to give her students, straight and nonstraight, information about lesbian culture, she nonetheless lauds herself for being one of those antihomophobic educators who "gave you the books/who let you know you were not alone. . . . You have a people" (181).

If Gail Griffin is no heroine of antihomophobic pedagogy, neither am I. Like the colleague I alluded to above, my poststructuralist feminism involves "reading for the absence," and for years I have integrated lesbian material, as well as material by other groups of women who are frequently excluded or tokenized, into all my courses. Nonetheless, I feel that I fail over and over again to deliver on the promises of an antihomophobic pedagogy, that is, one which questions and interrupts the operation of the binary heterosexual/homosexual so as to produce something more interesting than tolerance. It always feels like the first time to me, and I hope to do better next time, that is, to work with my class toward a thorough and convincing deconstruction of the binary so that they get a sense of how it operates in our social and cultural texts, all the while keeping the trauma of doing this work from being completely overwhelming for me and the class.

My most dramatic failure to do this work occurred when I deflected an angry rhetorical question of a feminist student in an upper-level women's autobiography course. Thirty female students, nearly all of them white and straight English majors, were concluding their discussion of the anthology of writing by radical women of color, *This Bridge Called My Back* (Moraga and Anzaldua 1983). The tense but polite classroom atmosphere was interrupted by the voice of an angry and agitated white student who indignantly asked, "When are we going to start reading and talking about normal women?" There was an audible gasp from the whole group.

Startled, angry, and fearful about how my course and by extension myself were being positioned by the student, I pretended not to know what she was getting at. I did not give her question a potentially and provocatively Lacanian reply: "But we already are!" Rather than reversing her question and giving it back to her in a displaced form, allowing "that which is said by one [to be perceived and articulated as] being already the reply" (Felman, quoting Lacan 1987, 55), I gave an informal lecture on "difference" and binary oppositions. Thus, that year's most important question remained unprobed and unworked through. I gave the students and myself a temporary reprieve in dealing with homophobia and racism, which is to say, lost opportunity to investigate how to rethink representational and reading practices. The theories I live and write by were not making it into my classroom.

However, the reprieve was bought at a high price; though the presence of "unpopular things"—in this case racial, sexual, and class difference—was always pervasive in my classroom, they were not quite "unleashed." Instead, it was a protracted standoff. The "normal" women held onto their subject positions, circled their wagons, and kept the "others" at bay. The Others felt, well, Othered. This course became a tour of the dreaded and exotic Other. On student evaluations, many of the women complained that the course was not really a course on women's autobiographies but was about "Blacks and lesbians." I was repeatedly faulted for allowing the "Black and lesbian" students (four out of thirty-five, however you count) to "dominate" discussions.

Because that student's question kept nagging me, the next year I attempted to address it through designing a new course with a colleague who specializes in antiracism and postcolonialism. We, the white lesbian and the straight woman of color, pledged not to do the "samo" of women's studies—take Mary Wollstonecraft as feminism's originary moment, lead up to the triumph of the white women's movement, and tack on a one week p.s. at the end about women of color and lesbians. Our course would deconstruct the normal/deviant, centre/margin binary as it operates in women's studies courses whose chief focus is gender rather than the production of social difference.

After some objections from the department, this multisectioned lecture and tutorial course was put on the books, retitled by them An Introduction to Gender Studies. My colleague and I were assigned two graduate student teaching assistants to lead tutorial groups, a white gay male and a straight white female, neither of whom had taught "political" courses before.

Along with all the predictable glitches which occur when teaching anything the first time, sickness forced me to miss the first semester. In my absence, my tutorial was taken over by a graduate assistant with no teaching experience and my colleague restructured the course. Since she had to do all the lecturing, she taught what she knew best. The first semester lectures were exercises in close reading, focused primarily on how racial and gender differences are inscribed in pseudo-universalizing discourses. Racism and sexism were treated as effects of difference rather than vice versa, and, though texts by Audre Lorde figured prominently, almost no attention was paid to sexuality.

My first day back, I learned from a variety of sources that my tutorial was in crisis. Unpopular things had been threatening. After one explosion about racism, the ideologically polarized group of fifteen women and men of diverse races, classes, and ethnicities, all of them ostensibly heterosexual, largely refused to talk to each other. Both the original tutorial leader and the group were defensive, keen to assign blame somewhere. Since the unstructured format of the first semester's tutorial had no chance of working as long as the silent treatment was in effect, I decided to have the students bring three questions in each week and work on them in small groups. While this format was an improvement, the crisis in my tutorial made me seriously doubt whether good intentions and a transformed curriculum in and of themselves would give me a better shot at replying to the assumptions about knowledge and identity which had informed my former student's angry question about normalcy.

Her question took on an added resonance when I learned that my tutorial had developed an official and punishing discourse about difference. The critique of pseudo-universals had been taken to mean that one must not generalize—never, about anything. Students also learned that one can speak only from and apparently about one's own subject position. They were prohibited from speaking for others and obliged to identify themselves according to their visible and obvious marks of difference, that is, by race and gender. Class and sexuality, being less patently visible, went unremarked. Our course on "gender, race, and class" had constructed a modified version of what Michael Warner calls "rainbow theory." We were missing a few colors—like pink and purple—but we had constructed a "fantasized space where all embodied identities could be visibly represented as parallel forms of identity" ("Introduction" *Fear of a Queer Planet*, xix) The white males tried to remember that they must always preface their remarks by indicating that they were speaking only as "white males." They nervously joked about how illegitimate and reprehensible they were as white males. The jokes were unfunny, involving as they did an unpleasant mixture of guilt and resentment.

The students' interpretations of the official discourse, or set of prohibitions, in "Introduction to Gender Studies" effectively put identities on trial. The tutorial was paralyzed by naturalizing assumptions that racial and other differences are fixed and obvious rather than constructed and fluid, as well as by the assumption that people are discriminated against because they are—*already*—different rather than the reverse (Scott 1992). The tutorial felt like a courtroom in which students had learned how to testify, whether as victims or as perpetrators of racism and sexism. Given their limited options, they struggled to see themselves and to be seen as victims of oppression, or, reluctantly and ashamedly, they admitted their complicity and privilege as perpetrators.

It took me a little longer to understand that, although the students had been restrained from speaking for others, they took this caveat to apply only to race and gender, the categories of visible social difference that had been showcased and reified in the lectures. As a result, homophobic discourse about gays and lesbians, who were apparently unrepresented in the tutorial group, had become the release valve for prohibited speech. Ridicule and contempt for "fags," and to a lesser extent for lesbians, were easily and unselfconsciously expressed by almost all the students. When it finally came time according to the restructured syllabus to discuss gay and lesbian texts as gay and lesbian texts, the students' assumptions about the obviousness and visibility of identity markers had been reinforced by our course's apparent reification of identities. That meant that the hunt was on to make a checklist of the visible characteristics and behavior traits of that unrepresented identity group. Against our intentions, our course was predicated pedagogically on a form of what Edward Said called "Orientalism": we conferred "on the other a discrete identity, while also providing the knowing observer with a standpoint from which to see without being seen, to read without interruption" (Clifford 1986, 12) Our course had apparently confirmed what they already knew, that homosexuals were a despised and despicable quasi-ethnic minority whose distinguishing characteristics were not sexual practices so much as a certain style or set of mannerisms.

Because of my absence, lesbian (and gay) material was introduced, as it is (when it is at all) in most women's studies classes, only
in the final weeks of the year, when the class was reaching or had
already reached its saturation point about diversity groups. For me, it
felt like a re-run of "When are we going to start reading and talking
about normal women?" As a result, the lecture hall and some of the
tutorials became scenes of trauma in Felman's clinical rather than
moralistic sense. We concocted, mainly unintentionally, scandalous situations without a cure, wherein events in excess of our frames of reference produced a radical condition of exposure and vulnerability
(Felman and Laub 1992). A lecture I gave on the denaturalizing aspects
of Freud's thinking about sexuality was greeted with audible sounds
of disbelief and disgust.

Like Richard Mohr, the openly gay white male teaching assistant
decided to let a film do the initial consciousness raising about homophobia. Like my colleague and me, he too made a fetish out of what he
had added to the curriculum. The gay-themed and gay-directed com-
mercial film he had chosen to show our class, *Parting Glances*, was a
personal favorite, something he knew almost by heart and had come
to regard as a sacred text. In many ways, the film seemed a safe choice
for a "first-time" cinematic encounter with sexual difference. It was a
chaste, middlebrow, realist text about innocuous gay white yuppies
that presented gays as just like straights.

With no introduction, the lights went down, the film came on,
and the students began to act as students predictably do in teacher stories about showing that first film, whatever it is, in gay and lesbian
studies classes. That is, they gasped, clung to their friends, covered
their eyes, and let out loud "yucchs." A few walked out. As in Griffin's
account of how not to teach *The Color Purple*, there was "silence. And
the class ended." Actually, as bad as it was, it could have been worse,
as Mohr's account indicates.

The teaching assistant was devastated but hid his feelings enough
so as to field questions with his tutorial when the film ended. Because
he was out to his students, he was treated as a native informant, in
Lacan's terms, "the subject assumed to know." An implicit believer in
humanist pedagogy, he did not object to the way their questions had
positioned him, nor to their commonsensical assumptions that "knowledge . . . can be supported or transported by one alone." The "question-
and-answer" session was the opposite of dialogical because neither
teacher nor students recognized that everybody present, straight, nonstraight and antistraight, was implicated in the information the teaching assistant was imparting (Felman 1987, 79; quoting Lacan, 83).

This amiable and popular teacher was asked and for a while tried to answer questions such as: "Why do all gay men love opera?" "Do they all have classy apartments in New York City?" "How come they're all white and rich?" "Why is the one who plays the female role messier than the other guy?" And finally, "Why did the director stereotype those gays so much?" Eventually he was so traumatized he could no longer speak. He gave up and put his head in his hands. After a hushed silence, when he was able to speak again, he told the students that he could not answer any more of their questions just then because they made him feel like the "Other" and that felt terrible.

The teaching assistant named himself as the Other in a way in which our students by then were familiar, that is, in the sense of the marginalized and excluded subaltern, as the feminist and postcolonialist theorists we read in our course used the concept, rather than as Lacan's "true Other," "who gives the answer one does not expect," and in whose knowledge is constituted "the return of a difference" (Felman 1987, 82). Though each of these senses of the other does not preclude the other, the teaching assistant, perhaps because he, too, was under the sway of rainbow theory, did not think that the teaching of un/popular cultures requires the pedagogue to play the other in the Lacanian sense too. In any case, he did not think to question their questions. And so, as in Griffin's class, this painful exercise, not exactly a "wonderful interchange" in any but the most ironic sense, came to an end. Once again, "Silence. And the class ended."

This disturbing experience became another humanist moment. Perhaps the students learned something about good behavior toward and increased empathy for minorities, but it is just as likely that they concluded that they should not ask questions that disturb the teacher. Because of the course's emphasis on the visibility and obviousness of identities, especially marked identities, an opportunity for analysis of the production of knowledge about all identities was once again lost (Scott 1992).

My tutorial that week was no better and almost as surreal. Rather than treat me, the course director and an out and obvious lesbian, as a native informant, the students used the structuring device of our group, the asking of three student-generated questions about the text of the week (in this case the film) to discuss "How do you recognize a lesbian?" The question terrified me, perhaps because it reminded me of others constructed along the same lines; to wit, How do you recognize a witch, a Jew, a Communist, an alien from outer space? The question intrigued the students, so much so that the other two questions were immediately dropped and utterly forgotten in the gleeful and excited discussion that followed, a discussion in which all of the students were actively engaged. Lisa M. Walker's perceptive article, "How to Recognize a Lesbian: The Cultural Politics of Looking Like What You Are," was a few months away from publication, but her observations about her ambivalence concerning the trope of lesbian visibility would have helped me with my own confusion in light of the classroom crisis that erupted that day:

> I do not wish to diminish the fact that the impulse to privilege the visible often arises out of the need to reclaim signifiers of difference that dominant ideologies have used to define minority identities negatively. But while this strategy of reclamation is often affirming, it can also replicate the practices of dominant ideologies that use visibility to create social categories on the basis of exclusion. The paradigm of visibility is totalizing when a signifier of difference becomes synonymous with the identity it signifies. In this situation, members of a given population who do not bear that signifier of difference or who bear visible signs of another identity are rendered invisible and are marginalized within an already marginalized community. (1993, 888)

Before I could intervene and turn the question back to the questioners, asking why they wanted or needed to know how to recognize a lesbian, and were they interested in learning how to recognize heterosexuals, the group answer, arrived at collectively, was announced: she is short, wears glasses, and is flat-chested. Pretty common visual markers, two of which are routinely ascribed to "feminists," but in that group, the only woman possessing all three characteristics was me. Suddenly, a dissenting voice shot out; a female student, an "out" lesbian in other classes, but closeted in our "unsafe" tutorial, began to demand that they produce evidence for their claim. Taller than me, voluptuous, and gifted with good vision, she did not fit the description. Nonetheless, she too deflected the question. Instead of coming out and asking "Ain't I a lesbian?" her counter-claim led the discussion down predictable paths about the errors of stereotyping. Yet again, deflected questions produced "silence. And the class ended."

In retrospect, the traumatic questions posed to the gay male teaching assistant and to me in our tutorials seem not only structurally identical but produced wholly predictable outcomes—indeed seemed even to constitute measures of a cruel success in terms of our course's presentation of the logic of difference and normalcy. In accordance with the pluralist and humanist notions of "diversity" or difference as already unproblematically "there," only awaiting inclusion and representation as "subjects" on the syllabus and as "subjects" in the front of the classroom, by the end of the year, "hom(m)osexuality" (Irigaray 1985) too had been rendered visible and intelligible. Which is to say that "homosexuality" was rendered in terms of heterosexuality or sameness. My colleague and I had successfully taught our students how to "read for the absence" of gays and lesbians in a way that did not implicate the students themselves, nor therefore, did it teach them "how to recognize heterosexuality" either.

And still, the most instructive and endlessly deflected question was yet to be posed in our course. On the final exam, whose questions were collectively put together by the entire teaching team and distributed ahead of time at the last class, we asked the students to tell us how the course had challenged their understandings of gender, race, class, or sexuality. The correct answer to this question was valued at 10 percent of the final grade. And of course, we got it. Over and over again, members of one or another dominant group told us in unconvincingly vague abstractions how they had learned to tolerate minorities.

How they were implicated in their reading practices was a question they never addressed—unsurprisingly, since we had not posed it. And the institutionalization of "radical subjects" had done nothing to compel its asking. In our "progressive institution," we experienced and committed "radical teachers" unwittingly taught our students to give us the answers they thought we expected rather than the likes of those Lacan solicited from his seminar, the questions that might structure a lesbian and gay studies that could conceivably get beyond antihomophobia 101: "Let everybody tell me, in his [sic] own way, his idea of what I am driving at. How, for him, is opened up—or closed—or how already he resists, the question as I pose it" (Lacan, in Felman 1987, 83–84).

Notes

1. On February 17, 1995, Kathleen Martindale died after a prolonged and courageous battle with breast cancer, a struggle in which medical practice and identity position intersect in significant and significantly disturbing ways. Her article "Can I Get a Witness" (1994) describes and interrogates that intersection. The present chapter is excerpted from her book *Unpopular Cultures: Lesbian Writing in the Postmodern* forthcoming with State University of New York Press. Kathleen Martindale has left both an enduring intellectual contribution and a no less enduring sense of her absence (editors' note).

2. A neologism coined by a gay psychologist on analogy with other psychological terms for irrational feelings, *homophobia* from the outset consigns and confines its analytic scope to the commonsensical and intrapsychic world of understanding of what many now refer to in a telling shorthand as the "'phobe." The term *phobe* also erases gender specificity. Attempts by some lesbian writers to inscribe the gender-specific *lesbophobia* into discussions of homophobia have met with little success. Only lesbians seem to know or use the term. Although the usual speculation is that *lesbophobia* is an unlovely word, verbal ugliness seems less likely the cause of its unpopularity than general inability to imagine the targets of such mistreatment.

References

Berg, A., Kowaleski, J., Le Guin, C., Weinauer, E., and Wolfe, E. A. (1994). Breaking the silence: Sexual preference in the composition classroom. In Garber (Ed.), *Tilting the tower: Lesbians teaching queer subjects* (pp. 108–116). New York: Routledge

Britzman, D. P. (1991). Decentering discourses in teacher education: Or, The unleashing of unpopular things. *Boston University Journal of Education, 173*(3), 60–80.

———. (1992, Summer). Structures of feeling in curriculum and teaching. *Theory into Practice, XXXI*(3), 152–158.

———.(1995). Is there a queer pedagogy?: Or, Stop reading straight! *Educational Theory, 45* (2), 151–166.

Chinn, S. (1994). Queering the profession, or Just professionalizing queers. In Garber (Ed.), *Tilting the tower: Lesbians teaching queer subjects* (pp. 243–250). New York: Routledge.

Clifford, J. (1986). Introduction: Partial truths. In J. Clifford and G. Marcus (Eds.), *Writing culture: The poetics and politics of ethnography* (pp. 1–26). Berkeley: University of California Press.

Cohen, E. (1991). Who are "we"? Gay "identity" as political (e)motion: A theoretical rumination. In D. Fuss (Ed.), *Inside/out: Lesbian theories, gay theories* (pp. 71–92). New York: Routledge.

Escoffier, J. (1992). Generations and paradigms: Mainstreams in lesbian and gay studies. In H. L. Minton (Ed.), Gay and lesbian studies issue. *Journal of Homosexuality, 24*, 7–26.

Felman, S. (1982). Psychoanalysis and education: Teaching terminable and interminable. *Yale French Studies, 63*, 21–44.

———.(1987). *Jacques Lacan and the adventure of insight: Psychoanalysis in contemporary culture.* Cambridge: Harvard University Press.

Felman, S., and Laub, D. (1992). *Testimony: Crises of witnessing in literature, psychoanalysis and history.* New York: Routledge.

Frye, M. (1982). A lesbian perspective on women's studies. In M. Cruikshank (Ed.), *Lesbian studies: Present and future.* Old Westbury, New York: The Feminist Press.

Garber, L. (Ed.) (1994). *Tilting the tower: Lesbians teaching queer subjects.* New York: Routledge.

Griffin, G. B. (1992). *Calling: Essays on teaching in the mother tongue.* Pasadena, CA: Trilogy Books.

Irigaray, L. (1985). *Speculum of the other woman* (Gillian Gill, Trans.). Ithaca, NY: Cornell University Press.

Martindale, K. (1992). Addressing heterosexism in women's studies classrooms. In D. Shogan (Ed.), *A reader in feminist ethics* (pp. 449–65). Toronto: Scholars Press.

Minton, H. L. (Ed.) (1992). Gay and lesbian studies issue. *Journal of Homosexuality, 24,* 1/2.

Mohr, R. D. (1988). The ethics of students and the teaching of ethics: A lecturing. In *Gays/Justice: A study of ethics, society and law* (pp. 293–311).

———.(1988). Gay studies in the big ten: A survivor's manual. In *Gays/Justice: A study of ethics, society, and law* (pp. 277–92). New York: Columbia.

Moraga, C., and Anzaldua, G. (1983). *This bridge called my back: Writing by radical women of color.* New York: Kitchen Table: Women of Color Press.

Nielsen, R. M. (1990). Page Dubois, Sowing the body: Psychoanalysis and ancient representations of women. *Canadian Review of Comparative Literature, XVII,* 3–4, 391–408.

Obear, K. (n.d.). *Opening doors to understanding and acceptance: A facilitator's guide to presenting workshops on lesbian and gay issues.* Amherst, MA: The Human Advantage.

Ontario Federation of Students Research Department and Rory Crath and Peter Regier. (1991). *The campus closet: Institutional homophobia in Ontario Post-secondary education.* Toronto, Ontario, Canada.

President's Select Committee for Lesbian and Gay Concerns, Rutgers University. (1989). *In every classroom.* New Brunswick, New Jersey.

Schulman, S. (1984). *The Sophie Horowitz story.* Tallahassee, FL: Naiad Press.

Scott, J. W. (1992, Summer). *Multiculturalism and the politics of identity*. October, 12–19.

Sedgwick, E. Kosofsky. (1990). *Epistemology of the closet*. Berkeley: University of California Press.

Walker, L. M. (1993, Summer). How to recognize a lesbian: The cultural politics of looking like what you are. *Signs*, 866–90.

Warner, M. (1992, June). From queer to eternity: An army of theorists cannot fail. *Village Voice Literary Supplement*, 18–9.

———.(1993). Introduction. *Fear of a queer planet: Queer politics and social theory* (pp. vii–xxxi). Minneapolis: University of Minnesota Press.

Yingling, T. (1991, Spring). Sexual preference/cultural reference: The predicament of gay culture studies. *American Literary History, 3*(1), 184–1997.

Zita, J. N. (1994). Gay and lesbian studies: Yet another unhappy marriage? In L. Garber (Ed.), *Tilting the tower: Lesbians teaching queer subjects* (pp. 258–276). New York: Routledge.

4

EN/GENDERING EQUITY:
PARADOXICAL CONSEQUENCES OF
INSTITUTIONALIZED EQUITY POLICIES

MARY BRYSON AND SUZANNE DE CASTELL

Recent critiques of purportedly "liberatory," "transformative," "emancipatory," or "critical" educational initiatives ask us to call into serious question the extent to which institutionally based attempts to emancipate themselves produce outcomes which are disabling, repressive, exclusionary, and silencing (see Delpit 1988; Ellsworth 1989; and Lather 1991). This essay interrogates our own involvement, as educators committed to radical praxis, in such contemporary policy initiatives, widely construed as emancipatory in intent, whose purpose is the promotion of "gender equity" in education. These initiatives, it will be argued, are contradictory not only logically, but ontologically. Such initiatives, that is to say, risk consolidating and reifying those very problems which they are officially sanctioned to champion, both by reifying and nominally solidifying categories with a shaky, partial, contingent, and positioned ontology (for example, gender, sex, and equity); and by obscuring the vastly unequal power relations within which such discursive turf is contested. "Gender equity," it will be further argued, is an inherently contradictory project, and one for which substantial conceptual clarification is necessary before any useful work can be done in its name. It will be argued here that the greatest danger of this discursive formation of *gendered* subjects, as the New Right mobilizes around family values and the "new masculinity," is that current gender equity theory, policy, and practice will then inscribe "women's ways" and other similarly preservationist liberal pluralisms (e.g., Belenky et al. 1986, or Gilligan 1982) as new regimes of truth (Foucault 1980) in educational policy, entrenching even further the very traditions they purport to overturn, and becoming instead the gender version of a precivil rights "separate but equal" policy justifying systemic discrimination.

"Gender Equity": A Contradiction in Terms?

For as long as the sexes are socially distinguished, "women" will be nominated in their apartness, so that sexual division will always be liable to conflation with some fundamental ontological sexual difference. So feminism, the reaction to this state of affairs, cannot be merely transitional, and a true post-feminism can never arrive.

—Denise Riley, *Am I That Name? Feminism and the Category "Woman"*

An obvious approach to the question of what fundamentally is meant by the term *gender equity* is to seek out a clear definition of these terms. But to attempt this, it turns out, is already to have begged some very significant questions.

Although in English "gender" is nowadays deployed as if it named a universal, contrary to any such presumption of semantic generalizability, recent feminist and poststructuralist research has amply documented the ways in which "gender" is local and particular and has argued that its meaning, therefore, can only be rendered concretely and historically, rather than abstractly and theoretically by means of a general definition (Davies 1989; Haraway 1991). In this respect, Braidotti (1991) argues, "gender" is, like "feminism,"

> neither a concept nor a theory, nor even a systematic set of utterances about women. It is, rather, the means chosen by certain women to situate themselves in reality so as to redesign their "feminine" condition. It would be dangerous to propose a purely theoretical representation of this multiple, heterogeneous complex of women's struggles. (264)

The concept of 'gender' was developed, Donna Haraway points out, in just this way, as a strategy for contesting the naturalization of sexual difference. "Gender," that is to say, emerged as a politically pragmatic alternative to the biologically determinist category of sex, emphasizing the socially constructed and hence alterable character of difference (see also Gayle Rubin's [1975] classic text on this subject). Indeed the distinction is today preserved relatively unchallenged in feminist discourses for this same reason. "Gender," concludes Haraway, "is at the heart of constructions and classifications of systems of difference" (1991, 1–19).

The term *equity*, as Chandra Mohanty (1990) and others (e.g., de la Luz Reyes and Halcon 1988; Kenway and Modra 1992; and Yates 1995) have powerfully argued, while nominally referring to a state of fairness and justice, typically refers *in institutional programs* to a state of sameness, quantitative balancing, uniform character, or equality of opportunity. Usually, "equity" is a term of concealment. In a progressive liberal masquerade, it announces the right to be or to become like the idealized subject of human rights; it re-asserts traditional rules, roles, and relations by announcing the right of nondominant, marginalized persons to assume the position of dominance, to hold the same jobs, go to the same places, have the same desires, and do the same things as the normatively sanctioned bourgeois subject of human rights. These become, then, rights of pseudo-membership in the group in dominance, rights to be like—but always impossibly so—those whose right it is to define the proper subject/s of rights. These are, of course, not rights as homosexuals, as indigenous people, as Asian, as poor, or as women. Such rights might in truth be "human" rights. Consider this, for example, touted in the press (*The Globe and Mail* 1991) as a "victory for gay rights": a Supreme Court decision to award spousal benefits to a gay male couple. The presiding judge in the case, Judge Roles, wrote, "The evidence is overwhelming that the petitioner and Mr. Garneau lived as husband and wife." Referring to an expert report filed in the case by psychiatrist Michael Myers, the judge said, "The evidence of Dr. Myers also suggests that the type of emotional bond between homosexual couples is no different than one between heterosexual couples" Such victories for gay rights, then, are achieved only to the extent that the state reconstitutes homosexuals as inevitably failing heterosexuals.

And, it is important to add here, others have argued that it has always been the purpose of state systems to equip diverse student bodies with the *habitus* universalized as normative (see, for example, Bourdieu and Passeron 1977; and Tyack and Hansott 1982). This compulsory submission of all children to extensive and intrusive state standards, according to Raymond Williams (1983) is the process whereby the state constitutes the subjects to which it then accords the rights that it then goes on to represent. This is what "equity" in education seems to have meant for minority students: the right to try but inevitably to fail to become white, male, and middle class. And this is what institutional "gender equity" policies seem to signify most often for girls and women: an impossibly contradictory injunction, on the one hand, to enact a series of characteristics designated as "gender-appropriate" in educational feminism's project (for example, to legitimate "women's ways") and, on the other hand, to embrace and participate ever more equally in the set of rules, roles, and relations established and maintained by a predominantly masculine power elite. In this impossible dream of gender equity, rights are accorded institutionally in virtue of, and to the degree to which, subjects approximate, instantiate, or simulate that which they can never in fact become. What kind of equity is that? Granted at last official rights to speak, we nevertheless do not receive rights to speak as Other, but only in the voice sanctioned by the dominant other. We gain rights to representation only to the extent that we do not represent ourselves as Other, but become, as Spivak (1988) has so persuasively argued, "subaltern" representatives of the dominant other.

Therefore, policies which make particular identity classifications a prerequisite to "equity" (for example, *gender* equity), necessarily function to *deny* rights more than to *affirm* them. That is to say, such policies accord rights only under conditions (in this case conditions of gender appropriateness) specified as normatively binding; hence they function as privative. Deployed as a basis of entitlement, identity classifications function both as technologies of normalization and, complementarily, as criteria of exclusion from the benefits in question (Foucault 1982). This does not amount to a pursuit of equity; it is better described as a pursuit of social order. Categories of entitlement to equity have for too long been deployed as barriers to equal educational rights. If public schools are indeed committed to equity, that entitlement is automatic; it is there from the start. It is a fully inclusive acknowledgment of and accommodation to diversity and difference. Taken seriously, it requires us to reverse the order of things: from identity as a condition of equity, to equity as a condition of identity.

If "equity" is to be possible, one might wish strategically to argue that the very fiction of any naturalized or unproblematic deployment of the identity category of "gender" must become the principal target of deconstructive analysis. In Judith Butler's (1990) groundbreaking work on "gender," the disruptive effects of this poststructuralist approach are clear. In this highly influential text, Butler works to "trace the ways in which 'gender fables' establish and circulate the misnomer of 'natural facts,'" and she argues that "the presumed universality and unity of the subject of feminism [women] is effectively undermined by the constraints of the representational discourse in which it functions" (41). Identity categories, such as "gender," created on the mistaken presumption of "universality and unity" of the female subject function, Butler argues, as "domains of exclusion" which "reveal the coercive and regulatory consequences of that construction even when the construction has been elaborated for emancipatory purposes" (41). This view of the exclusionary and normalizing function of identity-based classifications presents a serious challenge to such purportedly emancipatory projects as institutionally mandated ten-year plans to promote "equity" for particular target groups. Such inherently contradictory practices might better give way to more directly and self-consciously democratic activism in the pursuit of a species of equity predicated on, in Butler's words, "a critique of categories of identity that contemporary juridical structures engender, naturalize and immobilize" (73).

But there is little evidence of attention to any such poststructuralist deconstructions of traditional gendered subjectivity in educational discourses purporting to promote "gender equity." Contemporary feminist theorizing about "gender," it has been noted, provides a far richer conceptual resource than is accommodated within educational discourses on "gender equity. " It is almost as if the enthusiasm with which such undertheorized policies and programs are currently being pursued might operate as a blinder, a diversion, a way of concealing and suppressing what might be accomplished by such educational reforms. Certainly by treating gender as a basic ontological category, by construing it as theoretically unproblematic, and by insistently and enthusiastically pursuing the promotion of "equity" on that basis, it becomes possible to pre-empt and defuse any more radical understandings and practices which contemporary feminist theory might otherwise engender. The institutional practices by means of which such policies are negotiated—including such obvious considerations as the documentary prestructuring of debate and discussion, speech roles, rules of order, and not least the meager time allocated for working out a shared understanding of the problems at hand and for formulating that understanding in explicit terms—all operate within a taken-for-granted conception of gender, and as such, these constitutive factors operate from the start to preclude consideration of a range of ideas and information central to a fuller, intellectually honest exploration of the issues involved. "Gender equity" becomes a straightforward technical problem, rather than a question that has scarcely begun to be formulated, whose meaning has yet to be grasped, and indeed whose very existence as a question remains to be questioned. In Butler's (1990) words: "If the inner truth of gender is a fabrication and if a true gender is a fantasy instituted and inscribed on the surface of bodies, then it seems that genders can be neither true nor false but only produced as the truth effects of a discourse of primary and stable identity" (337).

Poststructuralist theories open up the possibility that "gender" is nothing over and above its significations; that what we call "gender" is an effect, not of sex or sexuality or cultural formation, but of the power of discursive regimes of language and representation which, to borrow Michel Foucault's (1980) words, "seep into the very grain of individuals, reaches right into their bodies, permeates their gestures, their posture, what they say, how they learn to live and work." What if the very thing we presume in these institutional discourses of remediation as the basis for a policy of equitable entitlement, we in fact create in and by these same discourses? Then in truth it becomes more than just a tactless *ad feminam* observation to point out the ways in which institutionally structured discourses of amelioration function more as blinders than as lenses, blinders whose effect is to render actual differences invisible, and thence to entitle only those who conform to pre-established conditions of entitlement, while disenfranchising the rest who have by this means become invisible.

A significant implication of poststructuralist analysis, then, is that it is in these very discourses of "empowerment" for women that we *create* gender, we define, delimit, and specify what it is to be "of gender." Cornel West (1987) speaks of the impermissibility of effacing, through our theoretical deconstructions, those material aspects of oppression which we "cannot not know." West's point is that there is a kind of "studied ignorance," which can no longer be permitted as an excusing condition for our failure to see, to make visible, and to act on what, in clear, concrete, and material terms, we know to be, not subtly, but grossly and obviously, inequitable. Conversely, though, the kind of intellectual paralysis which repudiates theory, and in particular, contemporary poststructuralist theory, as too difficult, remote, abstract, and irrelevant to the "practical" work of educational policy and program reform, is also a kind of culpable "not knowing." Where institutional policy is enacted on the basis of impoverished and inadequate theory, and where institutional practice continues to silence, exclude, demean, and disable those same groups that policy purports to empower, we "cannot not know" that there is a problem of professional ethics involved here.

It is inevitable, given the present sociocultural climate, that we will become increasingly often involved in institutional "initiatives" advancing "gender equity" as their goal. But the manner and contexts in which such work is supposed to be done will without doubt preclude and preconstrain much of what otherwise might be thought and said. There comes a point when no more can be done by making do, working within essentially misogynist conditions, acquiescing to the silencing and suppression in order to slip feminist agendas into antifeminist policies, hoping that the contradictions will not be noticed before they have had time to do their work. Where the discourse on "gender" is itself the engenderment of what becomes yet another normative order (and one not so very different, after all, from its predecessor), it is our practical duty to work together to oppose the inequities (which are, after all, not very hard to see); but our scholarly obligation is to persistently refuse to advance the agenda, to disrupt it by insisting on introducing the complexities that have been overlooked up to now. Where gender equity is construed as a species of technical fine tuning, and where structural arrangements within which such policy is negotiated effect a refusal to interrogate the traditional character and exclusionary consequences of taken-for-granted assumptions about how "gender" should be conceptualized, it seems very likely that the best we can do to advance "gender equity" is to obstruct its discursive formulation in policy and to disrupt and impede its institutional promotion in practice.

Here, then, is at least a *prima facie* case for seeing institutional projects of gender (stressing difference) and equity (stressing sameness or similarity), as these terms are currently operationalized, as inherently contradictory; as a kind of "squaring the circle." Granted, this is not an argument of any philosophical weight. But our intent is not to generate conclusions; rather it is to reveal questions and complexities in unproblematized and naturalized conceptualizations of gender, complexities which, for Haraway (1991) and other contemporary feminist theorists (e.g., Collins 1990; Fuss 1990; hooks 1984), fundamentally require us to call into question any assumptions about the necessarily emancipatory effects of identity-based ascriptions of rights.

The next section of this chapter proceeds to boldly go where no feminist should dare. What follows is an angry and highly critical account of the impact on one of us (de Castell) of the contradictory workings of a Ministry of Education–initiated gender equity committee, a committee, it is important to note, that was composed entirely of white people, almost all of them (us) women, who came prepared to work together to promote "gender equity." Anger, here, is narrated anecdotally both as a kind of knowing that is highly familiar to members of oppressed and in/subordinate groups and, it is important to note, as conferring a kind of agency through dissent that we cannot afford to repress. As Elizabeth Spelman (1989) suggests:

> If we recognize that judgments about wrong-doing are in some sense constitutive of anger, then we can begin to see that the censorship of anger is a way of short-circuiting, or censoring judgments about wrong-doing. As Peter Lyman has recently pointed out, anger is the "essential political emotion," and to silence anger may be to repress political speech. (272)

This "cautionary tale" (Van Maanen 1988) is intended to illustrate what might be termed "the return of the repressed" in feminist theory and praxis: it is about the subtle and not-so-subtle ways in which even the best-intentioned of our efforts to deal both intellectually and concretely with issues of gender and equity are as yet beyond our collective capacities. It is about the perilous contradictions of doing such work, about signposting its inherent pitfalls, and about describing the traps into which we fall, all too often, without our even recognizing how our conceptions and practices work against our stated intents in a kind of "hysterical paralysis of the intellect."

Imagine the following scenario:

I should have known, when I first walked in and saw those bowls of mini-lifesavers around the table, that I was in trouble.

The first meeting (October 1991) of the Ministry of Education Advisory Committee on Gender Equity began, as I knew it would, taking for granted that least clear, most contested, most fragmented conception: *gender*. The mood was to be of purposeful, optimistic consensus. We all, it seemed, knew who we were and why we were here: we had a job to do, and an unprecedented opportunity to do it. We were here to advance, together, a hitherto neglected human rights agenda, the agenda of "women." We were here to ensure the provision of equal rights to women, and our job was to work on the ways in which this mission would be carried out.

I put it this way, because our job was assuredly not to discover or to invent the ways in which this was to be carried out, because this had already been done for us. Accordingly, our first agenda item was to approve the Ministry of Education's implementation plans for the next four of a ten-year gender equity implementation plan for the province's public schools, from 1990 to 1994. Now you may notice that the first year had already, if inconveniently, taken place. Undeterred, we were advised that this meant we could proceed at a faster rate to 1991—a kind of bonus right at the beginning of the game. I reached for the lifesavers . . .

We began, predictably enough, with a round in which we were instructed to identify ourselves and to share with the group our information about the initiatives for the advancement of gender equity presently under way at our respective institutions. This tactic served, of course, to cement the taken for grantedness about what gender equity meant and to illustrate the kinds of things gender equity initiatives were and what they looked like. This rhetorical short-circuiting of the main argument, which was dutifully carried out by each of us nonetheless, failed to effect a total ban on discussion. Because if I knew nothing else (and in fact I really did at that point know very little else) it was that gender and indeed gender equity were not unproblematic terms. My knowledge had not been gained, at least at this point, from books. Mine was a very personal motive for speaking. I did not know who "we" were; that is to say, it was already all too apparent that I was not part of the we who were there, in skirts, in jewelry, in salon-styled hair, in wedding rings, in nail polish, in smiling, lipsticked lips. Nor was I part of "we men," the two who joined the first meeting, one young, in jacket, collar, and tie, with a boredom you could taste, and a resentment you could feel on your skin, the one who was told to be there, who never came back; then there was the older one, the jovial human-rights-in-the-school administrative activist, enjoining us all to work for the advancement of women, berating his absent, unsympathetic colleagues for their failure to see how gender equity was so necessary for us *all*, how it was necessary for men, oppressed themselves by sex-role stereotyping, their wives' careers impeded by the glass ceiling, their sons' emotional development obstructed by the burden of expectations on being male, who were not allowed to cry (the pinnacle of women's achievement in the affective domain). I was not part of "we women," nor part of "we men": I was instead—and this was the primary source of trouble for "us" from that day—one of the hitherto unthinkable, one "differently gendered."

The first task was getting people to see that there was actually a question to be asked here. Because the ministry of education had not seen the concept of 'gender' as much of a puzzle. The committee's work was quite straightforward: to approve the first four years of the ten-year gender equity implementation plan. So it seemed almost an impolite intrusion, a disruption, to ask "What do these documents mean by gender equity? It seemed to resemble the question, "What is the goal of this committee?" But that question, I was to discover, nearly tore the committee apart, because, of course, people came with very different understandings of what "gender equity" meant, and some had never really thought about its meaning. This critical omission, and the ambiguity it enabled, functioned to expedite a process of legitimation of a pre-ordained policy, a policy that had the surface features of progressive reform, but which in fact was conceptually bankrupt. Devoid of meaning, "gender equity" functioned as a placeholder, an unwritten, but nevertheless a regulative, fiction. This conceptual vacancy was covertly occupied by an operational definition of "gender equity," established *de facto* by distributing to all members of the advisory committee, along with the first meeting's agenda, a "status report" on "gender distribution" in the educational system, written by a firm of management consultants commissioned by the ministry. In this report, predictably enough, the term "gender" was operationally defined as "sex," and "equity" as "numerically equal distribution of men and women across a range of targeted roles, statuses and occupations." Accompanying this report was a memo to the effect that the report would enable the committee to identify its "baseline goals." This made it quite clear to us where we, who were supposed to be the "advisory group" on gender equity, were to be headed.

Completely ignoring the enormous conceptual contradictions it produced, the "women's ways of knowing" agenda was introduced as centrally important to the work of the committee. From there on, we embarked on the construction of a contradictory regime of truth, a regulative fiction in the name of emancipation, apparently blind to the likelihood that such a regime, whatever emancipatory illusions it might create, would operate repressively as a technology of standardization and normalization.

Rethinking This Text: Counter-Narratological
Speaking "Out" and the "Return of the Repressed"

The cat came back
Thought he was a goner, but the cat came back
On the very next day. . . .

We want to do our work, we want to create and be critical too. But how can we create if we know that our theoretical tools, our handholds, our rewards and also in part our unconscious images of what it is to be a creative person are produced by a culture which has excluded and devalued us? This is the question: how can we create? How can we create ourselves?

—Nancy Minnick, cited in Braidotti, *Patterns of Dissonance*

Our critical analysis of institutional gender in/equity policies is, it is important to note here, primarily motivated by the vastly inequitable and often impossibly contradictory conditions of our everyday existences as "campus dykes," "queer theorists," or "lesbian lecturers" in the faculties of education where we work, live, and teach, implausible and fundamentally unworkable identity positions which we have described elsewhere (Bryson and de Castell 1993) as "unten<ur>able discursive postures." Increasingly in these times of the proliferation on university campuses of seemingly liberal institutional equity ventures (the likes of which Mohanty [1990] refers to as the "diversity management industry") we find ourselves being drawn in, like moths to the open flame, without any choice, to become part of collective efforts to "empower" the oppressed. To that end, both of us (authors) have participated in significant long-term institutional ventures aimed at addressing and redressing systemic inequities in the conditions and practices of the university campuses where we work and in Ministry of Education–sponsored attempts at curricular restructuring. Yet it has invariably turned out, in our experience, that these ventures have the underlying purpose and effect to further silence, contain, and repress those people of difference with whom we are of necessity identified, even when it is in our own name that the committee's efforts are purported to be deployed. Likewise, as lesbians, we are called upon to represent our "position" and yet are systematically silenced on every opportunity where we try to avail ourselves of the opportunity to speak out. The anger and pain that are expressed here, then, arise within the vivid realization that we cannot not participate in this work, while knowing that, typically, to participate is to collude actively in the further undermining and impoverishing of the living conditions and opportunities for agency of those whom we originally wished to protect, liberate, or empower. We construe this kind of analytical work, then, as theory deployed strategically in order to envision and create a place (if only a place in the text) where the daily routines of institutional life might be rendered just a little less horrendous, brutal, demeaning, and terrifying—or, perhaps it might be more accurate to say, just a little more explicit in their implausibility as constitutive of "emancipatory" practices.

Perhaps one way to start to make (non)sense of the seemingly incompatible cacophony of voices that emerges within the contested turf of authoritative speaking, defining, ordering, and the like that characterize such discussions of gender equity is to engage the tools of discourse analysis in order to uncover as differently constructed a range of conceptualizations of "gender" implicit in contemporary understandings of gender equity. A preliminary procedure for explicating and critiquing such implicit presuppositions, then, is *tentatively* to order the conceptual field by means of a classification of conceptions of gender in terms of four theoretical paradigms (explicated further in Bryson and de Castell 1995) more or less historically represented in the order of their emergence in feminist discourse: first a positivistic conception of gender as biological sex; second, a constructionist conception of gender as socially produced and sustained; third, a critical conception of gender as the ideological product of a repressively patriarchal hegemony; and, fourth, a poststructuralist conception of gender as a noncohesive, open-textured pastiche of characteristics, aptitudes, and dispositions whose ongoing construction and reconstruction it is a central task of feminist praxis to enable and encourage. The historically emergent meanings of "gender equity" in educational discourse, accordingly, may be situated along a parallel conceptual continuum, at one end of which are biologically based conceptions of gender difference; at the other end, explanations of gender difference as socially constructed.

"Gender equity," positivistically conceived, for example, targets as its goal the achievement of numerically equal distributions of men and women across all sectors of society, although usually only certain occupations and professions have been selected for attention. Existing disciplines, occupations, and practices are left intact, affirmative action policies are instituted, and a concerted effort is made at resocializing girls and women to take up their (equal) positions in intellectual and vocational pursuits.

From the constructionist perspective, on the other hand—centrally the assumption that there exist clear, distinctive, and identifiably different "women's ways of knowing" which are currently being ignored or suppressed—there is no reason to attempt such resocialization; rather, disciplines (usually the physical sciences are invoked here) and occupations (administration and nontraditional labor being typifications) require gender-sensitive reconstruction directed toward greater inclusiveness. Much is made, on this view, of the benefits to men as well as women of this inclusion of "women's ways" and the values of "reproduction" as a necessary and desirable supplement to traditional educational emphases on production. Such gender equity policies would target the modification of existing curriculum, instruction, assessment, and social conditions of schooling to achieve a better fit with these "ways of knowing" attributed to women and might include programs for male students to enable and encourage their emotional development, for instance, or to equip them with the kinds of domestic competencies traditionally the preserve of women.

Different again would be critical conceptions of gender equity, which, quite the reverse of the inclusiveness model, not infrequently endorse a species of separatism (girls' groups, same-sex instructional arrangements, and so on). Out of a critical theory perspective might most readily emerge the insight that since it is principally misogyny which is the problem for women, the solution lies in courses for males that directly address this (often in men's groups predicated on alliance, rather than on the retooling of masculinity)—not in special policies, curricular modifications, counseling, additional training programs, or pedagogical approaches for women and girls.

A critical conception would, on the one hand, analyze "gender," and the more specific categories of "woman" and "man," as expressions of inequitable sociopolitical arrangements, and would endeavor, on the other hand, to make clear the ways in which being "of gender" understood in these terms would function to entrench that inequality. The idea of "mutual benefit" promoted in constructionist conceptions would therefore be inconsistent with a critical view; however, critical theory's enlightenment agenda could fit well with the positivist model, in the specific sense that efforts would be directed towards providing women and girls with increased opportunities to develop the skills and understandings traditionally distributed in far greater measure to boys and men. The argument here would of course be the counterhegemonic one of resisting traditional gender identification and simultaneously asserting rights to have access to resources traditionally linked to power and traditionally monopolized by males. The normative ideal in this case might well be androgyny, with separatism as a necessary intermediary step, in terms of concrete educational arrangements.

A poststructuralist agenda would construe "gender" as a set of "gender effects," as a set of manifestations, expressions, displays, and representations, not as an inner aspect of persons. Such a deconstruction of gender follows from poststructuralism's deconstruction of the autonomous, coherent, and stable self associated with enlightenment ideals of liberal individualism. Poststructuralism's "subject" is understood as shifting and repatterning itself in relation to the contingent conditions of location, place, and circumstance, gender being no more a privileged site of difference than race, class, or any of a host of other possible differences. In such a case, gender equity would have to give way to a more generalized policy of equity with respect to a vast range of kinds of difference—with, of course, all of the attendant dangers to a specifically feminist project that might involve. Although one would be hard pressed to find many pedagogic policies or practices predicated on poststructural conceptions of gender, it is worth considering how these might take shape.

Distinct conceptions of gender, as based on biological difference, on social-environmental condition, on hegemonic distortion, and on poststructural deconstruction and disruption, give rise to four correlatively distinct kinds of policy, all nominally (and confusingly for the practitioner) in the service of "gender equity." This renders such a policy treacherously self-contradictory in its net effects. In the absence of a conceptual and operational clarification that includes an analysis of its power effects, teacher advocates of gender equity, although seeming to be working toward the same goal, will inevitably be working against one another. Being without the conceptual resources to comprehend the problem adequately means being at a loss either to explain or to change inconsistent and mutually undermining orientations to the problem in practice.

Even the briefest look at these different operationalizations of gender equity, then, indicates quite clearly that to promote one conception of equity can effectively undermine others. Gender equity is conceptually contested terrain, and of special note for us are the contradictions between transformative aims (for example, to initiate a set of social and pedagogical practices aimed toward gender identity [re]formation) and preservationist presuppositions (for example, that female students necessarily operate through relations of connection and caring). These fundamental but unrecognized internal contradictions within and among competing conceptions of gender equity can result in a situation in which certain attempts to promote equity may function instead to promote repressively stereotypic norms of gender appropriateness. One particularly disconcerting example is the way in which contemporary conceptions of "women's ways," far from being emancipatory, work themselves neatly and tidily into the new masculinity, the return to family values, and decidedly antifeminist agendas. Another example is the strategic deployment of "gender employment equity" which fulfills the "letter of the law" by appointing female candidates but violates its spirit by favoring conservative candidates and/or preserving all other gendered institutional conditions and practices intact. This practice has the net effect of undermining liberatory agendas, even as it lays claim to purportedly progressive intents.

Concluding Thoughts

> Perhaps this is the time to stress technique again? . . . A detour into strategy, tactics, and practice is called for, at least as long as it takes to gain vision, self-knowledge, self-possession, even in one's decentredness.
>
> —Luce Irigaray, *Speculum of the Other Woman*

What follows from our analysis as presented thus far? There is an alternative to the paralysis created either by the naive deployment of a hopelessly liberal-pluralistic, or relativist re/presentation, of different-but-equal conceptions of "gender equity," or by the reckless assumption, in anger, of an insubordinate attitude of mere disruption and outright refusal to participate in this kind of work. Our confidence in persisting in working on "gender equity" reforms is based in the belief that it is precisely and only through participation that traditional gender mythologies will be understood and overcome, but that such change will be slow, arduous, and often accidental and piecemeal. On such a view, the work that was accomplished by the committee here reported on, despite the frustrating conditions of its enactment, actually works as a counterhegemonic mode of engagement, and thus was work worth doing. However, it is important not to commend a species of naive optimism that would have us diving cheerfully into what we have tried to argue is most often a riptide, against which our best efforts and all our good intentions are powerless: in a riptide, there is not much you can do. You can swim with the tide, but you are still carried out to sea.

The distinction between strategy and tactics is a central one for our purposes here. Strategy is an overall plan of action that consists in finding effective ways to impose the preferred time, place, and circumstances of an engagement most advantageous for one's purposes. Strategy refers to the overarching plan of action that both prescribes and limits lower-level tactical options. Tactics constitute a kind of "bricolage," an ingenious making do under conditions not of one's own choosing and not to one's advantage, which is the preserve of the relatively powerless—those who, because they cannot hope to displace hegemonic organizations and practices, look for weaknesses, accidents, or opportunities that may be seized in the moment and turned to the ends of precisely those whom the hegemony has excluded, disenfranchised, or rendered invisible (see Chafetz 1990; and de Certeau 1984). We believe that the time for the tactics of the weak is past and that it is time for a greater attention to strategy.

A place to begin might be with setting terms and conditions on our participation, setting conditions on the concrete contexts in which and the discursive terrain in terms of which gender equity (in institutional terms) can most productively be investigated. Equity agendas have become unavoidable, but the face validity of certain gender equity initiatives (which so often appear to us to constitute a calculated political staging of the ways liberal values can be embedded within patriarchal practices) will be severely in jeopardy if, as Modleski has argued (1991) feminism is enacted *without* the participation of feminists. Women are now, if perhaps not for long, in a position to refuse to participate in this work unless *we* are given the power to set out the time, place, and conditions of feminist policy making. At the very moment that we do this, we begin to cross over from the domain of tactical maneuvering to the arena of strategy. This is a major step, and a critical one, if "gender equity" work is to be anything besides collaboration with the enemy.

There is, indeed, much to do, but there needs to be time in which to do it. We need to renegotiate the circumstances and arrangements (including meeting "rules of order") within which the work is to be carried out. We need to take equally seriously both the goals and the practices by means of which we are to attain such seemingly, but not necessarily, liberatory ends as "gender equity." We need, above all, to take ourselves seriously in terms of our own preconstructed gendered, raced, and classed identities and material positionings within these contexts of the production of so-called emancipatory discourses.

To that end, Jana Sawicki (1991) argues for a kind of radical pluralism to take the place of liberal pluralism in negotiating difference/s within institutional contexts. Radical pluralism, she suggests, is characterized by the following principles:

1. It operates with a relational and dynamic model of identity as constantly in formation in a hierarchical context of power relations at the microlevel of society.
2. It politicizes social and personal relationships usually overlooked within liberal theory. Indeed, radical pluralism politicizes theory as well.
3. It challenges hegemonic power structures. (9)

For feminists to begin to specify conditions for radical social restructuring would be the first step in converting what have thus far been merely tactical engagements into strategic ones. To do this is, in an important sense, to seize control of the means of discursive production, and to turn that production to the ends of a *radical* or perhaps a *post*feminism, rather than, as has hitherto been done, subordinating nominally feminist agendas to the greater ends of orderly and hegemonically controlled institutional reform.

This is where the specificity of a feminist theory may be sought: not in femininity as a privileged nearness to nature, the body, or the unconscious, an essence which inheres in women but to which males too now lay a claim; not in female tradition simply understood as private, marginal, and yet intact, outside of history but fully there to be discovered or recovered; not, finally, in the chinks and cracks of masculinity, the fissures of male identity or the repressed of phallic discourse; but rather in that political, theoretical, self-analyzing practice, by which the relations of the subject in social reality can be articulated from the historical experience of women. Much, very much, is still to be done. (Teresa de Lauretis, cited in Alcoff 1986, 314)

References

Alcoff, L. (1986). Cultural feminism versus post-structuralism. In Micheline Malson (Ed.), *Feminist theory in practice and process.* Chicago: University of Chicago Press.

Belenky, M. G., Clinchy, B. M., Goldberger, N. R., and Tarule, J. M. (1986). *Women's ways of knowing: The development of self, voice, and mind.* New York: Basic Books Inc.

Bourdieu, P., and Passeron, J. (1977). Reproduction in education, society, and culture. Beverley Hills, CA: Sage Publications.

Braidotti, R. (1991). *Patterns of dissonance.* New York: Routledge, Chapman, and Hall.

Bryson. M., and de Castell, S. (1993). Queer pedagogy?/!: Praxis makes imperfect. *Canadian Journal of Education, 18,* 285–305.

———. (1995). Sexing the texts of educational technologies. In Jane Gaskell and John Willinsky (Eds.), *Gender in/forms curriculum* (pp. 21–43). New York: Teachers College Press.

Butler, J. (1990). *Gender trouble.* New York: Routledge, Chapman, and Hall.

Chafetz, J. (1990). *Gender equity: An integrated theory of stability and change.* London: Sage Publications.

Collins, P. (1990). *Black feminist thought: Knowledge, consciousness and the politics of empowerment.* London: Harper Collins Academic.

Davies, B. (1989). Education for sexism: A theoretical analysis of the sex/gender bias in education. *Educational Philosophy and Theory, 21,* 1–19.

de Certeau, M. (1984). *The practice of everyday life.* Berkeley: University of California Press.

de la Luz Reyes, M., and Halcon, J. (1988). Racism in academia: The old wolf revisited. *Harvard Educational Review, 58,* 299–314.

Delpit, L. (1988). The silenced dialogue: Power and pedagogy in educating other people's children. *Harvard Educational Review, 58,* 280–298.

Ellsworth, E. (1989). Why doesn't this feel empowering? Working through the repressive myths of critical pedagogy. *Harvard Educational Review, 59,* 297–324.

Foucault, M. (1980). *Power/Knowledge.* New York: Pantheon.

———. (1982). *Discipline and punish* . London: Peregrine.

Fuss, D. (1990). *Essentially speaking.* New York: Routledge.

Gilligan, C. (1982). *In a different voice: Psychological theory and women's development.* Cambridge, MA: Harvard University Press.

The Globe and Mail. (1991). 15 October, p. 12.

Haraway, D. (1991). *Simians, cyborgs, and women.* New York: Routledge, Chapman, and Hall.

hooks, b. (1984). *Feminist theory: From margin to center.* Boston: South End Press.

Irigaray, L. (1985). *Speculum of the other woman.* Ithaca, NY: Cornell University Press.

Kenway, J., and Modra, H. (1992). Feminist pedagogy and emancipatory possibilities. In C. Luke and Jennifer Gore (Eds.), *Feminisms and critical pedagogy* (pp. 138–166). New York: Routledge.

Lather, P. (1991) *Getting smart: Feminst research and pedagogy within the postmodern.* New York: Routledge.

Modleski, T. (1991). *Feminism without women: Culture and criticism in a "postfeminist age."* New York: Routledge.

Mohanty, C. (1990). On race and voice: Challenges for liberal education in the 1990's. *Cultural Critique, 18*(14), 179–208.

Riley, D. (1988). *Am I that name? Feminism and the category "woman."* Minneapolis, MN: University of Minnesota Press.

Rubin, G. (1975). The traffic on women: Notes on a political economy of sex. In Rayna Reiter (Ed.), *Toward an anthropology of women* (pp. 157–210). New York: Monthly Review Press.

Sawicki, J. (1991). *Disciplining Foucault.* New York: Routledge.

Spelman, E. (1989). Anger and Insubordination. In Ann Garry and Marilyn Pearsell (Eds.), *Women, knowledge, and reality: Explorations in feminist philosophy* (pp. 263–274). Boston: Unwin Hyman.

Spivak, G. (1988). Can the subaltern speak? In Cary Nelson and Lawrence Grossberg (Eds.), *Marxism and the Interpretation of Culture* (pp. 271–313). Urbana: University of Illinois Press.

Tyack, D., and Hansott, E. (1982). *Managers of virtue*. New York: Basic Books Inc.

Van Maanen, J. (1988). *Tales of the field*. Chicago: University of Chicago Press.

West, C. (1987). Postmodernism and Black America. *Zeta Magazine, 1*, 27–29.

Williams, R. (1983). *Keywords: A vocabulary of culture and society*. London: Fontana Press.

Yates, L. (1995). Some dimensions of the practice of theory and the development of theory for practice in relation to gender and education. In J. Blackmore and J. Kenway (Eds.), *Gender issues in educational administration and policy* (pp. 14–27). London: Falmer Press.

PART II

DISCOVERY AS IN<TER>VENTION: IDENTITY, AUTHORITY, AND RESPONSIBILITY IN EDUCATIONAL RESEARCH

❖

5

FROM CONFESSION TO DIALOGUE

FRANCISCO IBANEZ
V.I.D.A., Vancouver, B.C.

You can start by telling me who you are, where you're from, where you're going, what the meaning of life is for you.

[Laughs] All right, start with the easy shit.

[Laughs] Start with the easy shit, that's right.

Well, actually what you said before was, you know, "Tell me the things that you don't want to tell me, then we start there." I have no idea. I'd find very difficult to try and say what I don't want to talk about because you don't admit to yourself what you don't want to talk about. You kind of, you know when you get there, and all of a sudden you go, "Mmm I'm not comfortable here.". . . .

So where were we going? You asked me . . .

Well, we were trying to go, where else do you wanna go? What else do you want to ask? I'm kind of lost. I'm—we're sort of in a parallel universe, and I can't get out of it. We are going around. I have the impression we are going around something. We're not falling into something.

Well, you have to, you have to sort of peel away the layers before you get to—sometimes, I don't know if it's a conclusion, but you can't just . . . even if I were to say this is my type or something it would be out of context if I don't tell you a lot more. . . . I can't be summed up in ten words, so you tend to—you have to go and explain a lot to get to somewhere, to sort of get an idea of the broader picture, you understand?

Yeah

Takes a lot of tape maybe, but . . . (March 20, 1991)

What difference does it make to study our "selves" and not the "other"? In this chapter I discuss the ways in which identity, authority,

and power are transmuted and research practices radically reconfigured, when ethnographic investigation relinquishes the epistemological high ground gained in the disciplined interrogation of the other
and retreats to the all-too-familiar territory of the self-identity.

The research reported here was conducted primarily in British
Columbia, Canada, and Santiago, Chile. I visited ASOs (Aids Service
Organizations) in Toronto, Montreal, San Francisco, Seattle, and other
cities interviewing clients, staff, and volunteers. My purpose was to
explore the connections—and the total disconnections—between official HIV/AIDS prevention educational discourses[1] and the lived experiences[2]—sexual practices as contextualized within "everyday life" (de
Certeau 1984)—of a diverse sample of gay males. Second, by means of
a comparative, cross-cultural study, I sought to understand the *selective*
success of these official educational discourses and to make that
understanding available to HIV/AIDS educators for whom *all* lives,
not just those of, or most closely resembling, the group in dominance,
are important. Because of my own situation, such a study could not, by
any stretch of the imagination, be represented as the "disinterested
pursuit of knowledge." But of that, more later.

I worked with urban, middle-aged, body-abled, literate gay men
from a range of socioeconomic situations. Most of them have crossed
borders of one kind or another to live as immigrants, illegal residents,
or temporarily displaced, while holding jobs. Many Latino gay immigrants have died since the coming of AIDS without proper medical
attention and without access to HIV/AIDS prevention education.
Their experiences and their wisdom are my heritage.

Although flexibility was an essential characteristic of my
research schedule, I conducted a careful literature review (since 1990)
which was followed by a selection of methodological tools. I also
regarded my volunteer work in AIDS Vancouver in the educational
programs for gay and bisexual men ("Man to Man") as an integral part
of this research. In 1991 I interviewed men in Vancouver, B.C., and
Seattle, Washington. In most cases men were interviewed twice, and
full transcriptions of the first interview were mailed to the informants
before the second interview in which we discussed salient aspects of
the first. From October 1991 until February 1992 I did fieldwork in Santiago, Chile, on a CIDA grant. Thus, participant observation, community work, field note writing, and interviewing went all hand in hand.
Time limitations did not allow for a second interview of gay men in
Chile. In order to make up for the second interview more time was
given to the participants during the interview to listen to their own
recorded voices and to make changes to what had been said. The third

step in this research was the gathering and analysis of recordings, field notes, and related articles in academic and nonacademic magazines to produce a textual representation that does justice to its enormous significance.[3] This chapter is one such attempt at representation.

The dialogue excerpts that "interrupt" this text illustrate various research situations and informant opinions. This chapter traverses a range of epistemological and ethical considerations to end with conclusions about methodology that are applicable both to ethnographic practice and to HIV/AIDS prevention education. Issues of identity and representation are considered as those having a direct bearing on the ethnographic process of finding, gathering, and representing "data." Connections between the discourse of representation and practices (sexual and other) appear not only in the way gay men speak of their experiences in relation to safer sex language, but also in what they perceive this discourse is telling them, its insidious subtest. One does not always practice what one preaches; discourse and practice do not always enjoy goodness of fit.

What follows, then, is a discussion of some specific elements of research practices, interviewing, and participant observation: authority, identity, ethics, reciprocity, confidentiality, representation, and epistemological presuppositions. The cultural elements that determine each context are not explained in detail; important issues about cultural and sexual identities have been edited due to space limitations.

Identity, Authority

From where do I speak, for whom do I speak, and what gives me this authority when I write about ethnographic fieldwork, popular education, and HIV/AIDS prevention education? Saying "I'm a cultural insider" is not enough anymore; being "one of them" does not provide the key to a full understanding of their/our realities. Claiming "I'm doing research by invitation" is, at best, a suspect claim. Presumably, an ethical approach to the process of "doing" research necessitates the production of new methods of gathering data and new ways of turning it into "tales" that are morally and scientifically viable even though these may be tales about oneself and one's own social group. Most important, then, is to look for ways of building identities and authority and deploying power that are truly democratic, or at least capable of reflexivity and reciprocity with respect to the impact they have on those we "study."

If I wanted to be a "drama queen" and invoke raw "experiential authority" (Clifford 1988) I could say I do this work because I have been living with HIV since 1986.[4] I became seropositive as a Latino immigrant newly arrived to a Canadian city, at a great disadvantage, disenfranchised, with no access to intelligible information and no awareness about HIV/AIDS. I refused to get sick in angry silence. A decade and more into this plague I still perceive in the community the same sense of urgency and emergency, but the apathy has grown. The men and women who used to foam at the mouth are now dead, and the feeling that we have done everything we could is widespread.

Under these circumstances the current obsession for confessions might only backfire on good intentions to "educate" the population at large, leaving us in the realm of the stigmatized, victimized (if not always innocently) by images and tales that lie along the information highways like smelly road kills. Tragic stories are the stuff of North American tabloid popular culture these days, and they only contribute to a form of collective paranoia that paralyzes people and disables most social projects. We need to turn somewhere else to find a critical attitude toward AIDS and the identities it creates and to rebuild authority in a society that has learned to be absolutely cynical about power and its uses.

If I wanted to radicalize this identity, I would make charges of manipulation and abuse by the mass media, the health professionals, the pharmaceutical companies in North America, the scientific community, and the local government authorities (e.g., the Department of Immigration). Experience cautions me against this. Feisty activists are nowadays widely dismissed as obtrusive and disruptive, and their hands-on approach to AIDS politics is scarcely welcome. In fact AIDS politics in general is not welcomed that much anymore: it is as if we had liberated ourselves already and discrimination were a thing of the past. Long gone are the times when we would snatch away the microphones from lame epidemiological eminences to yell to the world that we were dying right there and then. People such as Larry Kramer are now portrayed as picturesque or simply as raving lunatics.

Invoking an "interpretive authority" to "thicken" (Clifford 1988) the ethnographic text with statistical analyses, pompous scientific commentary, and opinions well informed by politically correct standards is like preparing puff pastry without taking care of the stuff we put inside. I could analyze the situations and the people to death, another form of death by red tape—but do we not have enough of those? I could describe the phallocentrism that reduces HIV/AIDS education to condom usage, or the ethnocentrism of "white boys" who attempt to explain the various aspects of the AIDS crisis in reductionist terms such as "coming out" and "community."[5]

Finally, I could refuse to engage in HIV/AIDS prevention education because it is too late for some of us and the existing programs and policies are still based on the assumption that HIV positive people die at the testing site and do not need further education or training. This applies just as much, of course, to many other forms of physical and mental disability. We constantly hear in the media that people need higher education to obtain even basic jobs, but we rarely hear of new programs that allow people with disabilities to work *within* their limitations. Certainly, I refuse to be involved again in the mayhem of AIDS politics and funding. AIDS, like many other maladies, has been turned into another form of business that demands expertise and detached attitudes. Many of the ASOs that started as small, volunteer-run groups have turned into streamlined operations run by business school Ph.Ds and "accessory" community advisory committees. Still, let us give credit where credit is due: capitalizing AIDS into the AIDS "business" has compelled many NGOs (nongovernmental organizations) seriously to review and to reconsider their work and its ethical basis. The discussion—although often scarcely more than a mere mention—of ethnicity, gender, sexual orientation, and class, once almost unheard of, is now commonplace—however minimal it may still be.

The Body of the Subject

Experience is the flesh that dresses the skeleton of our identities, identities which overlap each other, cancel each other out, reinforce each other, and provide texture, a topography, of the "self." Identities are not static but are in constant interplay in public and private contexts. In validating observation and interviewing through participation, these multiple identities constitutive of our self have to play a key role. Sexuality, sex, pleasure, desire, anger, necessity, and power struggles cease to be regarded as mere experiences or "analytical categories." They are reconceptualized as expressions of the self and when surfacing and visible come to be recognizable as identities incribed in the body. It is in this way that the body is itself a text.

Marvin (1988) makes the point that the body is "squarely at the critical juncture between nature and culture. . . . The inscription of cultural codes upon the body is perhaps the principal means of detaching it from nature and transforming it into culture. The body and its actions [practices and identity/expressions], therefore, have richly ambiguous social meaning. They can be made to emphasize perceived distinctions between nature and culture as the need arises, or to reconcile them" (110). Thus, sexual identity "professes to inform us what we have in common, what makes us all alike and recognizable, what is true about ourselves" (187). In participant observation that specifically deals with sexuality and other expressions/identities of the body both points, nature and nurture, stand on a continuum. One cannot expect people to assert fully that they "were born to be this way" or that they "chose to be this way" the same way one chooses a career.

We face an odd dilemma when we interview a drag queen, to name just one example. Who should one interview, the diva or the man behind the make-up? Whose identity is more important? Whose purpose is my selection of identity serving?

One of my main concerns in this project was not to deny the experiences—expertise—of those people I interviewed. I acknowledge my control of the research, my biased language, my tenuous alliance with the academy, and my own situation within fieldwork. I acknowledged that by invoking various identities to construct experiential or interpretive authority upon those basis is a process at odds, and sometimes in opposition, to the identities of the participants. This process sometimes disregards and undermines the authority of the participants as "experts" and long-time inhabitants of their bodies. In a circular gesture, I attempted to shift from statistics and theories—interpretive authority—to our experiences—experiential authority—to build authority in a dialogue that allows various perspectives to co-exist.

Two identities inscribed in the bodily texts of Latinos are not usually considered when designing and implementing HIV/AIDS prevention education programs in North America; they are obscured by the HIV/AIDS prevention education discourse and discursive practices. One is a cultural identity, *el mestizo*; the second is a sexual identity, *el macho*. Both expressions are made more complex when Latino bodies cross borders (particularly into North America) and the immigrant identity—rarely a positive one—is thrust upon them.

Mestizos was the name given to the children of native women by Spanish men. Today *mestizaje* means a hybridization of races and blood. This is not only a biological process which began about five hundred years ago. It is an identity (often seen as political struggle) that has a crucial influence in the ethos of Latin Americans (Montecino 1991). The *mestizo* identity places an individual at the heart of a perennial conflict between what is mixed—*criollo*—and what is supposedly pure (European). The Latino body and its ethos are placed under siege and surveillance when we cross the border into North American countries. Bodies and ethos constantly collude and clash with the white ethos that is exuberantly deployed in mass media and reinforced in bureaucratic policies and regulations.

The second identity, el *macho*, embodies a specific Latin American sexual and social ethos. Various religious, cultural, and sexual themes such as the absent father, the dualism *virgin/whore*, and the dualism *caring mother/playful son* are contained within this identity. An exploration of the understandings and practices of Latinos and Gringos can help us understand the implications of this identity in the formulation of HIV/AIDS prevention education discourse, how this identity is deployed or constricted within the official HIV/AIDS prevention discourse, what happens with this identity when it encounters North American female and male identities, and what could be done to integrate this identity to the existing HIV/AIDS prevention education programs. Further exploration of the *macho* identity can also help us to verify the theoretical assertions of researchers such as Lumsden (1991), Montecino (1991), and Almaguer (1991). One of the most intriguing theoretical approaches explains that Latinos' sexuality is aim oriented and gringos' sexuality is object oriented. The former implies that *el macho* ultimately seeks to satisfy his sexuality as an *activo* [active] partner be it with a woman or a man; the choice of object does not diminish his sexual status in society. The latter assertion, that gringos are object oriented, implies that white Anglo Saxon men see their sexual status mainly based on the gender of those they have sex with.

Further exploration of the understandings and practices of Latinos and gringos can help us understand how these identities are deployed or constricted within the "official" HIV/AIDS prevention education discourse, what happens when they encounter North American identities and stereotypes, and what could be done to recognize them and their authority within the existing HIV/AIDS prevention education programs. It is only through participation in the form of dialogue and the sharing of authority—power—that theory can be checked against practices and lived experiences and more inclusive forms of education can be found. Programs of primary and secondary HIV/AIDS prevention need to be demedicalized and need to reflect the myriad of pressing needs and desires of nonmainstream social groups.

The Written Body of Evidence: Academic Text

Academic written texts are regarded as authoritative and legitimate. Embodied text—the bodies of our subjects—are perceived as "irrational" and "unreliable" and, so seen, they become the sites of "subjugated knowledges" (Foucault 1980). Appealing to both texts equally reminds us that "the personal is political"—"personal" not in an individualistic sense of the word, but in a dialectical sense, the body that is immersed in a web of social relations and within specific material conditions.

A primary methodological challenge here involved attempts to bring the other into my text—the body of the gay individual, the "contaminated" body of the person living with HIV/AIDS,[6] the voice of the immigrant with a broken accent, and the other identities at play in and on embodied subjects. This research practice does not necessarily make the final "product" more intelligible or better, but it provides enormous and all-too-often overlooked opportunities for dialogue, exploration, and discovery. The final text can offer more, and different, tales than a traditional academic exposition. This is why I gave transcriptions of the conversations to participants or I invited the participants to listen to the recordings of the first session. I recorded the second conversation and provided transcripts of that too. The participants thus had a better chance to rethink and alter what they said during the interview and to reshape the written text.

People in the margins and in social situations with greater plasticity are sensitive to issues on "both sides of the fence." I favored a form of "standpoint epistemology" to do justice to this sensitivity—"skills"—of the participants. This theory presupposes "that less powerful members of society have the potential for a more complete view of the social reality than others, precisely because of their disadvantaged position. That is to say, in order to survive (socially and sometimes even physically), subordinate persons are attuned or attentive to the perspective of the dominant class (for example, white, male, wealthy) as well as their own" (Nielsen 1990, 10).

> I could see all my friends going out with somebody and all that jazz, and I said to myself "What about me, I can't feel anything. I cannot go out [with somebody]." A series of questions were attached to this, you understand?
> How old were you?
> Nineteen. On one side I rejected all what homosexuality was, but on the other side it was my own sexuality that was demanding to be lived, you understand? Deep inside. It was a big conflict, you see. Something happened. I kept on working at the parish after I left the seminary
> What happened?
> I'll tell you in a second. At that time I was doing confirmation [catequesis], and there was a guy there I liked, you see. One day we went on a working retreat to the beach with all the guys of confirmation, guys between seventeen and twenty years old.

This seventeen-year-old guy had a story with me. We talked about it. This thing was well agreed, but this guy later let his tongue loose. He told the priest. He told a bunch of people, so . . .

What did he tell them?

Well, he told them that he was drunk, that I had raped him and lot of things, you see, although we had talked about it and had done it in common agreement . . . this brought a lot of stuff [upon me]. I was expelled from . . . All the responsibilities I had within the "pastoral" were taken away from me. I mean, I couldn't exercise as a *catequista* [a religion student who teachers others]. I couldn't do anything public, only to go to mass and goodbye, this caused an even greater frustration.

What did you say? . . . Never occurred to you to deny this or to accuse the homosexual goings on among all of them.

I didn't say anything . . . nothing, nothing, never, never. I never said anything because I felt guilty because I thought I was sick . . . so the others were right, not me. I started getting apart from all this church thing, and I started to participate a bit more in what was "social" stuff. I realized that the social and political stuff was just as traumatic and frustrating as the other. Apart from declaring themselves as liberals and all that bullshit, I was working with left wing parties, people said that the ultimate goal was to fornicate in peace, you understand? But it was for them, not for me. Now I realize all these things, you see. Many of these assholes, when "they had a story" with a woman, they were fascinated, you see, but when they got it, sort of, that I was gay, shit, there was a "trauma," a lot of stuff.

They told you something?

Well, no they wouldn't say anything in front of me, but, there were, I knew—comments would come to me that they had—I mean, there were a lot of comments behind me, you understand? This would screw me. It would screw me eternally, so I started all my working life—I started to have "stories" with some co-workers. I had a gay friend—I still have him—and we started to meet people like very, very isolated. The first was before I went to [a neighbour country]. We prepared a fashion show with my friend, and a hairdresser helped us. He was openly gay and new to the *ambiente* [scene] and the whole thing. I remember that the first time he brought an invitation to go to the [gay disco] I got angry. I said to my friend, "How can you even think about us going there? It's full of fags." Yes, like this in those words. (December 12, 1991)

In this work, it has been essential to adopt ethnographic procedures and theoretical stances that respect the diversity of opinions, perceptions, and expressions of the participants and are likely to cause the least harm to the participants and to oneself. A balance can be struck between censorship for the sake of the informants—treating people with velvet gloves—and the brutal description of the realities found in the field, a rabid form of tough love. Confidentiality and anonymity are not enough to protect people and accurately describe their realities. Participant observation and interviewing are obtrusive and *inevitably* alter the historical course of what is being observed; ethnography irrevocably influences the interests and lives of the people represented in them—individually and collectively, for better or for worse.[7]

Well, as you can see it is difficult to follow one's own train of thoughts in this house. In general in this city. It was a crazy week. I "graduated" in my course for leaders at the CChPS (with diploma and everything), worked with "pobladoras" in "Comuna El Bosque" (where P. and I used to teach, lots of memories there), worked with folklore cantores, etc. Going to the CChPS is addictive, like a drug. It seems almost strange to end a day without checking in at the old house in Porvenir 464. I guess this is because for the first time since I started this morbid business of AIDS I really feel I'm doing something that is not merely ritualistic. Some other days I feel differently, my usual schizoid personality swings, I feel that I could never get used to do this community work for a long time. All the educators around me have so much stamina and at the same time they are sort of resigned to their situation. I am ambitious, you know this. The work in poblaciones, in the NGO itself is slow and painful, it drags along, it eats the best of us. I think that this experience has made me change a lot but I still like the academic life and its middle class, sheltering, comfortable place in the world. What can I do, ¡¡las bonitas nacimos para vivir bien!! (Letter, December 2, 1991)

Interviewing: From Confession to Dialogue

In its design and implementation, a major goal of the project reported here was to look beyond the stiff academic standards for ethnographic research to a stance that could acknowledge and be responsive to the concerns and imbalances of any specific research situation. I was clear as I could then be about my research intentions, my choice of participants, my gain, and his/my rights and responsibilities. I tried to demystify the interview process by making it clear that this should not be perceived as a counseling session or a confession, but it could be a moment of reflection. Questions were presented as clusters of topics such that the participants would read and ask questions about them before the interview was recorded. Invariably, one of the first observations on the part of the participants was: "Will I have to talk about all of this?" to which I responded, "No, but when dealing with one point we will probably touch on many of the others." And so it happened; I explained that I did have "questions" in my mind, but I encouraged the participant to choose an area that looked interesting as a place to begin. Most topics included in the interview schedule involved subjects one usually hears discussed among gay men when dealing with HIV/AIDS, sexuality, and relationships. In Chile I devised a slightly different research schedule after consulting with a number of people about the cultural salience of the initial categories I had devised for English respondents.

My experience as interpreter for the Canadian Immigration Refugee Board was useful in deciding what I did *not* want these interviews to be: cross-examinations, the search for a "confession" of the refugee claimant's hidden truth. Indelible memories of my strict Catholic elementary schooling helped me decide that I did not want these interviews to be genuflected confessions to one's spiritual guide. I understand confession in the Foucauldian sense as a "one of the most highly valued techniques for producing truth" (Foucault 1980, 59). This "truth" is represented in social research texts in the form of answers to questionnaires, statistical analysis,[8] and structured interviews. Confession, when not obtained "spontaneously," is, says Foucault, "dictated by some internal imperative, the confession is wrung from a person by violence or threat; it is driven from its hiding place in the soul, or extracted from the body" (59). Sobbing confessions of persons living with HIV/AIDS that offer their tragedies for public scrutiny, wild descriptions of the "homosexual lifestyle," and figures that invest the number of sexual partners of gay men with a moral value are interpreted as the irrevocable "truth" of the sin of "promiscuity."

Listening to many stories, particularly stories of the first sexual encounter, "coming out," and romance, I found connections between confessions and sexual "preference" or "orientation" that were useful in interpreting the interviews from within a theoretical grid.

I have always thought that my personal history of how I became gay is rather confusing. Many aspects overlap. It is very clear for me that when I was eleven years old I felt or started to feel really in love with a girlfriend, a woman. This love feeling has followed me I think even until today. . . . Now I'm thirty-three years old, and I always feel—I have always felt—that I haven't loved anybody else but her, and today at thirty-three, sorry, thirty-six years old I understand that in some way she is still a person I admire profoundly, profoundly, and I always feel, even now, a little moved when I remember this love feeling I had because it was important. I feel that to a degree it marked me, and I don't know how I started to be an homosexual. I guess that maybe it's not incompatible for me to have loved a woman profoundly, but having desired men in a sexual way . . . I have felt full of illusions, tied. I think I have had an idea of love with several men, but the love or this love feeling that remains throughout time—I have not only felt it with her, careful, the love that I felt for her was absolutely platonic, maybe if it had been more carnal, more real, and more grounded maybe it would not have lasted what it has lasted because it was a love that ultimately moved in the world of thoughts. . . . In spite of the love that I had for this woman I felt homosexual anyway. Men excited me sexually in the buses, and when I was a child, a high school boy, or before maybe I was already getting profoundly excited by men, and I don't know when it was, what is clear to me that when I was little, six, seven, eight years old or at ten I thought how the hell homosexuality could exist, that whether it didn't nauseate homosexuals to be homosexuals, but I had a sexual awakening very violent and very strong. I was a very excitable type, and at twelve I had homosexual games with friends. . . . It was violent because I was starting to have sexual relations and it was something that I couldn't control, even more masturbation is still a frequent practice in me, but it was very much so when I was a child, as many times as I wanted a day. It was very easy. (January 24, 1992)

Foucault (1980) argues that "from the Christian penance to the present day, sex was a privileged theme of confession" (61). He adds that "the confession was, and still remains, the general standard governing the production of the true discourse of sex" (63). "Coming out," for instance, always involves a certain degree of power release to another person. Thus when interviewing, it is critical to acknowledge not only that gay men come out (as men who have sex with men and as men living with HIV/AIDS) from a position of lesser power, but also to reconsider the very concept of 'coming out' as an ethnocentric "white" notion with a whole embedded set of power relations of its own. This problem might not be entirely avoidable, but it should be explicitly formulated as Mercer and Julien (1988) have argued in order to give a safe space for "difference" to be spoken.

I have marked "confession" and "dialogue" as two opposing points in a continuum of communication. The term "dialogue" is here borrowed from Paulo Freire (1973). The term lends itself not only to popular education but also to critical ethnographic research. "Confession" represents a highly institutionalized location where practices are rigid and manipulative. One individual—the priest, the shrink, the scientist—asks questions, analyses, appropriates, interprets, and represents the bodily texts of others based on some vaguely understood inherent right to investigate. Patients get diagnosed and written up by doctors and nurses and their "objective" descriptions of bodies and situations become the "truth" about the individual. Dialogue represents the possibility of a greater power balance between individuals, the acceptance of more fluid social roles and a sharing of practices of representation.

There is some appropriation and co-optation of the "other" that one cannot escape,[9] and here again the golden rule of "the least harmful way to do research" applies. Bristow and Esper (1988) distinguish three dialogical processes in ethnographic research: "(1) the researcher's internal dialogue, (2) the dialogue between researcher and participant, and (3) the dialogue between researcher and society" (74). There is an ongoing dialogue between the researcher and segments of the society in formal and informal conversations with fellow students and teachers, in community work, in workshops, and in presentations. There is a strong dialogical instance in the form of urgency, anger, advocacy, and action.

Dialogue between researcher and participants occurs at various levels in this research and is not restricted to tape-recorded interviews. Intimate conversations, marginal commentary, accents, intonations, emphasis, gestures, laughs, and tears that give rich texture to the interviews are irretrievable. It is difficult to unilaterally assess the degree of dialogieity created with the participants. I can only provide indications of the atmosphere, involvement, and tone achieved in the course of recorded conversations. Instances of self-dialogue and reflection on the part of participants are included in these conversations

What other comments have you heard about HIV positive people?
From gay men, I don't really know because I don't know that many gay men. As matter of fact I don't know any other than

[my ex lover] and these people where he works, this other guy who has had AIDS for years and . . . he's there and he talks. I mean, I'm talking strictly as a person, never mind AIDS or no AIDS or whatever, he is not the most likable person or he is not the person you would talk to because probably he doesn't have much education or imagination or he talks very superficially about things, about the weather and about . . . stupid things. . . .

He's never talked about his experience?

No. I barely know him. I met him a few times in the bar, and we talked bla, bla, bla, a little bit here and there, and that's it. . . . What I'm trying to say that I don't know enough gay men that I have established some kind of relationship or friendship or lover or anything like that.

How does that make you feel? Well, that's a kind of loaded question I know, but . . .

It makes me feel sad because you know I see [a female friend]. She has so many lesbian friends, and I see women whether they are lesbian or not, they are capable—what I've seen—they are capable of making this bond between them. They become friends. They are together. They go here, they go there, they see each other, often, fairly often, and they don't fight, and the only thing I do not like in gay men is that the attitude is that I'm better than you are. I am more beautiful than you are, and therefore you don't deserve my friendship or you don't even deserve me talking to you, and I find so frustrating not to be able to establish at least a sensible, honest conversation with a gay man, because straight men, that's not a problem. I get along with them anytime, anywhere, a gay man, to establish, like you and I right now, it is very difficult for me or probably for everybody else, and yet I go to the bar and I see them coming, "Oh hi John," or, "Hi Mike," or "Hi whoever," and they go to another group and bla, bla, bla, and I wonder, Damn it, what is wrong here? Am I ugly? They think I have AIDS or something?" I try to talk to somebody and . . .

They look down on you or something.

Yeah, right, exactly.

The two things that surprise me the most about relationships here, and I'm afraid of saying it anymore because I have been chastised in the past for saying that this is an Anglo problem, might be a problem of the culture altogether—I mean Anglos and Asians and Latinos altogether in this mix, the problems that seem to happen or that I see, the lack of strong relationship and difficulty of establishing [a] long-lasting relationship and emotional friendship and the other—we talked about it the other day—is what I see as an incredible lack of curiosity. I mean they always ask you where you come from, is it very hot there, and all this "Andale, Andale!!" all this shit, but this lack of curiosity about.

You!!

You as a person, your experience, what you have been through and not because I'm HIV positive, but in general, I mean, how come you became gay.

I know—I know I've had two experiences. (September 20, 1991)

Qualitative research practices such as interviewing and doing participant observation have presented two other challenges that we have inherited from the traditional standards of reliability and validity: (1) people change their minds (Weeks, 1989); the research schedule and structure should allow them/us to do so, and (2) the material and historical conditions within which the research is carried out are unstable. We often hear so-called hard-nosed researchers describe ethnography as "purely anecdotal and circumstantial, one of the excesses of extreme relativism," or they say, "It would be impossible to replicate this study." However, the phrase *you had to be there* does not accurately deliver the significance of the punch line. There is a tortuous dialogue between academics and community workers, informants and researchers, and between researchers and society. The experiences of people living with HIV, for example, are irreproducible, but the ethical approach and its implementation are. Another criticism is that people might not be as empowered as the researcher would like to believe (Ellsworth 1989) and in such situations participants only "ventriloquate" the official line not to lose face. They say what we want to hear without any malicious intent on their part. The challenge here is to research and report the realities we find in a highly self-conscious form that allows for different voices and the complexity of their dialogue to exist in an academic text.

A moralistic judgment often is attached to the issue of consistency, coherence, and rationality in people's understandings and practices. When doing ethnography informants are expected to be truthful, consistent, coherent, and rational in their responses, and we utilize data-gathering strategies that seem morally sound and lock the participants into structures that are only useful to the researchers (see Clifford 1988, 55–91). Any departures from what originally was stated by the individual could be construed as unreliable, subjective, weak, moody, intuitive, and emotional. Any interventions outside the rigidly set boundaries of a questionnaire or scope of leading questions is described as insular wisdom, soft data, anecdotal information, in brief, as "subjective." It is argued that such data "should not infect objective truth—evaluative concerns of the subjective knower should be excluded" (Nielsen 1990, 4). Much of the stuff of participatory ethnographic research is contained in the bodily texts of those who are being represented. There is a need to secure a valid and legitimate place for these bodily texts in the textual representation of ethnographies. The final written text gives a mutilated fragment of such bodily texts, loose limbs that have to be considered as part of a more complex body. I consciously attempted to make the interview a moment of reflection, negotiation, and meaning making for all of us. This purposeful shift of emphasis from discovering what someone is hiding (i.e., confession) to negotiating representation not only serves the purposes and theories of the researcher (i.e., dialogue): there is a shift from the researcher's needs to the participant's needs, an emphasis on advocacy that is political and serves a collective purpose rather than an emphasis on individualistic scientific interpretation that is seemingly neutral. There is an emphasis on discovery, meaning making, and negotiation rather than on verification of a particular fact (Mishler 1986).

I wanted to speak about . . . I found it very, what I was going to tell you some time before, about being a bit effeminate. Is that the word?

Yes.

I love that!! Sometimes I feel, when one walks somewhere in front of so many men to appear like this, effeminate. I like it. I feel well.

I like it in the intimacy [of a place] but not in the street.

Well, depends . . .

I'm not comparing. I'm telling you my experience.

[Voice raises a couple of octaves] Oh, I'm sorry, sorry. [Laughs]

I'm telling you how I like it, in an intimate place. In the street I get scared, I get inhibited.

I see. I don't know, I might be very daring, but I like in the street, when I see a little group [of men] which looks interesting and "cool" I love it. I like to see their reactions. Not all of them have enough "personality" to say something to you.

Are reactions similar here in Chile and in the United States?

No . . . one can "break oneself" [be limp wristed] and be very effeminate there and no one says anything because it is very normal, it is very normal.

Well, my experience is that straight men are not going to pay attention to you at all.

Nothing, that's right, but here, you go in front of a [straight] group, one "catches the wavelength" when it is going to be comforting. One knows whom one is doing this with, but when I see a group like this, "cool" that I know they are not going to say anything, but I swear I love it, to be ambiguous, because it makes me feel good. It is a compliment. It makes me feel young, that I haven't lost my "spark" [Giggles]. (November 11, 1991)

The bodies of men (and women) living the critical phase of the HIV/AIDS continuum prominently flashed through the media during the 1980s came to feed these collective stereotypes. The bodies are the "flash-point[s] of conflict between desire, and the various institutions which regulate the look of the social world" (Watney 1987, 125).[10] Epidemiological studies have utilized the bodies of women and men to obtain confessions that support hard scientific truths. Women and men living with HIV/AIDS have volunteered in clinical trials and interviews in order to obtain what they needed at a certain point, a treatment, a cure, a hope. They have systematically been placed in situations where they are forced to misreport or to lie openly. Far too much of the research upon which HIV/AIDS education has been based is precisely of this character, and with irreversibly devastating consequences.

[In Chile] I never got the idea of having [the ELISA test] done here. . . . I don't know, never. . . . Maybe it's because I'm so sure about what I do, why do I have to go if . . .

In the United States you weren't so sure?

Yes, I was, but I did it more out of curiosity, because I read in a newspaper for Latinos. It said "If you want to have the AIDS test, it is with a translator, there is an interpreter here and bla, bla, bla, and it's free, and call us and O.K." So one day I said, "I'm gonna have it done." I did it because, now I recall, because I wanted to maintain relations with this poet [I have told you about,] . . . so I phoned, asked for an appointment and . . . at that time I was getting to know this poet. We were . . . I said "I like this man. I'm gonna do it just in case." I had heard through other people that it was asked, if you wanted to maintain relations with somebody and somebody asked you, "Did you have the test done," so I could say, "Yes, I had it done and here it is." So I went and had it done. There was a Chicano. I told him I wanted to have the test done out of curiosity. They asked me many questions, where I was from, what I was doing there. I was very honest. I told them that I had come with a tourist visa, that I was here working illegally.

How did they treat you?

They treated me very well. They told me that I was a person with a lot of courage to have gone like this to have this test done, that they admired this and went to have this famous test done. They asked me how my sexual life was, and I told them [Laughter] at what time I started. They asked me if I had prostituted myself. I have never done that. I have only done this for pleasure, because I like it, so that's that, so we did that. . . . So I was there with the doctor and this Chicano man asking me questions. Well, I have to make a great side comment [Giggle] I liked the doctor. I found him very attractive.

And you let him know this, I gather.

Of course. I told him, "If I had the chance to go to bed with someone I would do it with you, if you wanted to."

What did he say?

They were plop!! both of them.

The doctor was gay?

Gay. He said nothing. He looked at me like this. The Chicano was open mouth. I said, "Good things have to be told. When I find something good I say it, I feel it." The questions were very good. I liked them. . . . They asked me about my relations if one was "pasivo" or "activo," which positions I liked most, oral, if one maintained relations high or drunk, how were the relations that one had. I explained to him that I liked alcohol but not to go and get inebriated, a bit is O.K., I do not smoke, and if I go to bed is because I feel it and I feel desire, that innate desire one has, not that I need a stimulus. . . . After the test was done asked me if I wanted to fill out a form, answer a [written] test. I said, "Yes." He would pay me U.S. fifteen dollars, and it took two hours and something that I had to be there answering all these questions. After I left the "exam" [ELISA test], I went to another room to answer this test. I was relaxed, pretty curious, I felt O.K., I didn't have to speak English. I knew there was another person doing it for me at that moment. . . . The questions were about how I maintained relations, whether I would maintain relations with an active or passive person, whether I would use a condom or not, and after, what I told you about, if one met someone in the street, so one would say, "I'd like to be with you and maintain a rela-

tion, but we don't have condoms." Any of the two men had condoms, so one said, "Only masturbation," and . . . and so this man
asked me, "What else would you do?" I said—when I said that I
could suck it without [a] condom, well, I would do what I feel, so
he was accommodating this thing the way they wanted me to
answer.

How did you realize this?

Because the man translated this to me, "How come." First I
was speaking of safe sex, of taking all the precautions and think
about it all, thinking with my head, and then I said, "Well, if I like
this dude, why not do it without a condom?" So that answer
made them upset. . . . The man tell me, "You are contradicting
yourself. You don't have to answer like this." [He said] that I
have to follow my own standard . . . what I thought at the beginning, that the condom, and my head and later I come up with
this.

They were visibly upset or just like this?

I noticed the reaction. They were upset in both ways, but I
said to myself, Well, this is just a thing. They were the ones who
asked me to answer their form. I didn't ask to fill it out. I kept on
answering their questions. There was another thing I responded
to that they didn't like it very well, but at this moment I don't
remember. (November 11, 1991)

Conclusion

Let us now reflect on the different topics I have covered and how
they might influence educational understandings and practices. Striving for dialogue in interviewing and participant observation, this
chapter suggests, offers possibilities for reflection and explicitly politicized conscientiousness (awareness raising). Building a shared authority offers what Patti Lather calls "catalytic validity" (1991), which is
based on reciprocity and self-reflexiveness. Catalytic validity is a deci-
sive element in the construction of authority within the textual representation of participatory ethnographies. Neither ethnography nor
any other methodology might necessarily have any direct educa-
tional/pedagogical application. However, in the course of doing
ethnography there are many opportunities to do community work and
educational work. In reflexive and critical ethnography one acts from
within the community and with this community.

What we know about HIV/AIDS prevention education, its "official" discourses, and its discursive practices has little or nothing to do

with what is spoken/unspoken and practiced/unpracticed at the street level.[11] HIV/AIDS prevention education discourse describes the body; its identity/expressions; and its practices, actions, and roles in essential terms. There is a gap between the formal discourse of "what we ought to do" and the street talk with jokes, anecdotes, stories, whispers, and sarcasm that bluntly says "We do what we do," "I am what I am" and "Shit happens anyway." The experiences and understandings both of gringos and of Latinos who have crossed the borders bring to the surface—*deja a flor de piel*—the tensions between official discourse and street discourse, between reductionism representations of the body/self and the hybrid identities—*identidades mestizas*—of the skillful bodies (Delany 1991). Most men I interviewed had crossed borders to go into a different culture, a gay neighborhood, or a different social sphere. Most gay men cross a border to find a new life options. Until recently North American HIV/AIDS prevention education discourse was based solely on rigid perspectives of women and men and disregarded the culturally and sexually specific "ethos"[12] of those it intends to educate, thus succeeding only in delivering information. Latin American HIV/AIDS prevention education has mimicked North American HIV/AIDS prevention education discourse and discursive health promotion practices (e.g., posters, brochures, safer sex workshops) and has reproduced its essentialism. HIV/AIDS prevention education discourse is based largely on health promotion and social marketing approaches that make sense in the North American cultural context. Understandings and practices on and about illness, health, and sexuality have a theoretical (and theological) base that fits poorly both with street level understandings and with experiences of those who use it. North American HIV/AIDS prevention education discourse discriminates on the restricted basis of sexuality. It is task oriented toward predetermined goals (e.g., Alcoholics Anonymous' 12 steps program) and obscures gender, social class, and cultural identities. The official discourse attempts to occlude diversity behind a rhetoric that purports to be rational and nonjudgmental.[13] Through the conversations with gay informants in different geographical locations various elements emerge at the point of encounter of both cultures, the border crossing and the border dwelling. Recognizable identities are inscribed in the bodily texts of Latinos and gringos. They are fluid and should be problematized constantly to subvert the oppressive—and only *selectively* effectual—frames of HIV/AIDS prevention education discourse, and it has been the purpose of this chapter to consider ways in which ethnography offers significant possibilities for critical reflection and democratic praxis.

Notes

1. This is by no means the only discourse on and about HIV/AIDS. I single it out because of its institutionalisation through the medical, scientific, and nongovernmental organizations establishment. In Canada the official HIV/ AIDS prevention discourse has been defined in documents such as *Safer Sex Guidelines: A Resource Document for Educators and Counsellors*: Report from the Canadian AIDS Society consultation on safer sex, March 1988 (Ottawa, 1989). In the United States a similar publication illustrates this point: the public report by the Surgeon General—*Understanding AIDS*—widely distributed in 1988 both in Spanish and in English. In Chile a similar document entitled *Manual de Educaciòn para la Prevención del SIDA* was released by the Health Ministry's AIDS commission (CONASIDA0 in January 1992). The existence of these documents by no means "normalizes" the discourses on and about HIV/AIDS. The social construction (see *The Care of the Self*, 1984) and "polyvalence" (Foucault 1976) of any discourse has to be kept in mind at all times in order to avoid accepting this official discourse as the only legitimate one.

2. The scope of the project primarily encompasses individuals within specific sites of production and circulation of educational discourse: nonprofit, nongovernmental organizations (NGOs), and self-help groups. The description of understandings and experiences on and about NGO politics, the politics of funding HIV/AIDS prevention education, issues around living with HIV/AIDS, the relationship between the state and NGOs, ASOs, CBOs, and PWAs, and public policy aroundHIV/AIDS are beyond the scope of this chapter, although they are the foundations for the theoretical work presented here.

3. A separate analysis is required to deal with the issue of translation/interpretation from Spanish into English. Some of the participants are Chilean men who have lived in the United States and Australia. Some other Latin American men reside permanently (legally and illegally) in British Columbia or Washington State, United States These men are partially literate in English. My own experience as an interpreter for the Canadian Immigration Refugee Board (1989–1992) is useful when attempting accurate translations of the conversations conducted in Spanish (and Spanglish).

4. "Experience invokes a participatory presence, a sensitive contact with the world to be understood, a rapport with its people, a concreteness of perception. It also suggests a cumulative, deepening knowledge. . . . It is worth noting, however, that this 'world,' when conceived as an experiential creation, is subjective, not dialogical or intersubjective" (Clifford 1988, 37).

5. For an interesting discussion of white gay racism see Julien and Mercer's article "Race, Sexual Politics and Black Masculinity: A Dossier" in *Male Order: Unwrapping Masculinity*, ed. Rowena Chapman and Jonathan Rutherford (London: Lawrence and Wishart Limited, 1988).

6. This statement is redundant because the term *homosexual*, regardless of its HIV status has been construed as contaminated in order to secure the status of its alleged ontological counterpart: *heterosexual*. Fuss argues that "For heterosexuality to achieve the status of the 'compulsory,' it must present itself as a practice governed by some internal necessity. The language and law that regulates the establishment of heterosexuality as both an identity and an institution, both a practice and a system, is the language and law of defence and protection: heterosexuality secures its self-identity and shores up its ontological boundaries by protecting itself from what it sees as the continual predatory encroachments of its contaminated other, homosexuality" (1991, 2).

7. A continuum parallel to that between "dialogue" and "confession" can be marked between "consciousness raising" and "assistencialism," a "term used in Latin America to describe policies of financial or social assistance which attack symptoms, but not causes, of social ills" (Freire 1973, 15). In popular education and participatory ethnography practices the ideal to be attained is that of "facilitation." The researcher attempts to act as a catalyst for positive change. The other side of the continuum, "assistencialism" reproduces relations of dependency.

8. I side with Jesus Ibañez' (1991) assertion that "statistics has to do with the State: it is the science of the State. Through statistics, the State [*se reserva*] 'keeps a hold of' randomness [uncertainty] and [sets the norm] attributes to the norm. In Protocapitalism [statistics allows the state to] review the resources (descriptive statistics); in production and accumulation capitalism [statistics] allows [the state] to fight against entities without strategy (prescriptive statistics); in consumerist capitalism [statistics] allows [the state] to fight against entities with strategy (symmetric strategies . . .). Statistics allows for the domination of dominated classes without their being aware of such domination" (41).

9. In the analysis and textual representation stages of ethnographic research I am also unable to escape the capilarity of power relations. There is however a conscious attempt to part from absolute "editorial control" to "polyphony" (Clifford 1988, 51).

10. Some HIV/AIDS research has done nothing but revamp literary themes such as the contamination of blood (vampirism) by the other's desire (e.g., promiscuity). An interesting analysis of this theme is presented by Case (1991).

11. The formulations of the concepts of 'illness', 'health', and 'sexuality' have been made based on white concepts. The deployment of the infamous HIV+/HIV- dichotomy in the popular mind is an illustration of the circulation and reinterpretation of the authoritative discourse of the medical institution. This is a scientific distinction that ultimately is defined by counselors and physicians in the testing and diagnosis sites (Patton 1990).

12. Ethos is the way we inhabit a world and the sharing of some common elements such as time (history) and space (country).

13. "Safe Sex: Choices to Share." "If you already know about safer sex but feel guilty because you have unsafe sex, call AIDS Vancouver and ask about the sexual safety Support Group" (AIDS Vancouver brochure 1992).

References

Almaguer, T. (1991, Summer). Chicano Men: A cartography of homosexual identity and behaviour. *Differences: A Journal of Feminist Cultural Studies, 3*. Indiana University Press.

Bristow, A. R. and Esper, J. A. (1988). A feminist research ethos. *A Feminist Ethic for Social Research*. Nebraska Sociological Feminist Collective. Lewiston, NY: E. Mellen Press.

Case, S. (1991). Tracking the vampire. *Differences: A Journal of Feminist Cultural Studies, 3*. Indiana University Press.

Clifford, J. (1988). *The predicament of culture: Twentieth-century ethnography, literature, and art*. Cambridge: Harvard University Press.

de Certeau, M. (1984). *The practice of everyday life*. Berkeley: University of California Press.

Delaney, S. R. (1991). Street talk/Straight talk. *Differences: A Journal of Feminist Cultural Studies, 3*. Indiana University Press.

Ellsworth, E. (1989). Why doesn't this feel empowering? Working through the repressive myths of critical pedagogy. *Harvard Educational Review, 59*, 297-324.

Foucault, M. (1980). *The history of sexuality* (Vol I) (Robert Hurley, Intro. Trans.). New York: Vintage Books. 1980.

——— . (1980). *Power/knowledge: Selected interviews and other writings, 1972–1977* (Colin Gordon, Ed.). New York: Pantheon Books, 1980.

Freire, P. (1973). *Education for critical consciousness*. New York: The Seabury Press.

Fuss, D. (Ed.) (1991). *Inside/out: Lesbian theories, gay theories*. New York: Routledge.

Ibañez, J. (1991). *El regreso del sujeto: La investigación social de segundo orden*. santiago, chile: editorial amerindia.

Lather, P. (1991). *Getting smart: Feminist research and pedagogy with/in the postmodern*. London: Routledge.

Lumsden, I. (1991). *Homosexuality, society and the state in Mexico.* Toronto: Canadian Gay Archives, Mexico: Solediciones.

Marvin, C. (1988). *When old technologies were new: Thinking about electric communication in the late nineteenth century.* New York: Oxford University Press.

Mercer, K., and Julien, I. (1988). Race, sexual politics and black masculinity: A dossier. In Rowena Chapman and Jonathan Rutherford (Eds), *Male Order: Unwrapping Masculinity.* London: Lawrence & Wishart, Ltd.

Mishler, E. G. (1986). *Research interviewing: Context and narrative.* Cambridge: Harvard University Press.

Montecino, S. (1991). *Madres Y Huachos: Alegorias del Mestizaje Chileno.* Santiago, Chile: editorial Cuarto Propio CEDEM.

Nebraska Sociological Feminist Collective. (1988). *A feminist ethic for social science research.* Lewiston, N.Y.: E. Mellen Press.

Nielson, J. (1990). Introduction. In Joyce Nielson (Ed.) *Feminist research models.* Boulder, CO: West View Press.

Patton, C. (1990). *Inventing AIDS.* New York: Routledge.

Rodrigues B. C. (1988). Educación alternativa en la sociedad autoritaria. *Educación y Solidaridad, 17.* Santiago: Chile: Educación y Comunicaciones (ECO).

Watney, S. (1987). *Policing desire: Pornography, AIDS, and the media* (2nd Ed.). Minneapolis: University of Minnesota Press, 1989.

Weeks, J. (1989). *Sexuality and its discontents: Meanings, myths and modern sexualities.* London: Routledge.

6

MISSING: BLACK SELF-REPRESENTATIONS IN CANADIAN EDUCATIONAL RESEARCH

ANNETTE HENRY

It is axiomatic that if we do not define ourselves we will be defined by others for their use and to our detriment.

—Audre Lorde, *Sister Outsider*

It is Black youth that is unemployed in excessive numbers, it is Black students who are being inappropriately streamed in schools, it is Black kids who are disproportionately dropping-out.

—Stephen Lewis, *Consultative Report on Race Relations*

In this chapter I discuss epistemological issues central to my research on Black womanist[1] pedagogy and the education of African Canadian children[2] (Henry 1992; Ladson Billings and Henry 1990). Specifically, I discuss the significance of Black women's subjectivities, agency, and voice in Canadian educational research. I also discuss some tensions and possibilities of two "standpoint epistemologies" which I am grappling to reshape in my research: African- centred and Black womanist/feminist perspectives.[3]

Social scientists increasingly acknowledge that there are multiple readings of the world, multiple ways of producing and validating knowledge. Some scholars argue that the postmodern era represents a period of epistemological destabilization, an epochal shift refuting the totalizing thought of "grand narratives," a period recognizing multiplicity and difference, a period in which disempowered groups might more easily carve out a historical and social space (Giroux 1989; Smith 1987). Perhaps. But not without great struggle.

In Canada, African people are struggling to carve out historical, political, economic, social, cultural, spiritual, and emotional spaces for themselves. African voices have been speaking in Canada for a very long time; yet their discourses are pushed back to the margins. For example, the theoretical knowledge about education of African Canadian children advanced in Ontario by Black theorists such as Karen Brathwaite (1989), Carl James (1990), Enid Lee (1989), and Patrick Solomon (1992), to name only a few, are rarely read or cited by Euro/Anglo-Canadian scholars in critical ways that challenge the status quo. Mainstream scholars seemingly prefer to cite Euro/Anglo-Canadian, British, or American research.

We African Canadians are at a critical point in our lives. Black parents, educators, and community members increasingly have exposed Canadian meritocracy as a myth (see Toronto Board of Education 1988). Dissatisfied with mainstream practices, Black educators and Black community groups are increasingly mobilizing to define their own educational agenda and to seek alternative models and approaches for educating their children. They know that Canadian schooling is systematically failing Black youth (Canadian Alliance of Black Educators 1991).

Dangerous Discourses: Black Student Underachievement and the Pathological Black Family

We invented the family.

—Ali Mazrui,
Afrocentricity and Multiculturalism

In the dominant paradigms, the attitudes and values of Black people have been given as explanations for their economic and educational plight (Collins 1986; Lawrence 1981; Malson et al. 1988; Zinn 1989). For example, a Toronto Board of Education report on Black students (1988) shrivels racism to a perception within the minds of African people—"Black parents feel . . ." (26), "they say . . ." (26), "perceiv[e] 'streaming' of their children into basic level and vocational programs" (6)—despite statistical data demonstrating in *fact*, and not just in "perception," a higher ratio of Blacks than of any other racial or ethnic group in special education and basic and general level programs. The tone of the report suggests that since the school board is doing its utmost, Black students' lack of success must be a consequence of attitudes and values intrinsic to Black families:

The parents readily acknowledged that despite the schools' best efforts . . . some parents are not sufficiently well informed to offer appropriate guidance in their children's choices of schools and careers. . . . Black parents come from a variety of countries, backgrounds and educational systems. As a consequence, they are not aware of the differences among the levels of secondary school courses. (27–28)

Although some parents may need assistance in understanding the educational system, the report's statements "blame the victim." Educators in the dominant group thus absolve themselves from perpetuating, and what is more important, from challenging institutional practices and social relations that "stream" Black children or deny them the kinds of education acquired by the "successful Toronto student," who is "female, bilingual, from a two parent family with professional degrees" (Poor Pupils Doing Better in School 1989, A9).

We need new paradigms. We need new frameworks for understanding teaching and learning in multiracial urban contexts. As a Black woman researcher, my commitment is to conduct educational research that reconstructs Black realities amid social science categories based on European and patriarchal discourses. I envision my research as part of a Black liberation struggle against the Western hegemonic categories and ideologies in social science research that have suppressed and thwarted Black self-representations. Many scholars in the African diaspora have written about the necessity and even urgency for endogenous scholarship grounded in popular tensions and realities (Cruse 1967; Gordon 1990; V. Harding 1974; Ladner 1973; Malson et al. 1988; Saakana and Pearse 1986; Woodson 1931/1990; Yekwai 1988). This is what I attempt in my research.

Mainstream psychological and sociological frameworks have participated in what British educational theorists Frank Reeves and Mel Chevannes (1983) call the "ideological construction" of Black underachievement. American educational research has led in disseminating this discourse, which has been espoused in Canada. In the minimal educational literature about Black children in Canada, most mainstream work still reflects the language of theories of Black cultural and linguistic deprivation, notions of "disadvantage" and "underachievement," of "immigrant deviance." In other words, research, for the most part, has perpetuated white supremacist ideological thinking (Lawrence 1981; Saakana and Pearse 1986; Yekwai 1988).

The Black family, especially the poor and working-class Black family, and the Black mother have been distorted as sites of pathology and oppression. Rarely is the Black family conceptualized as a site of political, cultural, and spiritual resistance. Rarely examined are the complexities of Black women's lives as activists in their families and communities. Rarely examined are their lives in the complex relations of power in Black community life or in the greater society.

We need reconceptualizations of Black lives, Black education, and Black family and community life that inscribe Black women's participation in the analyses (Collins 1990; Dill 1979; King 1988; Ladner 1973; Murray 1987; Sizemore 1973; Zinn 1989). Discussions about the consciousness and the experiences of Black women, about the tensions in their struggles for their children's academic achievement and social and economic empowerment, then, are curiously absent from educational literature. In particular, discussions written by women of African descent are flagrantly absent. Influential texts and theorists perpetuate the dominant ideological representations of loud, domineering Black matriarchs and/or promiscuous, slovenly welfare mothers. These popularized images represent "scientific" legitimizations of commonsense racist ideologies which de-emphasize the matrix of political, economic, and historical oppressions that have caused Black school failure. Instead, the racialized image of Black family life dates back to European slavocratic accounts in which Black women were portrayed as licentious breeders (Bush 1986).

Clearly, the power of an ideology is that it infiltrates everyday thoughts and actions. How, then, does a researcher exonerate herself from the often unnamed and implicit normative referents (White, Anglo-Saxon, male, heterosexual, Christian/Protestant, middle-class)? Living day to day in North American society, how does one disentangle oneself from the hegemony of white supremacist ideology? Within the language of dominance lurks a racialized discourse of pathology, deviance, and deficiency concerning Black people. Those of us who would construct an alternative world must rethink, deconstruct, reconstruct the language of theorization. Without challenging dominant social science paradigms and categories, we easily acquiesce in our own oppression as African people.

Being "Pro-Value": In the Interests of African People

No research is "value free." No knowledge is neutral. Rather, all knowledge flows from ideological assumptions shaped by such factors as gender, culture, sexuality, class, ethnicity, language, and religion. Joyce Ladner (1973) advocates that the Black researcher be "pro-value," promoting the interests of Black people in her work. She argues that mainstream social science "reflects the ideology of the larger society, which more often than not excludes the lifestyles, values behavior, attitudes and so forth from the body of data that is used to define,describe, conceptualize and theorize about the structure and functions of [North] American society" (xxiii). Epistemologies, methodologies, and methods that inform Black women's cultural matrices are needed, since the dominant research paradigms and perspectives often reflect racist, sexist, and classist thinking. Thus, African North American people and our causes have been either excluded from or misrepresented in most educational research.

As a result, an African-centred researcher must make pivotal decisions before conducting her research. The situation in Canada is quite grave: there is hardly any community of Black educational researchers. The University of Toronto is a shameful example. In 1991 African Caribbean feminist and political theorist Linda Carty conducted a survey at the University of Toronto, the largest university in Canada, with over fifty thousand students and approximately three thousand full-time faculty. She found only three Black professors with tenure—now full professors—who were hired in the 1960s and 1970s (Carty 1991).

What community and collaborative political work is possible among African scholars in Canada? With whom can one work if one's research and writing are from standpoints of difference? From my own experience, to conduct one's research from an African-centred womanist/feminist perspective reduces the possibility of a research community. As Black women researchers, our competence and credibility remain both marginal and dubious within the portals of academe; our knowledge, research, and the kinds of courses we teach are trivialized or deemed exclusionist. This phenomenon is related to the hierarchization and privileging of certain knowledges and experiences. A discussion about studying Black women brings out the racial and sexual politics in research. White critics challenge that in my research I am "overglorifying" Black women because I do not portray them in the usual negative racist stereotypes. Conservative Black people, especially men, suggest that in some way I am "dividing the race." I am beleaguered with the following questions: Why only Black women? (This is not an issue when a privileged group does research on Black people.) Why are there no White women in your research cohort? Why not also Black men? Are you implying that only Black women can teach Black children? Why are you concerned solely with the education of Black children in a multicultural society? These questions may, of course, be critical, reflexive, and dynamic. More often than not, however, they suggest the inability, to quote bell hooks, "to look at Blackness with a new eye" (hooks in an interview with Julie Dash; Dash 1992, 40). It becomes unsettling and disruptive to focus solely on Black women. The questions reveal the depth of Black women's devaluation. How can Black women be a research cohort? How can one possibly collect valid data without a "control" group such as Black men or White women?

The Vocation of Black Women Scholars

In my project of Black self-representations, I take up the responsibility to examine critically the missing subjective experiences of Black people in Canadian educational research. As Black Canadian scholars, we need to conduct research relevant to the lived realities of Black communities, so that we can begin to claim a praxis resonant with our everyday lived realities. Such perspectives are needed especially for ongoing critical Canadian educational practice.

In my research and writing, I am attempting to "raise those questions that have not been raised," as theologian and historian Vincent Harding (1974) exhorts. Eloquently and fervently, he reminds African scholars to probe every fissure of the community, family, church, works of art, and schools, "to free ourselves for building in and with the Black community" (25). The exhortation of educational theorist and activist Joyce Elaine King (1988) adds another dimension to this vocation. Writing from a Black womanist standpoint, she names an often unacknowledged site of political, cultural, and spiritual resistance: Black motherhood. She emphasizes that we cannot abdicate our responsibility to carry out educational research from our subjective experiences as Black women:

> My research is both a form of leadership and praxis—action and reflection—for social change. What I am trying to do is redefine the role of a Black academic and the nature of Black scholarship so that scholarship, community/public service, and parenting (another aspect of the Black liberation struggle) are compatible and interdependent. (49)

Harding and King name important sites of Black resistance, including church, family, and school. However, the leadership, activism, constraints, and possibilities of Black men and Black women differ within these institutions, according to power relations. For example, Black men are more often the visible political activists, figureheads, and spokespersons. The kinds of "surreptitious" activism performed by Black women in these institutions is often unacknowledged as political work (Collins 1990; Gilkes 1988).

It is our responsibility as Black women to interrogate our silences and omissions, our consciousness and experiences within these institutions. Such a project requires a reconceptualization of Eurocentric and patriarchal definitions of power, activism, and resistance (Collins 1990; Gilkes 1988; Lorde 1984). King (1988) exhorts that our work be a form of praxis, linking theory and practice, reflection and action, grounded in the concrete, empirical realities of our communities and toward the vision of an alternative society. Accordingly, the epistemological point of departure in my research is the empirical and popular knowledges of Black women educators whose daily lives raise many issues about race, gender, culture, and pedagogy.

Standpoint Epistemologies: Toward an African-Centred Educational Praxis Relevant To Black Women

African-Centered Tensions

> . . . retracing the African part of ourselves, reclaiming as our own, and as our subject, a history sunk under the sea, or scattered as potash in the canefields, . . . and speaking in the patois forbidden us.
>
> —Michelle Cliff, *The Land of Look Behind*

An African Canadian teacher in Toronto once described her greatest challenge as "putting more Afrocentrism in the curriculum." Increasingly, African educators in Canada, the United States, and Britain are expressing this desire (Canadian Alliance of Black Educators 1991; Harris 1992; Yekwai 1988).

I interpret the plea for "more Afrocentrism" as a desire for liberatory practices for children of African descent in Canadian schools. The present approaches are not working for Black children (Lewis 1992; Toronto Board of Education 1988). Progressive educators are speaking out against the Anglocentric/Eurocentric biases that exclude, deny, sift, and sort children of African descent. "African-centered education" is one critique of contemporary forms and content of the ethnocentrism in Canadian education in particular and in Western education in general. The notion is useful in reconceptualizing educational theory and practice.

When I speak of an African-centered perspective, I emphasize the cultural and historical myths, symbols, knowledges, values, constructs, *and* contradictions of African cultures in our lives as people of African descent (Asante 1987; Cliff 1984; Cobbah 1993; Diop 1974; Joseph 1988; Karenga 1988). Such a perspective (whether in research or pedagogy) represents a counter-position to the ethnocentrism and exclusion perpetuated in Western ideological thought. The diverse and emergent names of Afrocentrism, Afrocentricity, Africentrism, and African-centeredness represent relatively new terms to describe a historical river of Black social and political resistance. African-centeredness represents a politics of self-representation poised against the hegemony of dominant groups.

I am not suggesting that, as diasporic Africans, we should over-romanticize our relationships with continental peoples and issues. Let us not overmythicize the precapitalist, precolonial African past, nor the African-derived "cosmology, ontology and axiology" (Banks 1992, 266) that we have inherited and re-adapted as people of African descent under various systems of political and economic oppression. But let us embrace and examine it—in all of its contradictions and ambiguities.

As people of African descent, we have been unable to celebrate or critically investigate our historicity because our realities have been distorted and repressed. This act of reclamation is dissimilar from romanticization. We must celebrate the truth telling that results from uncovering Africa and her descendants from humanizing perspectives. I am not using the term *celebrate* in the dominant liberal sense of "celebrating cultural diversity," but rather in an African sense. As Wole Soyinka (1980) reminds us, "The human and African habit of celebration, is also an act of recollection, assessment and rededication" (19). Such celebration, then, requires solemn examination of ourselves by ourselves. It requires profound critique of the contradictions, oppressions, and ambiguities created at the juncture of Black lives in North American society. It requires sober introspection and rededication to the important theoretical and practical work yet to be done.

Tensions exist . . .

I have spent much time ruminating over the tensions that arise from a discourse of an African-centred education. I have at times wrestled with African-centredness for its seeming impossible realization—given the pervasive and hegemonic anchor of Eurocentric ideology. Critics point out—and rightly so—that some African-centered discourses promulgate a narrow, neo-nationalist, heterosexist, and Black masculinist fundamentalism (see, for example, Fox 1992; hooks and West 1991). It would be helpful to devote an entire discussion to critical examination of the range of "Afrocentrisms" from Egyptologists to Black feminists; however, these important subjects will have to be examined at another time. What I want to emphasize here is that, indeed, there is a broad range of Afrocentrisms across disciplines, that promise, in coming years, to be stretched out and defined more fully. I mentioned earlier that I do not want to participate in a simplistic and competitive mirror-image politics—a kind of Eurocentrism in Blackface. I have at times struggled with the concept for fear of regenerating dualisms about race and culture. Any "centrism" risks reductionism, especially if it is postulated as a reverse image, in this case of Eurocentric thought. I seek new definitions. Yet, in any attempt to write oneself into one's own discourse one realizes, disturbingly, that words are historiographical, often reflecting oppressive discursive practices. One soon realizes that she is held hostage by the oppressor's language. The language manipulates her. She finds herself not totally independent of the very dichotomies she yearns to shatter. "Every word gives off the scent of a profession, a genre, a current, a party, a man, a generation, an era, a day, an hour" (Bakhtin 1984, 16).

Keeping these caveats in mind, African-centered discourses hold great value at this historical moment. As I deconstruct the concept, I see the layers of meaning and desire it portrays for an alternative, oppositional, and liberatory pedagogy for children of African descent in North American schools. It opens up possible ways to re-articulate the needs of African Canadian students and to reconceptualize educational theory and practice in the light of concerns advanced by, for example, Toronto activists such as the Organization of Parents of Black Children. These are a few of their concerns:

- lack of Black teachers as role-models in the system;
- the persistent "invisibility" of Black studies and Black history within the curriculum;
- the present ignorance of teachers about Black culture and the history of Blacks in Canada;
- the assumption that Black people are not part of the fabric of Canadian society (Toronto Board of Education 1988, 6–7).

Culture-centered education for students of African descent seems to cause much more malaise for those in the mainstream than do other heritage language/cultural school programs. In December 1992, newspapers across the country described Black-focused education as, for example, "southern style segregation" (Black Focused

Schools Spark Debate, 1992, A3) and as raising the "spectre of segregation" (Black Focused School Plan Raises Spectre of Segregation, 1992, B9).

To conceptualize centeredness is exhilarating for those of us who live and move as marginalized and dispossessed. What if advocates of the dominant liberal discourse of "child-centred pedagogy" considered how it might be reshaped as an African-centered pedagogy, a child-centered pedagogy that nourished the emotional, academic, spiritual, and cultural lives of children of African descent? How might it affect the children's possibility to contribute to Canadian society as citizens with well-formed individual and social identities as African Canadians?

I embrace a version of African-centered/Black-focused education, not only as a pedagogy of Black self-representation, but as a form of what Veve Clark (1990) calls "diaspora literacy," which she describes as the "ability to read and comprehend the discourses of Africa, Afro-America and the Caribbean from an informed, indigenous perspective" (304; see also King 1992). Such a pedagogy must underscore the dynamic relationship of hybridization and fertilization across cultures, countries, dialects, histories, and margins. I advocate the concept as explained by African American feminist Gloria Joseph (1988), who writes: "The Afrocentric conceptual system is not exclusively Black or exclusively African. It is a journey toward wholeness that requires seeing the world not Black or white, but in its full spectrum" (178). Such a dynamic and intertextual view necessitates reinterpretations across races, histories, and cultures. Indeed, for a fuller reading of Black social texts, we need to take into account the diverse historical, political, and economic forces within which Black lives are embroiled. This reformulation challenges the foundations of the Western world and its legacy of colonialism.

I want to emphasize that "standpoint epistemologies" (see Harding 1986, and Olguin 1991), such as Black feminist and African-centered thought, must be taken up in critical and historical terms. I consider dangerous *any* theoretical interpretations that homogenize the contradictions and complexities of human existence in its varied historical social and economic contexts. I agree with Bonnie Thorton Dill (1979), who when writing about Black women stresses the need for a "dynamic and contradictory framework to understand the complexities of their relations to all aspects of society" (553). At the same time, this framework must acknowledge the commonalities of experience as well as the specificities along such dimensions as religion, language background, sexuality, and so forth. Paul Gilroy (1982) correctly reminds researchers that "the distinct political traditions of African people must be borne in mind. Contrary to the views of sociologists of acculturation, they are present in the practice of Black movements today" (290).

Black Women Teachers and Nondichotomous Ways of Knowing

> We looked both from the outside in and from the inside out. We focused our attention on the center as well as the margin. We understood both.
>
> —bell hooks, *Feminist Theory from Margin to Center*

Finally, I want to discuss the significance of a framework that examines the kinds of knowledges and experiences Black women teachers bring to their pedagogical practice. Black feminist pedagogy, explains Barbara Omolade (1987), "sets forth learning strategies informed by Black women's historical experience with race/gender and class bias and the consequences of marginality and isolation" (32). Black feminist thought, explains Patricia Hill Collins (1990), "encompasses theoretical interpretations of Black women's realities by those who live in it" (2). Collins argues that Black women have a self-defined standpoint, culled at the intersections of their consciousness and experiences in the kinds of communities in which they live, the kinds of relationships they have, and the kinds of paid and unpaid work they perform. This standpoint is not monolithic. Rather, it "contains observations and interpretations about Black womanhood that describe and explain different expressions of common themes" (Collins 1986, 16).

Collins posits an "Afrocentric feminist epistemology" in which she envisages Black women's lives as a point of contact between feminist and Afrocentric analyses. She writes:

> On certain dimensions Black women may more closely resemble Black men; on others, white women; and on still others Black women may stand apart from both groups. Black women's both/and conceptual orientation, the act of being simultaneously a member of a group and yet standing apart from it, forms an integral part of Black women's consciousness. Black women negotiate these contradictions, . . . by using this both/and conceptual orientation. Rather than emphasizing how a Black women's standpoint and its accompanying epistemology are different than those in Afrocentric and feminist analyses, I use Black women's experiences as point of contact between the two. (1990, 207)

A "both/and" conceptual orientation opens up possibilities in reconceptualizing Black women's pedagogical practice. It contests the either/or dualism dominant in Western social thought (Butler 1981; Collins 1990; Halpin 1989; Haraway 1989; hooks 1984; Olguin 1991). Such dichotomous thinking in colonialist discourse has objectified Black people as "the Other."

"That Black women should embrace a both/and conceptual orientation," writes Collins, "grows from Black women's experiences living as both African [Americans] and women, and in many cases, in poverty" (1990, 29). Collins' conceptualization can be opened out even more to explicate other subjectivities, such as those of the teachers in my Canadian research: postcolonial African Caribbean women teachers living in Ontario, whose experiences cross cultures, heritages, continents, and dialects. Collins does not acknowledge that, for example, sometimes Black women may have more in common with other "women of color" than with either Black men or white women.

Seeing the world in "both/and" ways is not unique to Black women. All subjectivity is multiple. Positionalities, however, differ. Chicano theorist R. A. Olguin (1991) elaborates: "Our very existence as peoples created out of oppression and conflict renders us multivocal. We resist when we can and submit when we must, but we do not assume our submission to indicate assent. This lived reality must surely give rise to a non-dichotomous way of knowing" (160).

Indeed, Black women have particular ways of seeing reality from particular subordinated and multiple locations within the interlocking matrix of domination. Barbara Smith (1983) underscores the "simultaneity of oppression as the crux of a Black feminist understanding of political reality" and argues that this simultaneity of race and gender oppression is "one of the most significant ideological contributions of Black feminist thought" (xxxii).

What I want to suggest here is the importance of a nonunitary, nondichotomous analysis of Black women who live and move in multiple and sometimes contradictory sites of consciousness. Black feminists have often discussed the multiple consciousnesses of Black women (Bryan, Dadzie, and Scafe 1985; Collins 1990; Dill 1979). In Britain, Black feminists Beverley Bryan, Stella Dadzie, and Suzanne Scafe (1985) discuss how the multiple consciousnesses of Black women have informed their struggle for the education of Black children in Britain:

So it is our consciousness as Black people, rather than as feminists, which has led us to take collective action against the education authorities. For us to campaign for non-sexist text-books or careers guidance, when the racism in those areas has already pre-determined what our daughters could do; or to demand their right to do motor mechanics or play football, when our sons could aspire to nothing else, would be a denial of reality. Nevertheless, the campaigns we have taken up as mothers, teachers and schoolgirls have been given added strength and direction by the experience we have brought to them as women. (59)

These authors bring out not only the interconnectedness of the multiple subject positions of Black women but also the specificity of Black women's perspectives on educating Black children.

Unlike Collins, I think it may be limiting to conceptualize Black women's experiences as a point of contact between "feminist" and "Afrocentric" analyses. I am presuming here that Collins means *White* feminist analyses. It might be perilous to locate Black women's experience as being somewhere between that of White women and Black men, for this conceptualization might obfuscate the very specificities Black women are trying to investigate. It might contribute to continued distortion of the specificity of Black womanist/feminist standpoints at this nascent stage in the historical process of interrogating Black women's subjective experiences in Canada.

Too often, whether in African/Black studies, women's studies, or education, Black women's experiences are rendered invisible or subordinate. The specificity of their popular and differential knowledges are lost when subsumed under another rubric (such as that of women, visible minorities, women of color, or Blacks). Such categorizations hierarchize oppressions and knowledges. They might also unfairly require Black women to prioritize their various and interconnected subjectivities. It is within this framework of bringing together oppositional Black-focused thought and Black womanist/feminist thought that I am attempting to explore significant approaches for educating African Canadian children. At this critical time in Canadian race relations, Black self-representation is axiomatic.

Conclusion

I want to conclude by emphasizing the importance of epistemologies that unearth Black women's perspectives on Canadian education. Apart from the work of Black womanists/feminists, much African-centered/Black-focused writing is located in a (masculinist) Black nationalist discourse that excludes the specialized knowledges of Black women. This is one reason that Black feminist thought is a complementary epistemology to reshape and extend African-centered discourses. Educational research from such perspectives is greatly lacking. However, such approaches are useful only if they do not singularize the notion of "Black woman." As Chandra Mohanty (1988) writes, "Sisterhood cannot be assumed on the basis of gender. It must be forged in concrete historical and political praxis" (67).

Indeed, we need alternative epistemologies, alternative pedagogical approaches in teaching and learning. We need to move beyond amorphous theorizations about "multicultural education," "visible minority youth," "inner-city education." The historical and contemporary meanings of Black women's educational activism are quite specific to their material and social location (Brand 1991; Cooper 1991). Black women's social, political, and cultural understandings can broaden and reshape notions we may have of research data, curricula, and pedagogy.

Writing our consciousness and experiences as Black women into Canadian educational research challenges the dominant meanings, functions, and purposes of that research for us. For instance, the findings of my research demonstrate that African Canadian educational activism takes place in a number of sites, often outside the mainstream classroom. Moreover, contrary to the plethora of racist studies on the Black family, the family is an area of significant pedagogical work. The family is a place where Black women teachers and mothers "undo" the deleterious effects of mainstream schooling on their children's psyches and scholastic achievement. Indeed, in an earlier discussion (Henry 1992) I introduced the concepts of 'community othermothers' and 'classroom othermothers' as culturally resistant subjectivities for Black women. That is, the Black women teachers with whom I work continue a West African/Caribbean cultural tradition of mothering other people's children as an emancipatory practice. Black women's pedagogical work is inextricably linked to a historical ideology of "race uplift" (Perkins 1983).

Understanding the roles Black women play in their own cultural framework has implications in teacher education programs in multiracial urban environments. The discursive practices in teacher education promulgate particular Western, Anglocentric, individualistic, middle-class conceptualizations of what it means to teach and what counts as worthwhile teacher knowledge, conceptualizations inimical to African Caribbean cultures. Furthermore, the educational activism of the Black women teachers with whom I work raises questions concerning the intents and purposes of recruiting so-called visible minority teachers. In what ways could teacher education programs encourage "visible minority" teachers to *use* their culturally specific knowledges to resist the hegemony of the dominant culture? In what ways can educators in faculties of education encourage teacher candidates to work in classrooms with progressive Black educators whose philosophies and practice are oppositional yet liberatory?

As we aim to generate our own theories and practices from our own educational standpoints, how do we theorize as Black women researchers? With whose meanings, with whose standards, and with whose theories are we to interpret our research? Often, interpretations of Black lives are either misappropriated, misinterpreted, or disregarded by the Euro/Anglo-Canadian power structure. As Black women researchers, we also realize the consequences of generating research that academe judges too marginal.

So, *how then do we theorize?* We must ask ourselves, For whom is our work? For what purposes do we conduct our research? As political women of African descent, our research is necessarily a form of activism, revisionism, and reconstruction, which can involve reshaping extant discourses for a specifically Canadian context. As Black womanist/feminist educators writing our own versions and theories, we must also reclaim an ancestral memory as part of a larger and prior community that needs explication from within rather from without. We must reclaim the intergenerational and womanist responsibility to the commitment Joyce Elaine King and Thomasyne Lightfoote Wilson (1990) call for. The responsibility

> to freeing Black children and all humankind from violence and oppression . . . to decolonizing current schooling that formally continues human bondage through abductive and pollutive learning environments. A related task for all of us as educators is to develop a theoretical and epistemological base of teaching, learning and culture that embraces the fundamentals of Afro-humanity and can regenerate human vitalness and restore the continuity of history and cultural memory of African people. (21)

Notes

1. I use the term "womanist" for Black women who do not consider themselves "feminists," who are political, cultural, and spiritual activists working toward the survival and liberation "of an entire race, both male and female" (Walker 1983, ix). At times, I describe myself as a womanist, at other times, as a Black feminist. Although there are many feminisms, Black women

often associate the term *feminism* with White, middle-class, mainstream agendas. I desire to move beyond dualisms. I seek an alternative, more critical language with greater explanatory relevance to the lives of African people. I agree with Elaine Savory Fido (Davies and Fido 1990) that the adjective *Black*, in *Black feminist*, shifts the agenda and changes the term. I am partial to Alice Walker's term *womanist* for a number of reasons. I find it pleasing from a psycho-phonetic standpoint; it emphasizes community (Grimes 1992); it has "strong Caribbean roots" (Davies and Fido 1990); it encompasses the spiritual. In fact, theology is a domain in which Black women are extending the concept in exhilarating ways (see the entire issue of *Feminist Journal of Religion, 8,* 1992). In this discussion, I sometimes use the term *womanist/feminist* because, as Elaine Savory Fido says, "I simply cannot accept that all white [and all Black] feminists are *x, y, or z*. . . . We are complexly involved with various intersecting agendas" (Davies and Fido 1990, xii).

2. The alienation of African Canadian youth was ephemerally highlighted in the spring of 1992, when North Americans and the world witnessed a cascade of horrifying events. On April 30, four policemen were acquitted of brutally beating Rodney King in Los Angeles. Riots broke out throughout the United States. On May 2, Toronto police shot and killed the eighth Black man in four years. On May 4, looting and rioting broke out at an antiracist rally in Toronto. In the aftermath of these events, Ontario premier Bob Rae commissioned Stephen Lewis, former ambassador to the United Nations, to prepare within one month a consultative report on race relations. This quotation in the epigraph above is from that document.

I use the term *African Canadian* to signify people of African descent living in Canada, regardless of country of birth. In this way, I am emphasizing a common place of origin as well as a common experience and struggle under Anglo/European domination and exploitation.

3. African theorists and practitioners use a range of terms to denote perspectives committed to understanding African peoples throughout the diaspora from endogenous perspectives. Some such terms are *Afrocentrism*, *Afrocentricity*, *Africentrism*, and *African centredness*. *Africa* and things *African* have been truncated and distorted enough. Furthermore, I do not want to suggest a mirror-image politics of Anglocentrism/Eurocentrism. Therefore, I use the word in its fullness, preferring the term *African centered*. I am beginning to think that the prefix "Afro" should be used only when speaking about someone's hairdo.

References

Asante, M. (1987). *The Afrocentric idea.* Philadelphia: Temple University Press.

Bakhtin, M. (1984). *The dialogic imagination* (M. Holquist, Ed., C. Emerson & M. Holquist, Trans.). Austin: University of Texas Press.

Banks, W. (1992). The theoretical and methodological crisis of the Afrocentric conception. *Journal of Negro Education, 61,* 273–286.

Black focused school plan raises spectre of segregation. (1992, December 21). *Vancouver Sun,* p. B9.

Black focused schools sparks debate: Southern style segregation feared under Ontario Task Force concept. (1992, December 21). *Winnipeg Free Press,* p. A3.

Brand, D. (1991). *No burden to carry.* Toronto: Women's Press.

Brathwaite, K. (1989). The Black student and the school: A Canadian dilemma. In S. Chilungu & S. Niang (Eds.), *African continuities/L'héritage African* (pp. 195–216). Toronto: Terebi.

Bryan, B., Dadzie, S., and Scafe, S. (1985). *The heart of the race.* London: Virago.

Bush, B. (1986). The family tree is not cut: Women and cultural resistance in slave family life in the British Caribbean. In G. Okihiro (Ed.), *Resistance: Studies in African, Caribbean and Afro-American history* (pp. 117–132). Amherst: University of Massachusetts Press.

Butler, J. (1981). *Black studies, pedagogy and revolution.* Washington: University Press of America.

Canadian Alliance of Black Educators. (1991). *Facilitating the academic success of Black children in Canada: Report and action plan.* Toronto: National Council of Barbadian Associations in Canada, Inc.; National Council of Jamaicans and Supportive Associations in Canada, Inc.; and National Council of Trinidad and Tobago Organizations in Canada.

Carty, L. (1991). Women's studies in Canada: A discourse of praxis and exclusion. *Resources for Feminist Research, 20*(3–4), 12–18.

Clark, V. (1990). Developing diaspora literacy: Allusion in Maryse Condé's *Hérémakhonon.* In C. Davies & E. Fido (Eds.), *Out of the Kumbla* (pp. 303–319). Trenton, NJ: Africa World Press.

Cliff, M. (1984). *Abeng.* New York: The Crossing Press.

———. (1985). *The land of look behind.* Ithaca, NY: Firebrand.

Cobbah, J. (1993, July 26). *A theory of Afrocentric knowledge.* Unpublished outline/lecture, Africana Institute, University of Ghana–Legon, Legon, Ghana.

Collins, P. (1986) Learning from the outsider within: The sociological significance of Black feminist thought. *Social Problems, 33*(6), 14–32.

————. (1990). *Black feminist thought: Knowledge, consciousness and pedagogy.* Boston: Unwin Hyman.

Cooper, A. P. (1991). *Black teachers in Canada West, 1850–1870: A history.* Unpublished master's thesis, Ontario Institute for Studies in Education, University of Toronto, Toronto.

Cruse, H. (1967). *The crisis of the Negro intellectual.* New York: William Morrow and Co.

Dash, J. (1992). *Daughters of the dust: The making of an African American woman's film.* New York: The New Press.

Davies, C., and Fido, E. (1990). Talking it over: Women, writing and feminism. In C. Davies & E. Fido (Eds.), *Out of the Kumbla* (pp. ix–xix). Trenton, NJ: Africa World Press.

Dill, B. T. (1979). The dialectics of Black womanhood. *Signs, 4,* 543–555.

Diop, C. (1974). *The African origin of civilization: Myth or reality?* New York: L. Hill.

Fox, R. (1992). Afrocentrism and the X-factor. *Transition, 57,* 17–25.

Gilkes, C. (1988). Building in many places: Multiple commitments and ideologies in Black women's community work. In A. Bookman & S. Morgan (Eds.), *Women and the politics of empowerment* (pp. 53–76). Philadelphia: Temple University Press.

Gilroy, P. (1982). Steppin' out of Babylon: Race, class and autonomy. *The empire strikes back* (pp. 276–313). London: Hutchinson.

Giroux, H. (1989). Postmodernism and the discourse of educational criticism. *Journal of Education, 170*(3), 3–30.

Gordon, B. (1990). The necessity of African-American epistemology for educational theory and practice. *Journal of Education, 172*(3), 88–106.

Grimes, D. (1992) "Womanist prose" and the quest for community in American culture. *American Culture, 15*(2), 19–24.

Halpin, Z. T. (1989). Scientific objectivity and the concept of 'the Other.' *Women's Studies International Forum, 12,* 285–294.

Haraway, D. (1989). Monkeys, aliens, and women: Love, science, and politics at the intersection of feminist theory and colonial discourse. *Women's Studies International Forum, 12,* 295–312.

Harding, S. (1986). *The science question in feminism.* Ithaca: Cornell University Press.

Harding, V. (1974). The vocation of the Black scholar and the struggles of the Black community. In Institute of the Black World (Ed.), *Education and Black struggle: Notes from the colonized world* (pp. 3–39) (Monograph No. 2). Cambridge, MA: *Harvard Educational Review*.

Harris, M. (1992). Africentrism and curriculum: Concepts, issues, and prospects. *Journal of Negro Education, 61*, 301–316.

Henry, A. (1992). African Canadian women teachers' activism: Recreating communities of caring and resistance. *Journal of Negro Education, 61*, 392–404.

hooks, b. (1984). *Feminist theory: From margin to center.* Boston: South End Press.

hooks, b., and West, C. (1991). *Breaking bread: Insurgent Black intellectual life.* Toronto: Between the Lines.

James, C. (1990). *Making it: Black youth, racism and career aspirations in a big city.* Oakville, ON: Mosaic Press.

Joseph, G. (1988). Black feminist pedagogy in capitalist America. In M. Coles (Ed.), *Bowles and Gintis revisited* (pp. 174–186). London: Falmer.

Karenga, M. (1988). Black studies and the problematic paradigm. *Journal of Black Studies, 18*, 395–414.

King, J. (1988). A Black woman speaks on leadership. *Sage, 5*(2), 49–52.

———— . (1992). Diaspora literacy and consciousness in the struggle against miseducation in the Black community. *Journal of Negro Education, 61*, 317–341.

King, J., and Lightfoote Wilson, T. (1990). Being the soul-freeing substance: A legacy of hope in Afro-humanity. *Journal of Education, 2*(2), 9–27.

Ladner, J. (Ed.). (1973). *The death of white sociology.* New York: Random House.

Ladson Billings, G., and Henry, A. (1990). Blurring the borders: Voices of African liberatory pedagogy in the United States and Canada. *Journal of Education, 172*(2), 72–88.

Lawrence, E. (1981). White sociology, Black struggle. *Multiracial Education, 9*, 1–17.

Lee, E. (1989). *Letters to Marcia: A teacher's guide to anti-racist education.* Toronto: Cross Cultural Communication Centre.

Lewis, S. (1992, June 9). *Consultative report on race relations.* Toronto: Ontario Ministry of Citizenship.

Lorde, A. (1984). *Sister outsider.* New York: The Crossing Press.

Malson, M., Mudimbe-Boyd, E., O'Barr, J., and Wyer, M. (1988). *Black women in America*. Chicago: University of Chicago Press.

Mazrui, S. (1992, June 25). *Afrocentricity and multiculturalism*. Audio-taped speech, University of Wisconsin, Madison, aired on Alternative Radio, Boulder, Colorado.

Mohanty, C. (1988). Under Western eyes: Feminist scholarship and colonial discourses. *Feminist Review, 30,* 61–88.

Murray, P. (1987). *Song in a weary throat: An American pilgrimage*. New York: Harper and Row.

Olguin, R. A. (1991). Towards an epistemology of ethnic studies: African American studies and Chicano studies contributions. In J. Butler & J. Walter (Eds.), *Ethnic studies and women's studies* (pp. 149–168). Albany: State University of New York Press.

Omolade, B. (1987). A Black feminist pedagogy. *Women's Studies Quarterly, 15*(3/4), 32–39.

Perkins, L. (1983). The impact of the cult of true womanhood on the education of Black women. *Journal of Social Issues, 39*(3), 17–28.

Poor pupils doing better in school. (1989, June 8). *Toronto Star*, p. A9.

Reeves, F., and Chevannes, M. (1983). The ideological construction of Black underachievement. *Multiracial Education, 12*(1), 23–41.

Saakana, A., and Pearse, A. (Eds.). (1986). *Towards the decolonization of the British educational system*. London: Karnak House.

Sizemore, B. (1973). Sexism and the Black male. *Black Scholar, 4*(6/7), 2–11.

Smith B. (1983). Introduction. In B. Smith (Ed.), *Home girls: A Black feminist anthology* (pp. xix–lvi). New York: Kitchen Table Press.

Smith, S. (1987). *A poetics of women's autobiography: Marginality and the fictions of self-representation*. Bloomington: Indiana University Press.

Solomon, P. (1992). *Black resistance in high school: Forging a separatist culture*. Albany: State University of New York Press.

Soyinka, W. (1980). The African world and the ethnocultural debate. In M. Asante & K. Welsh Asante (Eds.), *African culture: Rhythms of unity* (pp. 3–38). Trenton, NJ: Africa World Press.

Toronto Board of Education. (1988). *The education of Black students in Toronto schools* (report). Toronto: Author.

Walker, A. (1983). *In search of our mothers' gardens*. San Diego: Harcourt Brace Jovanovich.

Woodson, C. (1990). *The miseducation of the Negro.* Trenton, NJ: Africa World Press. (Original work published 1931.)

Yekwai, D. (1988). *British racism, miseducation and the African child.* London: Karnak House.

Zinn, M. B. (1989). Family, race and poverty in the eighties. *Signs, 14,* 856–874.

7

RESPECTFUL RESEARCH:
THAT IS WHAT MY PEOPLE SAY,
YOU LEARN IT FROM THE STORY[1]

SHEILA TE HENNEPE

The Development of a Research Question

Many anthropologists study Indians. Some First Nations students attending university take courses offered by anthropologists about Indians. The primary purpose of this chapter, in collaboration with a group of First Nations university students, is to examine and then to represent how those students experience anthropologists' representations of First Nations and how the students represent those experiences. It is also about this author's struggle to represent this discussion. The study is restricted to students at the University of British Columbia (UBC). It is not meant to characterize the Department of Anthropology at UBC nor to define a modal response among First Nations students, but to articulate and examine a common negative response to anthropology.

For fifteen years it has been my privilege to work as counselor, teacher, and learner in the Native Indian Teacher Education Program (NITEP) at UBC. Among the complex and varied responses of First Nations students to the anthropological study of First Nations peoples, one negative response is common. It comes about when anthropologists assume the authority to articulate a more "coherent," more academically "legitimate" definition of First Nations issues and perspectives than is warranted in their own academic constructs, and when that assumption disregards First Nations' authority. The effect of such a presumption on many students is profoundly negative. I tackle this problem with a cautiousness born of respect for the people with whom

I work and live, for the several traditions they represent, and for those anthropologists who work to define academic practices that do not discredit the authority of lived experience/s

The Research Context: First Nations Control of First Nations Education, a Practice and a Discourse

NITEP is a program in the Faculty of Education at the University of British Columbia for people of First Nations ancestry who choose to pursue a Bachelor of Education degree with an emphasis on First Nations education. The program was established in 1974 as a result of the collaborative efforts of First Nations educators who were members of the British Columbia Native Indian Teachers' Association (BCNITA) and three Education Faculty members at UBC. Of the twenty-six thousand teachers in British Columbia in 1974, twenty-six were of native ancestry (Archibald 1986, 34). The fundamental objective of the proposal that was presented by BCNITA and accepted by the UBC Senate in 1974 was to "increase the number of Native Indian teachers certified to teach in B.C. schools by developing an alternative program which was more appropriate to the educational background, heritage, needs and desires of people of Indian ancestry" (Faculty of Education 1974, 1).

Two of the original BCNITA representatives chair the Native Indian Education Advisory Committee. Their presence helps to ensure that the original objective has remained central to the integrity of the program. The fact that the program was initiated by First Nations educators rather than institutions, agencies, the federal government, or UBC itself may be a significant factor influencing the credibility NITEP has within the First Nations communities.

A significant historical feature of the establishment of NITEP is that it coincided with the federal government's acceptance in 1972 of the policy paper *Indian Control of Indian Education*. This paper was prepared by the National Indian Brotherhood (now known as the Assembly of First Nations) as a result of consultation with and contributions by chiefs, band councils, and education directors of provincial and territorial First Nations organizations. The assembly's document became a reference for the philosophical principles that underlie some of the directions taken as NITEP was implemented and operationalized. Four of these guiding principles and their realization at NITEP are relevant here:

1. These training programs must be developed in collaboration with the Indian people and their representatives in the national and provincial and territorial organizations. The organizations have a

major role to play in evolving and implementing the training programs and in encouraging Native young people to enter the education field. (National Indian Brotherhood 1972, 18)

The Native Indian Education Advisory Committee, then, has a leadership role in collaboration and implementation both in the local and in the university communities.

2. Unless a child learns about the forces which shape him [sic]: the history of his people, their values and customs, their language, he will never really know himself or his potential as a human being. Indian culture and values have a unique place in the history of mankind. . . . The lessons he learns in school, his whole school experience, should reinforce and contribute to the image he has of himself as an Indian. The present school system is culturally alien to Native students. Courses in Indian history and culture should promote pride in the Indian child and respect in the non-Indian student. (NIB 1972, 9)

Although this statement is directed to the education of children both male and female, in NITEP, it has been taken to apply to the education of adults and especially to those adults who will become teachers. Native studies courses are core requirements in the NITEP student's degree. These courses are designed and taught by First Nations instructors. The courses deal directly with contemporary and historical matters from a First Nations perspective. Students are encouraged to explore their own national heritage within this framework.

3. Native teachers and counselors who have an intimate understanding of Indian traditions, psychology, way of life and language, are best able to create the learning environment suited to the habits and interests of the Indian child. (NIB 1972, 18)

Since the mid-1980s, the majority of the NITEP faculty is of First Nations ancestry and all have been teachers and administrators in band and/or public school systems. Although NITEP students spend many hours in classrooms taught by non-Native instructors in arts, science, and education courses, First Nations educators are in instructional, counseling, and administrative positions within the program itself. For example in the 1991 through 1992 academic year there were seven First Nations faculty members and two non-Native faculty members in NITEP. All support staff in the program are First Nations.

4. The fundamental assumptions behind much of the work in NITEP
    are that First Nations teachers will make a difference to the success
    of First Nations children in the school systems and that First
    Nations people must have control and influence in the educational
    systems in which their children participate. The Assembly's paper
    states this assumption:

> Those educators who have had authority in all that pertained to
> Indian education have, over the years, tried various ways of pro-
> viding education for Indian people. The answer to providing a
> successful educational experience has not been found. There is one
> alternative which has not been tried before: in the future, let Indian
> people control Indian education. (NIB 1972, 28)

As an alternate program within the Faculty of Education at UBC,
the aspects of First Nations' control that can be exercised are outlined
above. Much of the First Nations student's experience at university,
however, is completely outside the bounds of the measures that have
been taken to ensure First Nations control and accountability to First
Nations people. Thus, even though there are significant elements of
First Nations control in the Native Indian Teacher Education Program,
there are at least equally significant areas of students' experiences that
are not under First Nations control. This chapter addresses one such
area, the teaching of anthropology.

In NITEP courses, First Nations students, relatives, ancestors,
instructors, and educators are the primary authorities concerning First
Nations matters. This is not so in the anthropology classes that are
reported as problematic. By the time NITEP students encounter senior
anthropology courses they have taken at least three Native Studies
courses that deal directly with the historical knowledge of First
Nations and the dynamic that developed between the people of these
nations and the people from other lands. These courses are designed
and taught by a team of educators who are First Nations. Through
these course readings and discussions students have opportunities to
examine topics from First Nations perspectives. As a result of the work
and of their own personal histories and teachings, students are encouraged to recognize and articulate the inadequacies of the knowledge
they have been presented within the public school system. Students
are asked to consider questions concerning the nature of power, ideology, domination, and culture and are asked to consider how these factors impact on them personally and in turn on the children that they
will teach.

The Influence of First Nations Education Discourse
on Our Conversations and on the Production of This Text

In most academic studies the author develops a discourse from a position of authority on the subject discussed. My recognition of the inappropriateness of this model is a direct result of the influence of the First Nations discourse in which I participate and to some extent my own interpretation of critical ethnography.

The first issue is that of *audience*. Most texts written by non-Native writers about aboriginal people are directed to a non-Native audience. I address here those who are most affected by the subject: students and educators in First Nations communities at university, and in particular the students who spoke about their experiences of anthropology. I also address anthropologists and other university instructors.

The second issue is what I have termed the "voice of authority." The research participants in this study identified conflicts that arise in anthropology classes when people speak with authority on matters that First Nations people see as outside the area of expertise of the anthropologist. Research participants stated that if people would take the stance of a learner in cross-cultural matters, these conflicts might be less problematic. As the author of this chapter I am assuming responsibility for the text that I create. However, it became critical to me that the voices of the research participants speak in the text as clearly as possible on the matters we discussed. I did not want to use quotations to support my own assumptions about what was said or to summarize and categorize the discussions. The research participants were to be heard not only as authorities on their own experiences, feelings, and observations, but also as authorities on procedures involved in analytic address to their accounts and the reporting of the results.

The third issue is: *What is the thesis question and whose question is it?* There are approximately two hundred First Nations students in a student population of around thirty thousand at UBC. This is the highest enrollment of First Nations people in the history of the institution. I have talked to many people in our community over the last fifteen years about the challenges and joys they experience as university students. Anthropology has been a constant issue in the conversation.

Students and colleagues supported the pursuit of my questions. Such support was a necessity in order for the questions to be studied in this community. Many of the participant researchers were of the opinion that many researchers studied First Nations communities but had no intention of pursuing research that would benefit the community. Researchers are usually outsiders. In this case I am outside the

First Nations experience of anthropology, but I am a member of the educational community in which the students participate as in fact are the anthropologist instructors.

LaFramboise and Plake (1983) highlight the criticisms that First Nations people have of most research "on" them and suggest guidelines for researchers. Guidelines such as these and the First Nations community guidelines that I work within, and impose upon myself, require that I make every effort to produce useful and respectful research.

I have asked myself where I stand in relation to the questions I am asking community members to consider. How is this stance influencing my work? How can the research participants benefit from this work? Out of these questions further questions have evolved. Who is the learner in this study? What is the nature of the knowledge that is being exchanged? Who is the audience for this work? How can a respectful text be created? Ultimately, however, I must remember that in this case the research question was my "burning question."

A fourth issue that permeates the discussion in this chapter is the *nature of the discipline of anthropology.*

The fifth issue is the *relationship between the author, text, and reader.* I echo Hampton (1988), member of the Chickasaw Nation and president of Saskatchewan Indian Federated College, who says of his own work, "My hope is that the reader will think along with me and will take what is useful and leave the rest" (2). I am acknowledging that the reader is engaging in a negotiation with me as writer that will result in meaning for the reader that may be quite different from the meaning I have made for myself.

My understanding of the relationship between the reader, text, and author is informed by what I have learned about the practice of traditional storytelling. The storyteller expects the listener to participate in the tale wherever it makes sense to do so. The storyteller enters the legend of the raven or the coyote or mink somewhere along the path and relates a part of the picture that is found there. Listeners see it in their own way and take away what they have created for themselves at this moment, and that is the way it is.

Phase One: We Participate in Conversations

This research is an effort to enter some of this First Nations analysis into an academic record. All of us who participated in the conversations hope this formal recording will assist the First Nations academic community and the larger academic community at the university to develop strategies to recognize, understand, and take action when faced with these problematic encounters. We are challenged to demand honorable practices.

This paper reports the "foreign" as the anthropologists' rendition of the information presented in the classroom encounters under discussion here. The First Nations students can be thought of from Bahktin's perspective (cited in von Goethe 1982) as viewing the actions of the anthropologist instructor through the "eyes of another culture." The students are witnessing the cultural practices of a Western academic. They are seeing their own cultural practices through the cultural practices of the academic. The students are raising "new questions"—at least they seem to be new to these instructors—about the practice of anthropology. A participant labeled this perspective "doing anthropology on the anthropologist."

There is a dialogue envisioned in Bahktin's cross-cultural encounter. He imagines participants are mutually enriched as they either stand outside their own culture and look inside another in order to ask questions of the newly encountered, or as they stand outside their own culture and look back at it through the eyes, the questions, of the foreigner. In Bahktin's discussion there is an assumption that all participants agree to the encounter. In the classroom situations the students describe as problematic, this tradition of dialogic encounter is not occurring. These students would have difficulty accepting that the manner in which their cultural ways are being described is "mutually enriching." The original anthropologist researchers must have had questions of their own that they asked in the field, but the translation into the classroom is seen to be partial in at least two senses of that word. The professor is described as taking the authority and as the master of the language used to describe the other. The First Nations student's experience as other either is not acknowledged in the legitimizing of the discourse, or if it is, the language used by the student is criticized as not being the appropriate academic language. Opportunities for creative understanding might exist in anthropology classrooms, but if the instructor frames discourse in a way the students perceive as disrespectful, such opportunities are unlikely to occur. First Nations students identify a discourse about First Nations created by Westerners that does not correspond to the First Nations experience or to the discourse that they themselves would relate.

Fourteen people participated directly in this study. The national heritages represented are Sto:lo, Nle'kepmx, Cree, Haisla, Heilsuk, Chilcotin, Carrier, and my Scottish-English. Four of the participants are bilingual. The average age is mid-thirties. At the time of the study all of the people were attending UBC. Ten were students in the third or fourth year of NITEP, one was a law student and former NITEP student, and one was a NITEP graduate and a graduate student in the educational administration master's program, Ts"kel. Jo-ann Archibald is the current Director of the FRS Nations House of Learning at UBC. All the student participants had taken anthropology courses at UBC, and some had also taken anthropology courses at community colleges. All except the law student had taken at least four courses in Native studies. The law student had spent one year in NITEP and had taken two Native studies courses taught by First Nations instructors.

Nine women and three men participated. This is typical of the female-male ratio of First Nations students at UBC; for example, in the 1990 through 1991 academic year, eighty-one women and seventeen men were enrolled in NITEP.

The Conversations:
We Discuss What You Heard and What It Meant

The four questions that I asked were as follows:

1. Why did you choose to take anthropology courses?
2. Were these courses the kind of study that you anticipated?
3. Can you think of specific instances where you felt discomfort of any sort in anthropology classes?
4. If you could give advice to future NITEP students about taking anthropology courses, what would you say to them?

Questions 1 and 2 were asked so that the students would think about the anticipatory set they had when they began the courses. From my experience as a course counselor I knew that students chose to study anthropology for a number of quite varied reasons. Some students, for example, simply sought courses where they thought other First Nations students would be. Others thought that as First Nations people they would know something about the study of First Nations people and would therefore be somewhat better prepared for senior course work in anthropology than in, for example, English literature or mathematics. On the other hand, some students felt that as First Nations teachers they were unrealistically expected to know about the First Nations of Canada and felt that anthropology courses would help to increase their knowledge. The reasons for choosing the courses, then, would influence to some degree how students felt about the academic study that they actually encountered.

Question 3 was asked in order to focus the stories that were going to be told on problematic areas, to isolate incidents for examination. Some of the stories I had been told before and others I would hear for the first time.

Question 4 was asked because students continued to choose anthropology courses despite the fact that so many seemed to encounter difficulties. I knew that students often make choices based on the advice of others, so I was curious to find out what advice was given.

The students were asked to isolate instances in their experiences in anthropology classes that were problematic for them. I expected they would choose to highlight and discuss instances of what I, as the researcher, from my previous encounters with students' stories considered to be examples of hegemonic practices. Brodkey (1987a) states that scholarship is normally defined as unbiased or objective. Negative critique on the other hand is "at once a story of cultural hegemony and an argument for social change. Critical narrators then, are narrators whose self consciousness about ideology makes it necessary for them to point out that all stories including their own, are told from a vantage point and to call attention to the voice in which the story is being told" (71). In the sense that Brodkey describes, our conversations could be considered negative critique and the participants in this research encounter critical narrators. The story I am telling of my experience as a participant in the negative critique is told from my understanding of the vantage point of the First Nations students.

That's What My People Say: You Learn It from the Story

Freire (1985) insists that "theory or introspection in the absence of social action is escapist idealism or wishful thinking" (5). In his view, genuine theory can only be derived from praxis rooted in historical struggles. This classroom encounter is rooted in a historical educational struggle. There is an obligation implied in Freire's words to develop some genuine educational theories rooted in this struggle. Hampton (1988) states that within a theory of First Nations education there must be an appreciation of the facts of Indian history including the loss of the continent and continuing racial and political oppression. First Nations students have encountered difficulties in mainstream education since contact, and higher education is no exception. The historical struggle is genuine. What action is implied?

Action research is the systematic collection and analysis of a particular topic for the purpose of informing political action and social change. The research participants acknowledge their biases from the beginning of the study. They are not outside observers who will document the action from a stance that can be described as academically objective. The research they undertake is for their own benefit. The issue to be addressed arises from the community's interest to investigate it.

As we discussed and recorded stories about the problems in anthropology classes, the challenge for me soon became how to translate praxis, reflection leading to action, into text, a thesis, and how to imagine the text in relation to future action within this community context. My challenge was also to create a story about this struggle that is respectful to the lives of all of the characters.

I asked myself "Why would a non-Native graduate student attempt to complete research about First Nations students' reported perceptions of anthropologist instructors' 'realist tales'?" My answer was that I wanted to document and to enter into a broader public forum certain kinds of stories that I have been told over and over and over.

Initially I labeled this section "Anthropology as Storytelling." It seemed to me that the title might help to demythologize the authority of the knowledge that is passed there. Certain anthropologists create or borrow stories to tell about a tradition they encounter. They acquire the knowledge somewhere along the levels of abstraction described in the Agar (1986) theory. They talk about facts and theories and academic audiences and lived experience and micro and macro views as positivists and as critical ethnographers, but ultimately they have a story to tell. Sometimes the storyteller has it wrong and sometimes the storyteller admits to telling a little bit of what he or she knows. Sometimes the storyteller is a trickster, and sometimes storytellers do not think of themselves as storytellers. I submit that we are all constructing tales based on our truth as we know it in order to relate what we have to say to others. In many cases we want to teach others something about the way we see the world.

A story told to me about an anthropology class. "Shaman understands and respects the power of the universe, the interconnectedness of man, animals, plants and oceans" (Shuter, personal communication 1990). I will attempt to relate the conversation that took place between us, Sarah. I hope it reveals how these matters are integrated into a more comprehensive conversation and relationship. We had been doing a seminar with student teachers, and you were asked if you would offer one piece of advice to your fellow teachers in training:

"Just remember when you go to teach in a village like mine you will be the only stranger. Everyone there will speak with the dialect of our village. There are so many things that you can teach. Standard English doesn't have to be the most important thing. Why should all of us learn to speak like you do?"

You later told me that you could not get accustomed to the view of monolingual people. You said that they do not seem to know that bilingual people have the ability to think in two languages and that because of their bilingualism they have more ways to see the world. "English doesn't even sound as good as my language. Our sounds are happy. We describe things differently. A snowflake is a blanket for a chickadee." I asked you if you ever considered writing about the work you are doing to revitalize your language in your community. You had just returned from giving a three-day workshop for teachers. You said you did not feel like sharing your cultural self with most of your professors, and then you told me about your anthropology class.

My prof. dressed up like a shaman, and then the class was supposed to ask him questions. He had a paper headband with a paper feather in it on his head and a green shawl over his shoulders.

What did you think about that!

I just pretended that it wasn't happening. I tell myself that it isn't real. He is just doing something but it isn't real. There was another Native student in the class, and she just kept looking at me. We went for coffee, and she couldn't stop crying. She asked me why I was so calm, and I told her that I pretended that it wasn't real, that it wasn't happening.

The other woman said, "How could they be doing this? How am I supposed to feel? Why do they think they could go up to him and just ask any question? They think that he would answer like that. He thinks that he can just be a shaman. How can he wear that paper headband in front of us? It makes me sick."

We talked about the violation of trust between the shaman and the ethnographer. You said you would never tell this professor anything about your people. I can't remember what else we talked about that day.

Seeking symmetry. In this section I have imagined a series of concentric circles. Everyone who participated in conversations about the issues that arise in anthropology is sitting in the inside circle. The conversation that we had is represented in the text that follows. A protocol has been devised for the facilitation of this textual conversation. I had spoken to everyone individually before this meeting, so I refer to previous conversations as a way of stimulating the conversation at this gathering. I also participate in the conversation as a facilitator. The readers sit in the next circle. I imagine them witnessing what is reported in the first circle. The third circle would be created when we sit together to talk about the meanings we made and the breakdowns that occurred for each of us as we read the text. I submit that some of the issues discussed arise because historically the study of anthrolpolgy at university has been done in the absence of First Nations witnesses. In this section I direct my commentary to the people who participated in the conversations, the people who spoke to me. I did not want to create a text in which the audience is anonymous. For the sake of clarity for all readers, I will further explain some of the decisions I have made about the format of this section.

Concentric circles are introduced because the circle is a point of reference in much of our work in First Nations education. Recently I was traveling with a friend along a stretch of highway in Saskatchewan, and the circle orientation was pointed out to me. I have always thought of the prairies as flat and somewhat linear like the map of Canada. We were, in my mind, traveling across the flat land from east to west. My friend said he loved to drive out in the prairie because he was driving within the circle and he could feel its power. Suddenly the horizon surrounded us as we drove across a diameter.

The concentric circles then are introduced as a metaphor to locate the conversations in a First Nations context, to alert the imagination of the reader. The circles are an invitation to imagine how things might be interrelated. To consider how tension, balance, surface(terrain) and rhythm are components of symmetry.

The concentric circles are also introduced here as a visual metaphor to illustrate my understanding of another aspect of First Nations discourse. The discourse is embedded in a context that has as much prominence for the witnesses to the discourse, and to the participants in the discourse, as the discourse itself. It is necessary to locate the discourse. To locate the discourse in this section, first the circle of speakers and then a circle of witnesses is imagined. The witnesses (readers) are asked to engage in my interpretation of what Lightning (1992) terms "mutual thinking." Although Lightning is referring to listening to elders, the assumption of mutual thinking is that active attention, humility of the hearer, and respect for the speaker will put one in the frame of mind where the minds can meet. A multileveled story is then told by Jo-ann Archibald. Urion (1990) describes these aspects of First Nations discourse: "Like academic discourse, it is thus essentially empirical, and rests on observation. The major difference is the requirement—not just the acknowledgment—that the observer be part of the observation. Statements are not disembodied, but are evaluated in terms of multiple contexts, and further evaluated according to where the statements originate" (8).

For the sake of committing our discussions to print, I have imagined us gathered together to look at the patterns that emerged for me as I revisited the words on tape and thought about our conversations. One of the themes that has been very strong from the beginning of my work in this area is the notion of witness. As most First Nations readers will know, in some of the coastal nations the role of witness is clearly defined at ceremonial functions. People come to witness an important event, and it is their responsibility to remember it and to pass on the occurrences there to people who did not attend, to their children, and in some cases to a particular person whose role it is to remember. This practice reflects the function of memory in oral tradition. At many of these gatherings the stories, ceremonies, rituals, and protocols of the culture are performed.

People gather in anthropology classes to learn about Native cultural practices as told by the anthropology instructors. As I listened to your stories I began to hear the responsibilities you felt as you witnessed anthropologists talking about your people, your relatives, your ancestors. We discussed these responsibilities, the conflicts you felt as you experienced them, the reasons you believed these conflicts were occurring, and in some cases the action that you felt was implied. We have been formulating our own theories about the nature of anthropology as a discipline in the face of this particular audience. I believe that we are involved in what Lather (1986) labels "research as praxis." "For researchers with emancipatory aspirations, doing empirical research offers a powerful opportunity for praxis to the extent that the research process enables people to change by encouraging self-reflection and a deeper understanding of their particular situations" (263).

The main critique in this chapter is of the language, texts, and behavior of a few anthropologists in academia. The hierarchical nature of academic discourse is discussed. The conversation amongst us that follows in the text was not examined for disagreements, contradictions, and omissions. This strategy was not to elevate First Nations discourse or to idealize it. This level of interrogation did not occur because the conversational style that is displayed has its own rules. As speakers we were not asking each other to defend our positions. We were exploring and developing our perspectives.

I begin reporting our reconstructed conversations with a story that Jo-ann Archibald told me one night as we were sitting on a log surrounded by the ocean and the mountains and the sunset, thinking about her travels to Navajo country and my travels through these words. The story is included here for a number of reasons. First it was a gift. Jo-ann gave me the telling of this story because she thought it reflected the work we were attempting to do as we discussed the practice of anthropology and students' experiences with it. Second, most gatherings and many meetings I attend that concern the welfare of First Nations people in education begin with a prayer. An elder would normally take this responsibility. In this case, no one participated as an elder, so the telling of the story takes this position in the text. Third, because one of the recurrent themes in the conversations is Whose knowledge is the most credible in the circumstance described? it seemed appropriate to begin the transcript conversations with a story told to me by a First Nations person, a story she told because she thought it reflected some of the issues that I was encountering in my work. Also, in my own experience of being told this story, I was reminded of the temptation to take at face value the stories that we tell and hear. The participants in the conversations were selecting from their experiences in anthropology classes and I was selecting from the stories they told me. The story reminded me that we were engaging in a discussion based on this selected version of the participants' experiences. Perhaps if we interpret the created text too literally, we will miss the spirit from which the words have come.

Jo-ann: I'm thinking about a story that Barre Toelken (1979) tells of his experience with a Navajo elder, Little Wagon, whose grandson asked him where snow came from. Little Wagon told a story about an ancestor who found some beautiful burning material which he kept burning until the owners, the spirits, asked for it. The spirits wanted to reward the finder, but because the material was so precious, they asked him to complete very difficult feats to test his endurance and worthiness. After he successfully completed them the spirits told him in return for his fine behavior they would throw all the ashes from their own fireplace down into Montezuma Canyon each year when they cleaned house. "Sometimes they fail to keep their word; but in all, they turn their attention towards us, here in Montezuma Canyon." After a while the grandson asked why it snowed in another area. The elder told the boy that he would have to make his own story to answer that question. Much later, Little Wagon told Toelken that it was too bad that his grandson did not understand that the story was about moral values, about the reciprocal relationship between himself and nature, a fact which Little Wagon attributed to the influence of white schooling. (Archibald 1991, 95)

From the left we are:

Linda:	Nle'kepmx
Betty:	Cree
Harry:	Nle'kepmx
Sally:	Waglisla
Marie:	Chilcotin
Justine:	Nle'kepmx
Shannon:	Nle'kepmx/Okanagon
James:	Haisla
Thomas:	Carrier
Lorraine:	Chilcotin
Jessie:	Nle'kepmx/Okanagon
Mary Smith:	(a relation created to say some things that are best left anonymous)
Sheila Te Hennepe:	Scottish/Irish/English

Student as Witness: I am a mother.

Sheila: "Marie and I talked about the notion of witness first some years ago. You said: "I am a mother." You explained that when you sit in an anthropology class you are there as a student but at the same time you are a representative of all of your people that have come before you.

Marie: Our approach to life is to look after our children so they won't have to face the pain that we face. Anthropology should be brought up to date. It should be different because Native people are there in anthropology classes. If the curriculum is not revamped, I have children who are going to grow up and are they going to complain about these same things? When my children are at the age when they are trying to find out about themselves this is not going to help them in any way.

Sheila: Are students going there to find out about themselves?

Marie: Yes, I went there to find out about Athapaskans and Chilcotins. I think it is the way whites function to find out about other cultures. It stimulates their imagination in other ways. But we as Native people, we don't prepare ourselves for that [study of others]. Europeans go all over the place. It shows in colonization. They want to go to China to teach. Have Chilcotins done this? Europeans scientifically and logically study other cultures. I don't know how Indians do it. That is one thing we have to find out. How we analyze ourselves and other people.

We have been brought up to listen. What people say is of value. I have lived in my culture. I have not studied it. When anthropologists say things, I have to reflect to see what I know about this [topic]. If I don't know about the subject I just take it the way it is given. I take the position of not knowing where others take the position of knowing.

Sheila: Jessie, I think you also said something about your position as a representative of your people past, present and future.

Jessie: They talk about ancestors and the artifacts and things like that. Like it is a dead culture. They don't talk about it like it is alive, we are alive. We are sitting in the classroom looking at the professor, and he is looking at us like we don't exist. Like the Native culture is dead and it is history. It is not. We are here in the present, and this is what is painful, that they do not acknowledge that.

Sheila: When you say "We are sitting here looking at him," to you, it is obvious that you are all of those people he is talking about.

Jessie: Exactly. Yes.

Sheila: To him he sees Jessie.

Jessie: That is right, and Jessie only, as a separate entity removed from my whole tribe, my whole race, and all of the Native people in the world. . . . We don't. I consider myself as part of the whole like a little drop.

Sheila: Wouldn't it be great if he could see you with all of your ancestors. If the room was full of thousands of people, not just Jessie?

Jessie: Especially grandfather. If you say anything bad about Jessie, you will turn into a frog . . . [Laughter]

Sheila: Shannon you told me that your professor was misrepresenting some tribal practices and you felt a responsibility to influence the professor so he would change his statements.

Shannon: I had to ask my prof. questions even though I knew the answers. I felt that I had to ask these questions in order to . . . get it to come from him, and it made me feel angry and resentful to have to be in that position, the position of having to clarify on behalf of those people.

Sheila: Thomas related hearing about early tribal practices of the Cherokee, and he also, I think, suggested his ancestral connection with the people past and present.

Thomas: It is about them as a Native person. I think about myself and what I learn about, to me all Native people, are Native people and they are all my brothers and sisters, so I'm really there to learn about me, at least an extension, even if it is a remote part of the United States or an Eskimo.

Sheila: I believe that Marie, Jessie, Thomas, and Shannon are speaking as witnesses. As I looked through the transcripts of your words, you identified what I have labeled "voices of authority" from this position of witness. Who is speaking for whom and what is their authority to speak about this matter in this particular way to the people gathered here? Some voices are Native, and some voices are non-Native. They are voices from different nations and traditions and disciplines.

Student as an Authority: Someone asked me about Coyote and his similarity to Raven. I said, "I don't know, I'm Chilcotin."

Sheila: Perhaps the place to begin is with your own voices of authority. Many of you commented about your position as a Native person speaking in class as an authority on Native matters.

Jessie: The first time I got into this class, he wanted to say a Native word, so he pointed me out and asked me to say it in Scekwem for him . . . so that was the very first day in front of two hundred students. The other part was after class I had about fifteen students wanting to talk to me . . . talking to a real Indian I guess, and my classmates as well because we were pointed out as Native students.

Sheila: So people in the class wanted to talk to you about the subject [topic of lecture].

Jessie: . . . about the subjects, and they wanted to see if we could help
               them with their assignments and all of this, and it was nerve-
               racking. So I went to him and I told him, "You know I really
               don't want these people coming to me for expertise because
               I'm not an expert. I'm taking this course because I don't know
               a lot about Natives either. I am a Native, and I know some of
               my own background and what my ancestors have done, but
               I don't want to be considered an expert in anthro.

Anthropology instructors as authorities: The statements are said as
truths rather than as a reflection of themselves (as anthropologists).

Sheila: Many of you here identified professors speaking as voices
               of authority, as authorities, in Native matters and you felt
               that in these particular cases what was said was inappro-
               priate or incomplete in some specific ways.
Marie: Anthropologists have forgotten that they have come from
               another culture and that they are seeing through their own
               filter. The statements are said as truth rather that as a
               reflection of themselves. The prof. could say, "This infor-
               mation is based on x person's view on x research and x
               ideas," not the prof. as a person and his own ideas. Per-
               sonal conflicts arise because the context or the frame of ref-
               erence of the information is not presented. Is this the
               prof.'s terminology or Tait's?
Shannon: Anthro. is a science because they only accept their way and
               what is documented, what is written down. Nothing is
               validated unless it is written down, which goes against the
               Native culture.
Sheila: So by written down . . .
Shannon: In books, and they believe in the Bering Strait theory,
               whereas some Native people don't believe it. But as far as
               they are concerned there is no other way. Every year it is
               taught that way. That this is the way it happened. They
               never really mention that Native people don't really
               accept . . .
Sheila: Have a different view.
Shannon: The Native culture as oral history is not validated in
               anthropology, so it is almost like the Natives are seen as an
               inferior culture because they weren't literate.
Linda: One prof. is talking about her pet theory, but she never
               speaks of it as a theory. It is her opinion. She presents it as

fact. What she says is that anthropologists recreate Native culture, and I really have to object to that. I think it has been something that has been preserved since [a] long time ago. It is not being rediscovered or recreated. It has simply been going along on its own steam all this time. If you look at my mother or my grandmother or other peoples' grandparents, these are people who don't know how to read, many of them won't speak English, or they speak very little English. Many of them rarely come off the reserve, and many of them do not get involved in academic life.

So I don't know how they got involved with anthropologists in order to learn how to be Indian. I think that her saying this is not really basing her ideas on logic or fact. My mother or grandmother have never read books. They don't read anthropological books. There has never been an anthropologist on the reserve as far as I know. Their culture is not something that has been recreated. It is something that is ongoing. You can't just recreate something. The culture is not superficial. It goes very deep.

Sheila: When she said that, do you know what she is thinking about?

Linda: Yeh, things like the potlatch and ritual and house building, the door faces east, those kind of things. I don't think anthropologists have recreated it. Doing dances, singing songs, my family has been singing songs for a long time, and they still do. I don't think they went to the Smithsonian Institute to find their songs.

Sally: We went to the longhouse the other day, and we were looking at the totem poles, and he was talking about fillers. He said for some reason Native people don't like leaving spaces, and so they have fillers in their designs.

Sheila: Ovoids?

Sally: . . . and that they exaggerate the proportions . . . in looking at the size of the totem pole that he is describing and looking at the size of the beak and the size of the nose and looking at the size of the raven or the beaver or the bear; I look at it, and I say it is not exaggerated. It is the right proportion for the size of the animal. So when we go outside we don't see any fillers. There are hands or claws where there are supposed to be claws, and there are feet and eyes, and I was trying to look for the fillers he was talking about. He said you see them more on bentwood boxes than you do on totem poles.

Sheila: Do you see this as a disrespectful comment?

Sally: It is unclear whether it is undermining, to say they are fillers. It is to say they just put them there because they didn't know what else to do.

Sheila: What is your reaction?

Sally: . . . objection within myself. I ask him questions.

Sheila: Linda, Marie, Shannon, and Sally are concerned that their professors as voices of authority in classrooms be fair and speak accurately when they talk about the people. It is important that the professor as the voice of authority in the classroom be fair and accurate. I heard Marie and Sally feeling the responsibility of a witness and at the same time recognizing the institutional authority of the professor in this situation.

Marie: The students believe the authority of the prof. If the prof. was the first heard . . . if the Native person was first heard there would be more credibility in the academic environment.

Sally: There is this connotation, this implication, behind what he is saying [professor speaking about fishing rights without mentioning restrictions and regulations], and it is these implications that disturb me because it leaves a lasting impression on other people.

Sheila: So partly your concern is for other students in the class getting the right information. You said you didn't speak about it right away. You speak to other people.

Sally: I am wondering if my concerns are just my own, or do other people see it this way. They always encourage me to ask questions. . . . I am just trying to find a question that will help to clarify to me as well as to other people. I am concerned that other people get the right image about Native people and who they are.

Sheila: Betty and Marie, you told me that you question the confidence that anthropologists demonstrate in their knowledge of others given the amount of time that they spend participating in people's lives. Betty, you also spoke as a Cree, a First Nations representative.

Betty: With a lot of professors you can't go and say, "Hey, you're wrong on this point," and present your own facts. They would just say, "I'm the doctor in anthropology, and you can't tell me this, because I've researched it with written material." Well that's not including my elders. That's not including any of my people who they are writing about.

It's like me talking about my next door neighbor. I know nothing about my next door neighbor. To start talking about that person and saying well, anything, is like a lie. There is nothing to back it up. It's untrue. So any professor who does the same thing, talks about people without facts and understanding, shouldn't be there.

Sheila: So you know that is happening sometimes.

Betty: Yes. I don't like the feeling you get in those classes. Even if there are other Native students, I don't like the feeling, because I feel I am being pushed back below other cultures, because I don't feel I'm there. I'm unequal.

Sheila: What does that mean?

Betty: My presence not being recognized. My people are not being recognized as a First Nations people. We were here first, and we are First Nations. Here I am right now. I'm proof of that, and you can't be talking about something that was written in a book from someone who knew nothing about it. Just because they can stand on the outskirts of the reserve, going in and out and saying that they live in tepees and they are dirty outside. They don't know what the inside is like. You can't say to me that by observing the people for an hour, or a day, or a week, or a month or a year, you can't tell me something was wrong with these people when they have their own lives and values and ways of expressing themselves.

Marie: I have lived thirty-two years in white structures. I still don't understand it. I don't know how their structures work. I still don't understand it. How can an anthropologist live with people for one year and think that he knows them? Also, they come there with an agenda in mind to find out certain things. Who does it benefit? The local people? It doesn't seem to benefit. It only makes people confused or insulted. They can do that on any group. I don't think that Native people have done this to white cultures.

Language of authority: So I have to turn off my Chilcotin thinking and think in Western culture.

Sheila: The authority of language was mentioned. Linda talked to me about edited language as undermining the authority of elders. The editors, on the other hand, may think that the standard form carries more authority.

Linda: Something like the Lillooet stories and probably the
            Wendy Wickwire book in the future are examples of liter-
            ature that are not accepted in the language or literature
            classes because they are written in the language of the
            people who speak. That is, they are not edited into stan-
            dard English, and because they are written the same way
            the Native people told them, the stories, they are not
            accepted because the language is not up to par, and I
            think that the stories, written down exactly as the elder
            would tell them, would have more meaning than some-
            thing that is rewritten or retold. There are a lot of rewrit-
            ten or retold stories sitting on the shelf that nobody ever
            reads, and I think they don't really portray a true picture
            of Native life. Where something like the Lillooett stories
            would be an accurate portrayal even without the voice
            and body language.

Sheila: The title of Wendy's book is powerful (*Write It on Your
            Heart* [Wickwire, 1989]). I could hear a different language
            in the title.

Linda: Yes, that is it; you can hear the different language in the
            stories too when children are taught that this kind of lan-
            guage spoken by their elders is not acceptable. It is not
            going to do good for their self-esteem.

Sheila: Linda your concern for hearing the voice of authority from
            Native speakers in the literature led to a discussion of lin-
            guists' voices of authority influencing how Native lan-
            guages should be spoken. Another student reported a lin-
            guist saying that if it had not been for the efforts of the
            linguists in this province many of the Native languages
            would not be alive.

Linda: I have to disagree with that. If I look at the people on my
            reserve, they never learned their language from a linguist.
            It has been going down, and it is in the culture. It is being
            transmitted still. I am interested in speaking my language,
            so I approached some people from my home area who are
            in Vancouver, and they were not receptive to the idea, and
            they are influenced by linguists. They thought that I would
            not pronounce the words properly, and they thought the
            words could only be pronounced in a certain way in order
            for it to be true, but like a child they stumble before they
            can walk.

Textual versus oral authority : I am sort of the book he has written.

Sheila: The authority of the authors in the written texts in anthro-
          pology was mentioned. This was often described as a voice
          that did not respect the voice, the orality, of elders.

Jessie: When I think back on it now there was a bit of resistance, you
          know, having been a Native and being told to read *x* amount
          of books and to look at all of that background and history.
          There was a bit of resistance sort of saying, "I know it, and I
          don't need to read it." I sense that was what I was going
          through. Now reading Celia's book [*Resistance and Renewal*,
          Haig-Brown, 1988], I sense that there was resistance in com-
          ing from the academic and coming from the ancestors.

Sheila: I think it would be interesting to talk about that. Do you
          know what was at the heart of the resistance? You said the
          difference between what was in the books and what your
          ancestors said to you.

Jessie: Right. It just seemed to me that what was presented in the
          books was saying, "This is the truth. This is the right thing."
          Yet, in our minds, we sat in class, and we knew different,
          and we didn't have the courage at that time to stand up and
          say, "I disagree." At the same time you wonder, "I know
          my grandparents told me this, and this is how they do this,
          and then the prof. is saying this is what the anthropologists
          studied, and this is right, and this is absolutely true." The
          other aspect is when you try to explain what your ancestors
          told you, and you try to put it on paper, they won't accept
          it. They say, "I want you to refer to a book, this book." I say,
          "Well, who is he? What does he know?" You know?

Sheila: Yes.

Jessie: . . . I went to his office to talk to him, and I told him that
          my grandfather was a medicine man. He said "What proof
          have you got?" That really annoyed me because he wanted
          proof, and he said, "Tell me what he did." That whole
          thing about trust, trust with the people that were working
          with us and going through the system; now I would have
          second thoughts.

Respect: That is what my people say. You learn it from a story.

Sheila: In our conversation we have heard that cultural teachings
          and spiritual ways are strong forces in many people's lives.

Some of the breakdowns occur because the respect and authority that is expected in these matters is violated. One story that Linda told was, to me, a violation of basic human respect. Her solution seemed to rest in cultural teachings.

Linda: I had three students come to me to do research on the question: Are Native people human? The first time someone came in I didn't really think anyone would ask that . . . but the question was given to the whole class.

Sheila: Linda, you talked about how the students tried to cope with this question, but I will not document that. Personally, I find the question abhorrent, and the documentation of the discussion extends the abusiveness of the question. I remember how you decided to approach this situation though.

Sheila: Did you ever figure out why the question was asked?

Linda: I did speak to a few people about it later on with some of the people who were researching the question, and they suggested he might have asked it because he was trying to prove to the class that indeed we were human. I guess he didn't take into account that there was a lot of literature out there that says we aren't human. It suggests we are savages, barbarians, less than human. I think for him the only answer was yes.

Sheila: Hmm.

Linda: Respect of life . . . you have to take into account not only yourself but your neighbors and the world, your environment, the whole earth, everything.

Sheila: Marie talked about issues of respect.

Marie: Native people believe that certain aspects of culture should only be discussed at certain times. Anthropologists do not know or respect the rules. Instead of anthropologists giving the information, someone else could. The student could. They would know what to say. Native people from the larger community. Myth is not dead. It is real to people. They live by it. I don't like to treat them as dead museum pieces. There are some things that are closer to people's hearts, ways of thinking that aren't talked about in anthropology. Raven stories give me a feeling of ecstasy. It doesn't just explain history. It is more than that. It is trying to figure out the meaning of life. What they call legend doesn't have any sacred qualities.

Sheila: Thomas, this reminds me about the story you told in the lounge the other day about the lecture about the story about the woman and the dogs.

Thomas: It is left that way as if you were talking about a woman giving birth to dogs, and you leave it that way. The professor selected only this portion of the story to tell. Well, it is certainly different telling the legend in its entirety, the way it is supposed to be told. To me really what he did there, was, he is a showman. He wanted a laugh, and that is what he got.

James: I ask the prof. when we are going to the museum to start handling the artifacts, and this is obviously a taboo subject because they are specially treated and they are in a transparent box. There is a film. It is called *Box of Treasures*, which is the issue of the artifacts repatriated with the people around Alert Bay. One old woman that they interviewed said that it is like it has been locked up and now it has been let out of the box.

Sheila: So there is some live thing there?

James: Yeh, it is still alive yet. It has been locked up all this time. Everything has life, a life span, and I don't think that life ever ends because once it is disintegrated into dust it goes back into the soil, food for new life. I don't like going to the museum because of that.

Sheila: What does it feel like?

James: When I first went there I almost started crying. I looked at these masks, and they looked really sad. Like it was locked there. The original purpose was being used, and it was moving. It had life and whereas in the museum now it is still. It is not doing anything. It can't be touched. Why are these big monuments bolted to concrete? The cultural society in Alert Bay, the masks aren't treated as . . . like, they are not in cases. They are on stands, and people can go and touch them. They can take them off, and they can use them as part of the teaching of the dance of the culture which is what the masks were for; they have a purpose. They were not made to be collected and put on a shelf and never used. The way the missionaries viewed the totem poles has stuck in everybody's mind.

Sheila: What is that?

James: They see the totem pole. Do they think about what the significance of the totem is, other than a carving? It is a living

| | history. It is a living storybook. I don't think it can be really explained. It is there. You understand it. It is not just the thing that you see. It is almost like they acknowledge myth but with a little chuckle. |

Sheila: What does that mean?

James: Maybe that is just the way they present themselves, just a myth, but that is all that it is. It doesn't really have anything.

Sheila: You mean like a fantasy?

James: He compared everything to a fairy tale which, to me, I kept saying, "How dare you?"

Sheila: Fairy tale?

James: In a lot of stories Native people have people of rank, and he says, "When you look at a fairy tale it has a king and a princess . . . ," but I don't see legends and fairy tales side by side. A legend has a very strong human message; where you look at a fairy tale and it is for enjoyment. It is like only kids read fairy tales. Legends, it is kids, and goes into adulthood and old age. Like the whole thing of Raven being able to transform into Coyote. Raven takes on a different type of human form, and in the Western fairy tale they have talking animals, but that is sort of done in a chuckle. It doesn't really happen. But with the Native people it is innate. It is just the way it is. It is accepted that is the way it is. You almost do not question what is being told to you, and this has to do with respect.

Lorraine: A friend of mine went to a camp where a prof. from here was teaching Athabaskan spirituality and teaching people how to dream. I was flabbergasted because you can't teach people how to dream. . . . I got real sarcastic and said if you want me to do that, I can do that to you too, teach [fake dreaming], and you can get the same experience. I don't have any powers. I was real angry because they were playing with something.

Sheila: She doesn't understand if she is trying to teach dreams?

Lorraine: . . . I said that playing with something like that about dreaming, while the spirits are around—it's not good to play around with because it is dangerous because something could happen . . .

Linda: It is kind of funny here. All these experts teaching us about ourselves. But we already know about us, but we are studying to be us.

Sheila: Throughout this conversation we have heard many of the strategies that you use to deal with the breakdowns that you face. Mary, you and Thomas talked about this too.

Thomas: I see it the way Native people are perceived in society. It just bounces off me, and I leave it like that. It is my shield, and I am really overprotective. It is sort of like you fall in love and you get hurt and then you are tough. The next time, tougher, right? You don't get burned the next time. I think that is just the way it is.

Mary: When a Native student goes into a classroom, part of you is removed and sort of your Indian spirit is put apart from you, so you are separated so you can deal with the mainstream society values. When you try to talk about the Native matters that are in the text without using the eyes of your Indian spirit . . . When you look at it with your wholeness all that emotional stuff wells up. You try to see it through their eyes. When you leave the room your spirit is back. This is how I deal with pain. Remove yourself from your body. Your spirit is up there waiting for you. You are up there and looking at yourself. You look back, and you see compliance. You comply.

Sheila: Mary also told me about working with a legend in a rather subtle way.

Mary: The prof. did not agree with my interpretation of a legend from my culture. Maybe I didn't give her the answer she wanted. I don't know what they figure legends are used for, but each one has a different story. So the next time my friend and I chose a particular legend and we translated from our language. There was a lot of stuff in there. You have to translate the whole story. I remember my friend and I laughing our heads off because we thought it would bother them.

Sheila: I was thinking [about] what you said before, and I wonder what the difference is in your mind between deciding not to talk about your cultural knowledge, and in this case you have decided to actually give them more than they have, and you say you are doing that to bother them.

Mary: I guess where we get it from is from the legends themselves, because in some teaching in the legends what they do is instead of doing the right and proper thing they do the opposite. You can see it more clearly when the other person is doing it than when you do it yourself.

Sheila: Is it a little bit like Raven's character?

Mary: Yeh. I see that things a lot of times aren't the proper way to
             do it, and he [Raven] is . . . people laugh at him and see he
             is wrong, but it is not that he is dumb or anything. It is just
             that you see him do it, and you know you're not supposed
             to, or people will laugh at you.
Sheila: This is kind of tricky here. I want to make sure. I feel what
             you are saying. I can sort of sense it. [Mary and I talked
             about this some more, and one of the things that she meant
             was that Raven is acting through the prof. The prof. is
             "doing it wrong," and people are laughing at the prof. The
             prof., of course, is unaware of Raven's manipulation.]
Mary: That is just the way it is. We gave them the stuff. We were
             laughing as we were doing it. It sounds like she was get-
             ting more than she asked for because she was supposed to
             learn something else too from the legend itself, not my
             interpretation.
Lorraine: Well, that is what my people say. You learn it from the story.

We have been throwing stones across the surface of a pond. As they
skip, circles form and intersect with circles from other stones. Each
stone will eventually sink below the surface. Each story in this section
could be examined, but first the stories need to be told.

  How do the questions change as we create First Nations control
of First Nations education? I think of the Navajo grandfather's story.
Maybe you have been describing the snowflakes in the hope that we
will begin to understand the fire.

Note

  1. This chapter is a significantly abbreviated version of an article presented in Te Hennepe, S. (1993). Issues of respect: Reflections of First Nations
students' experiences in postsecondary anthropology classrooms. *Canadian
Journal of Native Education*, 20(2), 193–260. Readers are urged to consult this
article for a full account of the research recounted here.

References

Agar, M. (1986). *Speaking of ethnography*. Beverly Hills, CA: Sage.

Archibald, J. (1986). Completing a vision: The Native Indian Teacher Educa-
    tion Program at the University of British Columbia. *Canadian Journal of
    Native Education*, 13(1), 33–46.

———. (1991). To keep the fire going: The challenge for First Nations education in the year 2000. In R. Case (Ed.), *Educational perspectives: A critical analysis of British Columbia's proposal for educational reform.* (pp. 181–200). Burnaby, BC: Simon Fraser University.

Brodkey, L. (1987a). Writing critical ethnographic narratives. *Anthropology and Education Quarterly, 18*(2), 67–76.

Faculty of Education. (1974). *A proposal for a NITE Program Report to the Dean's Committee on a Native teacher training program.* Vancouver, BC: University of British Columbia.

Freire, P. (1985). *The politics of education.* South Hadley, MA: Bergin and Garvey.

Haig-Brown, C. (1988). *Resistance and renewal: Surviving the Indian residential school.* Vancouver, BC: Tillacum Library.

Hampton, E. (1988). *Toward a redefinition of American Indian/Alaska native education.* Unpublished doctoral dissertation, Harvard Graduate School of Education.

LaFramboise T. D., and Plake, B. (1983). Toward meeting the research needs of American Indians. *Harvard Educational Review, 53,*45–51.

Lather, P. (1986). Research as praxis. *Harvard Educational Review, 53, 257–277.*

Lightning, W. (1992). Compassionate mind: Implications of a text written by Elder Louis Sunchild. *Canadian Journal of Native Education, 19, 215–253.*

National Indian Brotherhood. (1972). *Indian control of Indian education: Policy paper presented to the Minister of Indian and Northern Development.* Ottawa: National Indian Brotherhood/Assembly of First Nations.

Native Indian Teacher Education Program. *NITEP Annual Report (1990–1991).* Report presented to NITEP Advisory Committee, University of British Columbia. Vancouver: Author.

Toelken, B. (1981). *The dynamics of folklore.* Boston: Houghton Mifflin.

Urion, C. (1990). Changing academic discourse about native education: Using two pairs of eyes. *Canadian Journal of Native Education, 18, 1–9.*

Van Maanen, J. (1988). *Tales of the field: On writing ethnography.* Chicago: University of Chicago Press.

von Goethe, J. W. (1982). *Italian journey 1786–1788* (W. H. Auden & E. Meyer, Trans., M. Bahktin, Intro.). Harmondsworth, UK: Penguin. (Original work published 1962).

Wickwire, W. (1989). *Write it on your heart: The epic world of an Okanagan storyteller/Harry Robinson.* Theytus Books: Penticton, B.C.

8

WHAT IS THIS THING CALLED LOVE?: NEW DISCOURSES FOR UNDERSTANDING GAY AND LESBIAN YOUTH

DEBORAH P. BRITZMAN

In dealing with an open-secret structure, it's only by being shameless about risking the obvious that we happen into the vicinity of the transformative.

—Eve Sedgwick, *Epistemology of the Closet*

Over the last twenty-five years, educational researchers have concerned themselves with theorizing the structural dynamics and lived experiences of inequality in education. This critical literature—now encompassing structuralist, Marxist, feminist, and antiracist orientations—explores the not-so-hidden relations among education, cultural reproduction, and social regulation. Many of its early insights build upon Bourdieu's (1973) notion of "cultural capital": the antagonism between the cultural knowledge and codes students bring to school and the version of "culture" extolled and valorized by the formal and hidden curriculum. Bourdieu underlines the fact that schools award unequally the cultural dispositions of the dominant class: those who do not enter school with middle-class dispositions can neither exchange nor change their cultural capital for such things as social acceptance, school success, and presumably, social mobility.

Feminist researchers generally have been dissatisfied with disembodied theories of cultural reproduction and insist on the centrality of gender when accounting for what counts as inequality. Correctly, they argue that cultural capital cannot be abstracted from patriarchal relations and from the workings of gendered forms of subordination (Lewis 1991; 1993; O'Brien 1987; Weiler 1988). Likewise, antiracist and postcolonial scholars have rethought the concept of 'cultural capital' to account for its multiple and conflictive racialized dynamics: culture is analyzed as a significant site for producing codes of whiteness and discourses of Eurocentricity (McCarthy 1990; West 1991). Ogbu (1988), for instance, examines school knowledge as the embodiment of racialized relations of power since it depends upon the interests, values, dispositions, and discourses of the white power structure. His ethnographic work posits the view that many African American youth equate success in schooling with "the burden of acting white." These students articulate the painful contradiction that the accommodation of school knowledge requires a betrayal of one's culture and that, more often than not, position students of color as colonial subjects.

If educational researchers are just beginning to understand that schooling produces not just forms of knowledge and particular relations of inequality along race and gendered divides, but more immediately, must coincidentally produce and organize the racial, cultural, and gendered identities of students, the complexities of these matters in tandem and as social relations are not well theorized. Part of the problem is that the category of "identity" has not been bestowed with its kaleidoscopic qualities: there is more to identity than meets the eye, and individuals do not live their identity as hierarchies, as stereotypes, or in installments.

The difficulties of any attempt to sort one moment of an identity from the flurry of moments that make identity such an interesting, interested, and perhaps overcrowded and social space become somewhat more apparent when "sex" is theorized, but not as an add on to what Kobena Mercer (1991) termed as "the mantra of race, class and gender." Because theories of cultural capital, patriarchy, and "the burden of acting white" fragment one aspect of identity as separate from another, and because issues such as the development of heterosexuality and homosexuality may still be viewed as taboo topics by the research establishment, the last twenty-five years of educational research have been oddly silent about the polymorphous practices of sexualized youth. In fact, when identity is rendered as a hierarchy and when theories of development are thought to be rational and linear in chronology, identity as polymorphous and as polyphonous is repressed. In terms of educational research, more often than not, the idea of identity still remains tied to the mistaken view that identities are either given or received and not negotiated socially, politically, and within specific historical conditions. These absences result in the pinning of identity onto a straight continuum. And there, identities are paraded onto the stage of educational research as either suffering from accommodation or rendered pleasurable by resistance.

I want to argue for a more complex and historically grounded notion of identity, one interested in identity as fluid, partial, contradictory, nonunitary, and very social matters. To think about identity means examining how such matters are constitutive effects of both social relations and history *and* as able to rearticulate desire and pleasures. When it comes to questions of desire, of love, and of affectivity, identity is quite capable of surprising itself: of creating forms of sociality, politics, and identifications that untie the self from dominant discourses of biology, nature, and normality. This capacity and the labor of untying the self from normality in order to be something more than what the order of things predicts is an idea central to newer work in gay and lesbian studies and in what is presently termed "queer theory." (See, for example, Butler 1993; Fuss 1991; Gever et al. 1993; Warner 1993.)

Simon Watney (1991, 394) has theorized school as signifying: "a double threshold between the privacy of the home and public space, as well as between the categories of child and adult." Circulating within the terms of private and public, and within the terms of adult and child, are the given and possible meanings of sexuality: the rules, investments, and the inventions of discretion and display, the structures of the closet and the classroom, and the pleasures and perils of, as Joseph Beam (1986) put it, "making oneself from scratch." To understand the contradictory meanings of these categories in terms of sexualities requires that we address the availed and disavowed gendered and sexual representations that formally and informally circulate in schools. At the same time, we must also acknowledge that schools—in however stingy a way representations of identity are offered and policed—are not the only sites of identity. In the case of thinking about how lesbian and gay youth make themselves, or for that matter, how any youth of whatever sexuality makes herself, it behooves educators to consider the burgeoning availability of representations of queerness in popular culture and with what these representations might mean in terms of the struggle for youth and civil rights. In particular, we need to ask the following questions: What can be known about the relations among schooling, curriculum, popular culture, and particular representations of heterosexuality and homosexuality? How are these representations made sense of in and outside of school? What might it mean for educators to explore the dynamics of sexual subordination and sexual pleasure in ways that require the involvement of everyone? What do theories of sexuality have to do with theories of representation? Finally, what might the fields of Gay and Lesbian studies offer to the education of educators?

To extend the insights of cultural production, theorists require that one account for not just the painful stories of subjection and pathos that spring forth when gay and lesbian youth are typically spoken for. More centrally, one must also understand stories of desire and friendship that persist despite hostile conditions. Such an approach, then, requires neither a discussion or refutation of attributes of causality or origin, nor a debate over whether children are sexual. Just as the question of what "causes" heterosexuality makes no sense for vast and contradictory reasons, an examination of the causes of homosexuality—even as a political project—makes no sense. *No* sexual identity, even the most normative, is automatic, authentic, easily assumed, or without negotiation and construction. It is not that there is some stable heterosexual identity out there waiting to be assumed and some unstable homosexual identity best left to its own. Rather, every sexual identity is an unstable, shifting, and volatile construct, a contradictory and unfinalized *social relation*. As a social relation within the self and between others, sexual identity is constantly being rearranged, stabilized, and undone by the complexities of lived experience, popular culture, and school knowledge and by the multiplicity and shifting histories of such social markers as gender, race, generation, nationality, physicality, and popular style. My interest, then, is in "how adults respond to children's sexuality in ways that range from total denial to an untroubled acceptance" (Watney 1991, 398).

There are three dynamics or moments of sexual identity I want to hold on to. One concerns the social contexts and conditions of identity formation for gay and lesbian youth in education. These conditions are generally dismal, hostile, and repressive. What contradictory realities and discourses must be accounted for when these identities are "greeted" by school knowledge, pedagogy, and teachers? The second concerns the dynamics of popular culture as a significant site of sexuality and economies of desire. Such Canadian TV shows as "The Kids in the Hall," and North American mainstream magazine reports of "Lesbian chic," gay and lesbian rock and film stars, and the proliferating interest in media for transsexuals, transvestites, and cross-dressing have brought—in whatever problematic and pleasurable ways—new forms of visibility and access of queer cultural codes for mass consumption. What do representations of queer sexualities offer to youth? Finally, I want to link these two moments back to the education of educators and argue that teachers must know more about gay and lesbian sexualities than the pointing out of bad old stereotypes or the pathetic stories of victimness that presently bracket how sexual differences are lived in schools. Educators must do more than link gay and lesbian bodies to the problem of homophobia. What might it take for teachers to work with the constructs and conceptual orders of sexualities in ways that ethically commit to social justice and in ways that rearticulate pedagogy as a problem of proliferating identifications and pleasures not tied to the dynamics of domination and subordination?

To grasp the complexity of sexual identities requires a more radical understanding of the discursivity of knowledge, discourses, histories, and practices that allow the concept of 'sexual identity' to emerge as a problem and become what Foucault (1980) has termed "an incitement to discourse." It might mean, in the case of education, inventing theories of sexual capital. By sexual capital, I mean to signify a political economy of sexualities, a series of *necessary* relationships between, on the one hand, heterosexuality and homosexuality, and, on the other hand, the uneven and subordinating differences between the signs of use value and the signs of exchange value. The knowledges that organize and disorganize sexual capital and the conflicting representations of sexuality that are available, then, may well tell us something about how sexual identities become normalized and outlawed. As well, these competing discourses will also suggest the contradictory social practices and conduct that render as intelligible and unintelligible things such as affection, desire, and the erotic. In exploring the problematic of sexual capital—the contradictions of exchange and of currency—my concern is not just to consider why heterosexuality is normalized and rendered through pedagogy. Rather, the concept of 'sexual capital' should signify something more transgressive: the lived experiences between and within those forms of sexuality that are valued and exchanged for social acceptance, social competence, pleasure, and power, and, those forms which have no currency *yet still promise pleasure even when they cost social discouragement and ostracism.*

A Brief Genealogy of Boundary Crossings

When it comes to the subject of sex, there is an odd contradiction between the ambiguity of language and the dominant insistence upon the stability of practices. Cindy Patton (1991, 374) points out that "the language of sex is so imprecise, so polyvalent that it is 'hard' to know when we are talking about sex and when we are talking about business or politics or other weighty matters." Double entendres notwithstanding, the referential power of sex offers speakers and listeners infinite pleasures and perils. Yet playful and dangerous linguistic drag becomes forgotten when sexual practices are inserted into discourse. Whom one has sex with, as Jeffrey Weeks (1986) states, "matters." It matters so much that one's imagined and real sexual practices become synonymous with one's identity and with one's gender. Weeks continues:

> Gender, the social condition of being male or female, and sexuality, the cultural way of living out our bodily pleasures and desires, have become inextricably linked, with the result that crossing the boundary between proper masculine or feminine behavior (that is, what is culturally defined as appropriate) sometimes seems the ultimate transgression. (45)

This collapsing of gender and sexuality seems to be most noticed when, for whatever reason, certain bodies cannot easily be "read" and fixed as yet another confirmation of the discourses of universality and nature. Here, I am calling attention to those bodies that are taken as betraying the "naturalness" and hence normality of gender and of sex. The troubling question, "Are you a boy or are you a girl?" may also mean, "Are you gay or are you a lesbian?" The universal assumption, until it is disturbed, is that "everyone" is, or should be, heterosexual and that heterosexuality is marked through rigid binaries of gender. Transgressing gendered boundaries is likely to result in the social interrogation of one's sexuality and in the punishing insistence that forms of masculinity and femininity must be rigidified as opposite and as capable of transcending social construction. But how does the insistence on gender and sex stability work?

Gay Community News (1991) reported on a fight between parents during a girls' soccer game. A ten-year-old goalie was playing so well that a father of the opposing girls' team stopped the game to demand "proof" of the goalie's gender. Even after viewing her birth certificate, the father, now joined by other fathers, demanded to "see" for themselves. The report continues:

> After the game, Linda Dennis [the girl's mother] said she took her daughter over to one of the men who had questioned Natasha's gender. "I said, 'Excuse me, but I would like to take the opportunity to introduce you to my daughter Natasha.' He looked at Natasha real funny and said, 'Good game, boy.' I said, 'No, it's good game, girl.' He said, 'Good game, son,' and started to walk away." At that point, another mother . . . also began arguing with the man. (2)

Later, the soccer association banned these fathers and mothers, as well as the coach who did not intervene, from attending future soccer games.

The above story suggests not just the question of what qualities fathers draw upon to render gender intelligible and normalized but the more disturbing question of the deep investments—the sexual capital—these fathers spend in getting gender right. But what happens to Natasha's ten year old sexual capital? How can she make sense of the sociality that diminishes what she might do? One might wonder if Natasha will stumble upon such texts as Kennedy and Davis' (1993) ethnographic study or Joan Nestle's (1992) collection, *The Persistent Desire: A Femme-Butch Reader* and read the oral histories of women who transgressed gender to make new desires and new styles. Can Natasha find as interesting Leslie Feinberg's (1993) Bildungsroman, *Stone Butch Blues*, and if she does, where and how might these texts be encountered? One might also consider that at this particular soccer game, Natasha's desire for a conduct untied to gendered policing is being constructed as deviant, and the discourses that are being made available do not offer confidence, risk, and pleasure.

To pull the zoom lens back for a moment, Valerie Walkerdine (1990) offers the insight that pedagogy produces not just particular versions of the knowledge of subjects but the very subject presumed-to-know. She comments on how pedagogy coincidentally must construct representations of children along with the knowledge deemed appropriate to that construction: "The school, as one of the modern apparatuses of social regulation, not only defines what shall be taught, what knowledge is, but also defines and regulates both what 'a child' is and how learning and teaching are to be considered" (32). This is reminiscent of Simon Watney's observation that schooling mediates between private and public spaces and it must do this in order to do something more: offer representations of socially normalized versions of adult and child, of woman and man. The "child" of any pedagogy is coincidentally already coded as a normalized gendered, sexed, and racialized child. In this sense the child becomes one of the most normalized and regulated constructs in education.

To return, then, to our ten-year-old goalie, Natasha will probably become some teacher's "pedagogical project." Some of her teachers, for example, will probably attempt to "refeminize" her, rewarding her if she wears a dress, lipstick, and so on, and dismissing her if she does not. The gestures, tenor, and affective offerings of teachers and of students within Natasha's world may well be contingent upon whether they view Natasha as capable of "getting gender right." Within such category maintenance work, then, resides a hierarchy of identity correctness: ostensibly, this logic asserts that first one "gets" gender right and then one "gets" hetero-sexed. It is a logic that insists upon the collapsing of categories of gender with sex. And for Natasha, and for those like her, social acceptance will depend upon a particular exchange of sexual capital recognized by an excessive performance of female heterosexuality. However, this normalizing exchange, perhaps best termed as "the burden of acting straight," is also dependent upon how knowledge about heterosexuality is conveyed informally—through social relations and scarce economies of affection—and through the formal means of the school curriculum of sex education, a site where heterosexuality is normalized.

If addressed at all, classroom knowledge about sexuality is typically made synonymous with heterosexual reproduction although even this knowledge is rendered banal. Still, so-called technical information about sexual reproduction remains highly contested because information about sex is viewed as the cause of increased sexual activity. This dominant theory of sexuality supposes a theory of representation: simply put, students are constructed as copy cats. The more they know, the more they will practice. This fear of contagion brackets the ongoing debates about school personnel availing condoms to high school students and, of course, about discussing representations and practices of gay, lesbian, and bisexualities. Questions of desire are not a part of this mimetic theory since children are constructed as in need of protection from sex education.

Michelle Fine's (1988) analysis of the antisex discourses of sex education in schools suggests three intertwined problems that result: "Within today's standard sex education curricula and many public school classrooms, we find: (1) the authorized suppression of a discourse of female sexual desire; (2) the promotion of a discourse of female sexual victimization; and (3) the explicit privileging of married heterosexuality over other practices of sexuality" (30). Consequently, girls do not have opportunities to understand and to explore the meanings of their bodies, nor are lesbian and gay adolescents acknowledged, and they, therefore, have no opportunities to explore their identities and desires or even to look to institutional support for intervening in violence against them. What is being constructed are identities susceptible to sexual victimization and a discourse of protection where ignorance circulates as knowledge. However, the effects of this discourse are not lived in uniform ways.

What Is Heteronormativity?

As Eve Sedgwick (1991) reminds, there is no manual for "How to bring your kid up gay." Just the opposite is availed, namely proliferating advice to parents and to educators about how to "cure" gayness, how to avoid what the medical establishment is now terming "Gender Identity Disorder of Childhood," and how to organize against curricular reform that addresses gay and lesbian lives. In the following section, I want to suggest three common and quite contradictory myths about the homo/hetero divide and situate these myths not in identities but within what Michael Warner (1993) terms as "heteronormativity" or the obsession with normalizing sexuality through discourses that render as deviant "queerness."

First, for significant numbers of heterosexuals who imagine their sexual identity is "normal" and "natural," there is the fear that the mere mention of homosexuality will encourage homosexual practices and cause youth to join gay and lesbian communities. The idea is that information and people who give it work "to recruit" innocent youth. Part of this myth is quite correct: sexual identity is social and depends upon communities and sites of common practices, representations of those practices, and discourses. As Jeffry Weeks (1986) states: "Sexuality only exists through its social forms and social organizations" (24). But this myth structures the dual assumption that without knowledge of communities, students may decide it is better to be heterosexual than to live the lonely stereotype of the isolated homosexual. This fear produces two kinds of homosexuals: the predator and the pathetic. Within this complicated myth is also the anxiety that whoever does offer gay and lesbian representations in sympathetic terms is likely to be accused of either being gay or of promoting an outlawed sexuality. In both instances, knowledge and people are deemed dangerous, predatory, and contagious.

A second kind of myth concerns the fantasy that adolescents are either too young to be gay and lesbian identified or that adolescents of any sexual conduct do not already engage in relationships with gay and lesbian forms of sociality. In the first instance, the myth supposes that Freud is just plain wrong about children and sexuality. In the second instance, it is supposed that adolescents do not already have lesbian and gay family members or friends. The concept of lesbian mothers or gay fathers is taken as an oxymoron. What is not an oxymoron is the normative heterosexual family. In fact, this myth offers a very narrow definition of family without ever having to admit it.

A third kind of myth supposes that sexual identities are separate and private: knowledges about homosexuality and heterosexuality are positioned as if they have nothing to do with one another. The assumption is that ignorance about homosexuality has nothing to do with ignorance about heterosexuality. This myth simultaneously asserts a severe notion of privacy, that what one "does" in private should be of little consequence in public. The fact is that schools mediate the discourses of private and public work to leave intact the view that (homo)sexualities must be hidden. Moreover, the insistence that sexuality is to be confined to the private sphere reduces sexuality to the literal and specific sexual practices one performs, as if experimentation with sexual conduct were an equal opportunity experience. Moreover, even if this were the case, which it is not, such a myth makes it impossible to imagine sexuality as having anything to do with aesthetics, discourses, politics, cultural capital, civil rights, or cultural power. The privatization of sexuality is perhaps one of the most insidious in that it is used to justify "the closet" as if such an imagined space could be a harmless and interesting choice.

Taken together, these myths work hard to produce normative notions of heterosexuality as the stable and natural sexuality. Such myths require significant mental gymnastics. But, more to the point, they impede significant numbers of heterosexual educators from educating themselves, in intelligent and sensitive ways, about sexuality as a contradictory and socially complex social construction. They have also prevented these educators from even considering how their social policing contributes to the denial of gay and lesbian civil rights. This latter point is significant since heterosexuals do vote about gay affirmative legislation and do educate youth about civic duties.

We must acknowledge that gay and lesbian identities act within the discursive regimes of normative discourses, symbolic and material violence, and policed invisibility (Butler 1993; Friend 1993; Khayatt 1992; Lorde 1982; Nestle 1987; Watney 1987). Throughout the United States, laws forbid positive discussion of homosexuality in public school classrooms, gay affirmative practices of safer sex in AIDS education, or the hiring of openly gay and lesbian teachers (Rofes 1989). According to Paul Siegal's (1991) review of lesbian and gay rights free speech cases in the United States, "lesbian and gay teachers seem to comprise a disproportionate high ratio of plaintiffs in employment discrimination cases" (236). Moreover, the legislative initiatives of the old and new Right, have resulted in the banning of safer sex practices for gay and lesbian youth in AIDS education units, the disavowal of gay and lesbian representations by any artist as a precondition for arts funding, and most recently, the canceling of funding for two sex studies of teenagers designed to assist in the development of AIDS education programs (Yang 1991).

Outside of schools, the family as well is a site of disciplining by the state apparatus that legalizes heterosexuality through marriage and that provides tax relief to those heterosexuals who comply. Nan Hunter (1991) analyzes the recent court cases affecting the most intimate moments of gay and lesbian life: who can and cannot constitute a family. It is worth quoting Hunter at length:

> Is there a place in the family for queers? For lesbians and gays, these debates have dramatic real life consequences, probably more so than with any other legal issue. . . . The unequal treatment is blatant, de jure and universal, as compared with the employment arena, where discrimination may be more subtle and variable. No state allows a lesbian or gay couple to marry. No state recognizes (although sixteen counties and cities do) domestic partnership systems under which unmarried couples (gay or straight) can become eligible for certain benefits usually available only to spouses. The fundamental inequity is that, barring mental incompetence . . . virtually any straight couple has the option to marry and thus establish a next-of-kin relationship that the state will enforce. No lesbian or gay couple can. Under the law, two women or two men are forever strangers, regardless of their relationship. (408)

Without the kind of economic, legal, and medical protection afforded to heterosexuals who organize themselves in sanctioned ways—that is, as the right to access material benefits that construct heterosexuality as synonymous with the state apparatus—gay and lesbian partnerships, from the birth of their children to their last will and testament, are socially obsolete. These institutional and social dismissals are very much a part of the sexual capital of gay and lesbian youth: such conditions shape not just the meaning of gay and lesbian sex but also the meaning of heterosexual sex. My point is that constructions of sexuality work discursively to normalize what is marked and what is unmarked.

With these kinds of institutional constraints—that is, the simultaneous legal invisibilities and outlawing of sexual practices, and the everyday avoidance of validating gay and lesbian concerns—it should come as no surprise that gay and lesbian youth may be constituted as one of the most isolated populations in schools. In an early research article in *Adolescent Psychiatry*, A.D. Martin (1982) suggests that much of the socialization of gay adolescents concerns learning to hide. The sexual capital that allows one to hide takes the contradictory form of discourse. Gay and lesbian youth must learn to cloak meanings, coding signifies in such a way that lesbian and gay practices are disguised from those deemed unaccepting. At the same time, these codes must also be made intelligible to those in gay and lesbian communities. Simply put, the codes are available to those with the knowledge and the desires to read them.

A different form of learning to hide is far more insidious. This concerns the double denial of the meanings of one's sexual practices and the pain of having one's body disciplined. While gay and lesbian youth are busily constructing their identities, they always encounter contradictory and hostile representations of their identity work. Moreover, they, like their heterosexual peers, are offered the view that children are either without sexuality or are already little heterosexuals (see, for example, Rofes 1989). Hiding one's homosexuality when it is already presumed not to exist may be the most reasonable response to larger social and state hostility toward homosexualities. Learning to hide thus becomes a part of one's sexual capital and one always has a relationship to "the closet" whether one wants one or not! As Eve Sedgwick (1990) points out, one does not "finally" come out. As a speech act, it is repeated throughout one's lifetime. Coming out, staying in, or outing others is always a momentary and unfinalized decision. The universal assumption of heterosexuality does not require heterosexuals to think about the self and its relation to others in these terms.

Educational researchers have yet to explore what Dank (1971) called the "cognitive dissonance" of gay and lesbian youth. "Most persons who eventually identify themselves as homosexuals require a change in the meaning of the cognitive category *homosexual* before they can place themselves in that category" (cited in Herdt 1989, 7). The very signifies of *gay* and *lesbian* must be rearticulated in ways that are pleasurable, interesting, and erotic. This is because of the historic persistency of coupling homosexuality with forms of pathology and disease; the assumption of homosexuality as being unnatural; the stigma and illegalities of gay and lesbian practices; and, the assumption of homogeneity, that same sex relations are all the same (see, for example, Altman et al. 1989; de Lauretis 1991; Patton 1991; Weeks 1986; 1991). Moreover, rearticulating the signifier *homosexuality* coincidently requires that heterosexuality must become uncoupled from discourses of naturalness or from discourses of morality. Heterosexuality must become viewed as one possibility among many. Those who can do this work, however, do so in contexts that place as a risk erotic possibilities.

This process of identification, disidentification, and rearticulation, of constructing a new discourse of the self, of others, and of desire, then, occurs in troubling and hostile contexts. As Herdt (1989) pointed out in his introduction to a special issue on gay and lesbian youth in the *Journal of Homosexuality*, gay and lesbian youth are betwixt and between worlds: "For lesbian and gay youth, this inbetweeness is represented by the ordinary heterosexual lifestyles of their parents, on the one hand, and the adult gay and lesbian community on the other" (21). These adult communities may be diametrically opposed, and when this is the case, one may be forced to rank one's identity and choose between communities. Such a forced "choice" significantly shapes how one experiences race, ethnicity, gender, religion, and generation and how one struggles against racism, sexism, and homophobia in a range of different communities.

At the same time, it must be understood that there is not just one gay and one lesbian community. In urban areas, gay and lesbian communities may be segregated by race, gender, ethnicity, and class, and by aesthetic, political, and cultural interests. Moreover, in terms of gay and lesbian youths' access to these very different communities, the generational dissonance within gay and lesbian communities—a significant effect of the legal terms of consent and of adulthood—is just beginning to be acknowledged and challenged.

Martin and Hetrick (1988) suggest three related kinds of isolation affecting gay and lesbian youth: (1) cognitive isolation, where knowledge, practices, and histories of gays and lesbians are unavailable; (2) social isolation, where gay and lesbian youth suffer from social rejection by heterosexual youth and adults and are isolated from each other; and, (3) emotional isolation, where being open about one's sexuality is viewed as a hostile act, while being closeted labels one as antisocial. I would add a fourth kind of isolation, aesthetic isolation, where, as previously described, gay and lesbian youth must rearticulate received representations of heterosexuality with their own meanings while imaginatively constructing gay and lesbian aesthetics and style. Joseph Beam (1991) describes this process as "making ourselves from scratch." Michelle Cliff (1980) posits identity work as, "claiming an identity they taught me to despise."

Yet the discursive isolation of gay and lesbian youth in places such as schools, communities, peer groups, and families, and in spaces such as official school curriculum and the state take a different turn when one considers the now visible presence of gay and lesbian activists in the medias. After all, the struggles of gays and lesbians are over representation and cultural power. Over the past decade, we have witnessed the combined militancy of gay and lesbian cultural workers in general and, in particular, over how both the AIDS epidemic and gay and lesbian civil rights are to be popularly represented. These

struggles have resulted in a significant increase in the public availability of gay and lesbian representations and cultural codes, the publicizing of internal community arguments over what kinds of representations should be asserted, and over publicizing racism and sexism
within gay and lesbian communities. Whereas, even a few years ago,
the national medias in North America censored the reportage of gay
and lesbian current events, in our recent present, everyday citizens,
including our gay and lesbian youth, can now read about or watch
marches, protest demonstrations, gay and lesbian films, weddings,
court cases, and, if fluent in the codes, read the obituaries of people
who are gay and lesbian.

From Rock Hudson to Pee Wee Herman, from Martina to
Madonna, from James Baldwin to Audre Lorde, from RuPaul to K. D.
Lang, from Queer Nation to ACT-UP, the increasing visibility of conflictive gay and lesbian sensibilities, at least in urban areas, intervenes
in how the previously described isolation might be lived and contested. Moreover, in small and large communities, citizens are now
debating and voting on gay rights legislation and gay candidates and
on whether and how to support equal protection under the law. The
more complicated issue is how to reconceptualize the distance
between sexuality as normalized through social convention and hence
refuse the imperatives of a heteronormativity to stand in for sexuality
and the very contradictory meanings of gay, lesbian, and bisexual
identities. What work might educators perform? Which categories
must they rearticulate to understand the sexual capital of any youth?
How might one explain the fact that in spite of the availability of new
questions and discourses, the public debates and the representations
that announce the presence of gay and lesbian identities have not been
accompanied by an increase in understanding or tolerance, or by the
gaining and the maintaining of basic civil rights. This queer paradox—
of emerging identities becoming more visible yet less understood—
needs exploration.

The Trouble with Gay Parties

On July 16, 1991, two diametrically opposed events coincidently
occupied the same public space in Binghamton, New York. These
events seem emblematic of the "open secret" suggested by Sedgwick.
On that July evening, despite threats of cancellation, the local public
broadcasting company (PBS) screened in its series of new video art the
award winning video of Marlon Riggs, "Tongues Untied." Viewers
were repeatedly warned of its controversies: the central one being that

the video represents the languages, lived experiences, and bodies of black gay men. Prior to its broadcast across U.S. airwaves, "Tongues Untied" was unevenly distributed, playing mainly in gay film festivals and reviewed in gay publications. That it was aired on PBS was a major victory for those who demand public access to gay representations.

Earlier that morning, there appeared, in the local newspaper's editorial page, yet another lament on the demise of Western civilization. This chronology of despair took a slightly different focus and an odd linguistic turn: much of the letter catalogued how multicultural education was ruining the editorial writer's own comfort with language. He complains: "We can no longer say we attended a gay party." Obviously confident in what this sentence means and in the convocative power of "we," yet oddly managing to acknowledge his own loss of confidence in being able to control language, the letter goes on to list other words "we can no longer say" because of feminists and African Americans. "They," he argues, "are ruining perfectly good words." What he does not say is that some of these words are ruining what Eve Sedgwick (1990) has called his "erotic identity" (81). I think that what the editorial writer means is that he can no longer say he has been to a gay party without being mistaken for being gay himself.

The sentence, *We can no longer say we attended a gay party* suggests something about the slippery work of words and the significant work of political practice: how, in the first instance, intentions collide with what others construct, and how, in the second instance, words, prior to the time they enter our heads and leave our mouths, are overpopulated with the identities and intentions of others. This sentence refuses to hold still as different speakers borrow what cannot be said, and as what cannot be said, in the words of Michel Foucault (1980), "speaks verbosely of its own silences [and] takes great pains to relate in detail the things it does not say" (8).

Let's return for a moment to our editorial writer. He assumes the signifier "gay" used to reference a state of abandoned happiness and that it is events rather than people that bestow this state of affairs. He infers that it is becoming increasingly impossible to uncouple the signifier "gay" from homosexual and lesbian identities despite his wishes that these identities just go away. And finally, he believes he can speak for us all.

The sentence—*We can no longer say we attended a gay party*—is overcrowded with contested versions of both secret and not so secret parties and in the case of the signifier *we*, hidden and not so hidden identities. Living in this sentence are sets of social practices: collectivities of gay and lesbian identities that are probably having a good time, and collectivities of heterosexuals who disparage this form of sociality. Coincidently, then, the "we" in this sentence is not easily contained. There is the editorial we that implies a community of heterosexuals who in no way want to be mistaken either as gay or as affirming gay sociality. There is also the gay and lesbian we who speak this sentence with a very different intent, signifying the practices of being in the closet, of erotic identities left untold, and of the contradictory ways such knowledge is rendered inaccessible and accessible because it is deemed dangerous.

These public debates between those who deny and those who affirm gay and lesbian identities are very much a part of the public discourse of education. One need only visit schools to understand that children and youth constantly produce, embody, and perform sexualities and their different urgencies for making sense of the detours of bodies and desires. Unofficial talk about sex, sexuality, and what it means to take up gender—in whatever form—fills the hallways, the toilets, the cafeteria, and sometimes even discourse in the classroom. While the need for and effects of not having a new discourse of sex in schools continue to be highly documented (Fine 1988; Patton 1991; Weis 1990), perhaps the most suppressed question concerns the education of the educator. If the educator is unwilling to engage with gay and lesbian cultural representations, how can it be possible for the educator to understand the conditions of self-fashioning and pleasures that youth make? The contours of this question go well beyond the "facts" of sexuality, if such things exist outside the truths of representation. This is particularly true of what it means to educate about AIDS and safer sex during a time when gay-positive government funding of education is prohibited while condoms are being distributed in public school. Cindy Patton (1990) puts the problem this way: "The impulse to provide more and more facts rests on a futile hope that some objective truth will constitute education about AIDS. Perhaps it reflects a wish to avoid actually talking about the 'deviances' around which both terror and passion circulate" (109).

In the context of public education, those of us who are gay and lesbian and those who may be interested in untying discourses of sexuality from discourses of normalization hardly have space to address questions of any sexuality, let alone discuss gay parties. And yet, as the beginning epigram of Eve Sedgwick suggests, it is precisely in these dangerous times when "risking the obvious" portends such contradictory effects that the cultural knowledge of things such as gay parties must be named and identities must be claimed and affirmed, even as they are precariously constructed.

Do You Know What I Mean?

In the introduction to *Brother to Brother: New Writings by Black Gay Men*, Essex Hamphill (1991) writes: "If I had read a book like *In the Life* when I was fifteen or sixteen, there might have been one less mask for me to put aside later in life" (xv).[1] It is not that as a youth, Essex Hamphill did not try to find out about gay sexualities. Like many gay and lesbian youth, he went to the public library to learn of private things. The few books he did locate, however, said nothing about gay love and nothing about black gay men. Hamphill is not alone in making a significant relation between sexualities and literacy. Sue-Ellen Case (1991) points to the unpredictability of making an interested lesbian self: "I became queer through my ready identification with a male homosexual author. The collusion of the patriarchy and the canon made Rimbaud more available to me than the few lesbian authors who [at the time of my adolescence] had managed to make it into print" (1).

Then, as now, searching the public library stacks for books about gay and lesbian identities is a strange affair. While many public libraries no longer catalogue homosexuality under the category of "sexual deviance," typically, books authored by gays and lesbians are shelved among texts on sexual disfunction, child abuse, prostitution, and other socially stigmatized practices. Things like dictionaries and thesaurus also produce these connotative chains of signification, thus culturally mapping deviance onto homosexualities. One effect of such category maintenance work is that the necessary interrelationships of heterosexuality and homosexuality remain obscured. This also works to represent heterosexuality in very particular ways. We need to acknowledge that information about heterosexuality is also a representation. While seemingly everywhere, heterosexuality is constructed as synonymous to the dominant morality of gender policing, the impossible cultural mythology of romance and happy endings, and the imperatives of patriarchy, the state apparatus, and the political economy of civil codes. And these representations are neither helpful nor pleasurable to significant numbers of heterosexuals. In fact, they may position heterosexuality as a site of suffering.

To return to our reader in search of gay and lesbian literature, if she can get past the ways lesbian and gay sexualities are institutionally coupled with deviancy and social disorder, other problems emerge. Persons under eighteen years old, for example, must have parental permission to take such "adult" reading out of the library. This rule works to censor access to whatever representations libraries may hold. Even if she could "pass" for eighteen, there remains the stigma of carrying such

books to the librarian's desk and the fear of being confronted with the
"open secret." This scenario, of course, assumes that our fictive reader
found the desirable book and that our fictive librarian is straight.

The difficulties and unequal relations of cultural and sexual
power that seem to ground the conditions gay and lesbian identities
confront are not the entire story. And yet, in recounting the difficult
conditions within which sexual identities are fashioned, there is the
risk of reinscribing the very conditions of normalization one attempts
to name. The problem is when gay and lesbian identities are reduced
to the effects of sad and depressing conditions, and as reinscribing, in
Judith Butler's (1993) terms, "that theoretical gesture of pathos in
which exclusions are simply affirmed as sad necessities of signification" (53). Consequently, there are two conceptual issues at stake here
for any effort that attempts social justice. One must be cognizant of the
complex dynamics of oppression and how these dynamics work in
ways that are intolerable. But one must simultaneously understand
that identities—however subordinated—are not lived as stereotypes.
To think about this second point, it is absolutely necessary that the
pleasures of desire, this thing called love, be encountered on its own
terms, on terms that do something more than suffer from the punish-
ment of dominant discourses.

Love on its own terms is imagined in a short story by Charles
Pouncy (1991), "A First Affair." Our narrator is Stanley. He is fourteen
years old, lives in Brooklyn, is an African American, comes from a religious family, and knows he is gay but is just beginning to figure out
what this means. Stanley meets the streetwise Stacy in a junior high
school detention room. The boys do not get to talk until the hall monitor momentarily leaves the room. Then Stacy asks Stanley, "How long
you been gay? . . . You want to go to a party?" (11). Stanley tells Stacy
he is not allowed to go to any parties because his family is religious. At
the same time, two voices argue in Stanley's head: his mother's authoritative voice, warning him to stay away from people like Stacy, and his
own internally persuasive voice, conjuring ways to go to the party.

That evening, Stanley's mother expects him to go to church. Stanley tells his mother he has to work on a school term paper, hoping his
mother does not figure out that term papers are due later in the school
year. His mother agrees to let him stay home alone and that evening.
As Stanley gets dressed for the party, he thinks: "A party with—all
boys! What might happen? Who might find out? What if somebody
got shot? . . . The worst thing that might possibly happen would be
that everyone in the neighborhood would find out, my father would
beat me viciously, and I would be sent to Cheraw, South Carolina" (16).

He wants to look good but only manages to patch together what he takes as his first party clothes. Stacy picks him up, and they go to the gay party, hosted by Willie the Woman. Now Willie the Woman is known in the neighborhood because he wears women's clothing and carries a purse. One day, while Stanley and his father were sitting on the porch, Willie the Woman walked by. After he passed, Stanley's father said, "All that ain't even necessary, you hear?" (13). But in his father's naming, Willie the Woman does, in fact, become necessary.

When they arrive at the party, Stanley is shocked to find that Willie's mother answers the door and graciously invites them inside. He quickly sits down, surprised that he recognizes many of the boys there. Willie's mother brings Stanley to the bathroom, combs his hair, and gives him a broach to wear. Feeling more handsome, Stanley returns to the party and eventually meets Paul, who also belongs to Stanley's church. They have a great deal to talk about, and when the party ends, Paul walks Stanley home. As they walk, Paul tells Stanley, "You know, I don't know a lot of gay people . . . but a lot of the ones I know are sort of strange. . . . It's sort of hard not knowing people you have things in common with, and trying to be—gay" (21–22). Before parting, the boys kiss in the doorway of Stanley's apartment building. The story ends with Stanley overhearing the voice of his mother ask his brother where he is. "'I don't know, Momma,' my brother yelled back. 'It looked like Stanley was kissing some man'" (22).

Charles Pouncy's story traces the pleasures and the dangers of young gay desire: of the need to find others and of the fear of being found, of the ways gay bodies are disciplined and of the unruly desires that dare to speak their name. As a precursor to the vogue house parties of New York black gay men, such parties imagine the possibilities made by a few gay youth. Despite Stanley's learned fears, the worst does not happen. He meets a parent who affirms her child's desires, and he meets another boy just like him. And while the last sentence portends something more, the story offers glimpses of pleasure and of young identities in the process of love and of friendship.

Navigating Cultural/Sexual Borders

Eve Sedgwick (1990) offers a way to consider the relationship between the knowledge and ignorance, a relation suggested by the gay signifier *the closet*. She makes a compelling case against the view that ignorance is a neutral or an originary state, arguing instead that ignorance is an effect—not an absence—of knowledge. Sedgwick writes, "Insofar as ignorance is ignorance *of* a knowledge—a knowledge that may itself . . . be seen as either true or false under some other regime of truth—these ignorances, far from being pieces of the originary dark, are produced by and correspond to particular knowledges and circulate as part of particular regimes of truth" (8).

The old binary dualism of ignorance and knowledge cannot address the fact that any knowledge already contains its own ignorances. If, for example, young people or educators are ignorant of homosexuality, it is a pretty good bet that they know little about heterosexuality. What, then, might it require of the knower to understand ignorance not as an accident of fate but as a residue of the known? In other words, what if we read ignorance about homosexuality not just as an effect of not knowing homosexuals or as another instance of homophobia but as ignorance about how heterosexuality is fashioned? The issue here is that the normative category of heterosexuality only becomes intelligible by defining itself in hierarchies of difference, what it is not. Jeffrey Weeks (1986), for example, traces the historical trajectory of the category of heterosexuality, dating its emergence, as a category of identity, to around 1870. This new historical category trailed a proliferation of new definitions of sexuality, all of which became a part of the medical/psychological apparatus. "Sex," as Michel Foucault (1980) writes, "was not something one simply judged; it was a thing one administered" (24). The problem is that while normative heterosexual identity coincidently requires constructing homosexuality as lack, what cannot be thought is that fact that all sexualities must be constructed, that one's practices and interests are socially negotiated throughout one's life, and that sexual fashioning need not be tied down to structures of domination and subjection.

The politics of understanding sexuality as a construction is presently being debated in the field of lesbian and gay studies. Many scholars (see, for example, Stanton 1992; Weeks 1986, 1991; Vance 1989) define two orientations to these debates: whether sexuality should be understood as essentially there or as socially constructed. However, the heuristics of essentialism and constructivism are more fluid than static in this field because, like Feminist studies, these academic arguments are meant to be read as political interventions rather than as literal representations of some originary state. Sedgwick (1990), however, offers a different formulation as a way out of this endless debate. She argues that acknowledging any side does not necessitate social change which, ostensibly, is the point of these debates.

Sedgwick prefers to pose the question of the meaning of sexuality in terms of "minoritizing" versus "universalizing" orientations. I believe these categories are relevant to educating educators. Minoritizing orientations approach the question of homosexual/heterosexual definitions as being relevant only to a "small, distinct, relatively fixed homosexual minority" (1). This orientation shuts out the fact that identity is, first and foremost, a social relation. The logic and criteria of a minoritizing orientation compels educators to deem homosexuality as a separate and discreet category, relevant only to homosexuals. For a different vantage, those who take a universalizing orientation approach the divide between heterosexual and homosexual as a particular construction and "as an issue of continuing, determinative importance in the lives of people across the spectrum of sexualities" (19). If educators are to be effective in working with every youth, they must begin to take a more universalizing view of sexuality in general and homosexuality in particular. So that rather than seeing questions of homosexuality as having to do with only those who are homosexual, one must consider how dominant discourses of heterosexuality perform their own set of ignorances *both* about homosexuality and about heterosexuality.

To engage with Sedgwick's views means that we are obligated to move well beyond the search for origins, in the case of essentialist views of sexuality, and well beyond the search for cultural and historical conditions, in the case of constructivist views, that may have given rise to gay identities. The pedagogical question minoritizing and universalizing approaches enable, Sedgwick states, is: "In whose lives is homo/heterosexual definition an issue of continuing centrality and difficulty?" (40). The power of this question is that everyone is implicated. It theoretically insists upon the recognition that the quality of lives of Gays and Lesbians has everything to do with the quality of lives of heterosexuals.

The field of gay and lesbian studies offers structuralists, feminists, and postcolonial theorists some rare glimpses into what it might mean to account for the simultaneity of identity and to act within the perils and pleasures of identity politics. Given that the struggle for gay and lesbian civil rights is a struggle for representation, and given that fact that all of us confront the slippery ways discourse turns against itself—as in the recent struggle under the confusing call against "political correctness"—I think educators would significantly benefit from acquainting themselves with the field of gay and lesbian studies, not because it would access some distant other, but more immediately, reading gay and lesbian scholarship, representations, and expressions might compel a second look at one's own constructed sexuality and a different look at what it is that structures how the sexuality of another is imagined.

The advice of Marlon Riggs (1991) offers educators a way to think about such cultural work:

What we as cultural theorists, historians, activists, and students of change are now challenged with is not just combatting the ideological Right,—whose consensus is crumbling, and whose days are decidedly numbered, no matter how much they posture, pray, bash, and sue. Our greatest challenge rests in finding a language, a way of communicating across our subjectivities, across difference, a way of navigating the cultural borders between and *within* us so that we do not replicate the chauvinism and reductive mythologies of the past. (19)

If education and the pedagogies it offers can "navigate the cultural borders" of sex and do so in ways that problematize and pluralize, then part of our work must be to rethink the representation and discourses of identity, knowledge, and cultural power that circulate in schools and within the knowledge/power apparatus. It means, on the one hand, understanding sexualities on as many terms as possible and still managing to signal sexualities as something fashioned in language and conduct. This means constructing pedagogies that implicate everyone and that can allow for less normalizing discourses of bodies, of genders, of social relations, of affectivity, and of love. On the other hand, to navigate cultural borders means something more: that educators must risk the obvious in order to access the transformative. This requires a more explicit and risky education, an understanding that education is already about risking the self and about the desire to be open to the idea that some risks make people more interesting.

Note

1. Edited by the late Joseph Beam (1986), *In the Life* was the first anthology of Black gay writers. The anthology edited by Essex Hamphill, *Brother to Brother*, continues the work of Joseph Beam.

References

Altman, D., et al. (1989). *Which homosexuality: Essays from the international scientific conference on lesbian and gay studies.* London: Gay Mens Press.

Beam, J. (1991). Making ourselves from scratch. In E. Hampill (Ed.), *Brother to brother* (pp. 261–262). Boston: Alyson Publications.

———. (Ed.) (1986). *In the life: A black gay anthology.* Boston: Alyson Publications.

Bourdieu, P. (1973). Cultural reproduction and social reproduction. Reprinted in J. Karabel & A. H. Alsey (Eds.), *Power and ideology in education* (pp. 487–511). New York: Oxford Press, 1977.

Butler, J. (1993). *Bodies that matter: On the discursive limits of "sex."* NY: Routledge.

Case, S. (1991). Tracking the vampire. *Differences: Queer Theory\Lesbian and Gay Sexualities, 3*(2), 1–20.

Cliff, M. (1980). *Claiming an identity they taught me to despise.* Watertown, Massachusetts: Persephone Press.

deLauretis, T. (Ed.) (1991, Summer). Queer theory: Lesbian and gay sexualities. Differences: A Journal of Feminist Cultural Studies, 3.

Feinberg, L. (1993). *Stone butch blues: A novel.* Ithaca: Firebrand Books.

Fine, M. (1988). Sexuality, schooling, and adolescent females: The missing discourse of desire. *Harvard Educational Review, 58*(1), 29–53.

Foucault, M. (1980). *The history of sexuality: Volume I.* New York: Vintage Books.

Friend, R. (1993). Choices, not closets: Heterosexism and homophobia. In L. Weis & M. Fine (Eds.), *Beyond silenced voices: Class, race, and gender in United States schools* (pp. 209–236). Albany: State University of New York Press.

Fuss, D. (Ed.) (1991). *inside/out: Lesbian theories, gay theories.* NY: Routledge.

Gaines, K. (1991, October 22). Girl soccer player's gender questioned. *Gay Community News, 2.*

Gever, M., Greyson, H., and Parmar, P. (1993). *Queer looks: Perspectives on lesbian and gay film and video.* Toronto: Between the Lines.

Hamphill, E. (Ed.) (1991). *Brother to brother: New writings by black gay men.* Boston: Alyson Publications.

Herdt, G. (1989). Introduction: Gay and lesbian youth, emergent identities and cultural scenes at home and abroad. *Journal of Homosexuality 17*(1–2), 1–42.

Hunter, N. (1991). Sexual dissent and the family. *The Nation 253*(11), 406–411.

Kennedy, E., and Davis, M. (1993). *Boots of leather, slippers of gold: The history of a lesbian community.* NY: Routledge.

Khayatt, D. (1992). *Lesbian teacher: An invisible presence.* Albany: State University of New York Press.

Lewis, M. (1991). Interrupting patriarchy: Politics, resistance, and transformation in the Feminist Classroom. *Harvard Educational Review, 60*(4), 467–488.

————. (1993). *Without a word*. NY: Routledge.

Lorde, A. (1982). *Zami: A new spelling of my name*. Watertown, Massachusetts: Persephone Press.

Martin, A. D. (1982). Learning to hide: The socialization of the gay adolescent. *Adolescent Psychiatry, 10*, 52–65.

Martin, A., and Hetrick, E. (1988). The stigmatization of the gay and lesbian adolescent. *Journal of Homosexuality 15*(1–2), 163–183.

McCarthy, C. (1990). *Race and curriculum*. Philadelphia: Falmer Press.

Mercer, K. (1991). Skin head sex thing: Racial difference and the homoerotic imaginary. In Bad Object Collective (Eds.), *How do I look? Queer film and video* (pp. 169–210). Seattle: Bay Press.

Nestle, J. (1987). *A restricted country*. Ithaca, New York: Firebrand Books.

————. (Ed.) (1992). *The persistent desire: A femme-butch reader*. Boston: Alyson Publications.

O'Brien, M. (1987). Education and patriarchy. In D. Livingston (Ed.), *Critical pedagogy and cultural power* (pp. 41–54). Massachusetts: Bergin and Garvey Press.

Ogbu, J. (1988). Class stratification, racial stratification, and schooling. In L. Weis (Ed.), *Class, race, and gender in American education* (pp. 163–182). Albany: State University of New York Press.

Patton, C. (1990). *Inventing AIDS*. New York: Routledge.

————. (1991). Visualizing safe sex: When pedagogy and pornography collide. In D. Fuss (Ed.), *inside/out: Lesbian theories, gay theories* (pp. 373–386). New York: Routledge.

Pouncy, C. (1991). A first affair. In E. Hamphill (Ed.), *Brother to brother: New writings by black gay men*. Boston: Alyson Publications.

Riggs, M. (1991). Ruminations of a snap queen: What time is it?!" *Outlook 12*, 12–19.

Rofes, E. (1989). Opening up the classroom closet: Responding to the educational needs of gay and lesbian youth. *Harvard Educational Review, 59*(4), 444–453.

Sedgwick, E. (1990). *Epistemology of the closet*. Berkeley: University of California Press.

————. (1991). How to bring your kids up gay. *Social Text, 29*(4), 18–27.

Siegal, P. (1991). Lesbian and gay rights as a free speech issue: A review of relevant case law. *Journal of Homosexuality, 21*(1–2), 203–259.

Stanton, D. (Ed.) (1992). *Discourses of sexuality: From Aristotle to AIDS.* Ann Arbor: University of Michigan Press.

Vance, C. (1989). Social construction theory: Problems in the history of sexuality. In D. Altman, et al. (Ed.), *Which homosexuality? Essays from the international scientific conference on lesbian and gay studies* (pp. 13–34). London: GMP Publishers.

Walkerdine, V. (1990). *School girl fictions.* New York: Verso Books.

Warner, M. (Ed.) (1993). *Fear of a queer planet: Queer politics and social theory.* Minneapolis: University of Minnesota Press.

Watney, S. (1987). *Policing desire: Pornography, AIDS and the media.* Second Edition. Minneapolis: University of Minnesota Press.

———. (1991). School's out. In D. Fuss (Ed.), *inside/out: Lesbian theories, gay theories* (pp. 387– 401). New York: Routledge.

Weeks, J. (1986). *Sexuality.* New York: Routledge.

———. (1991). *Against nature: Essays on history, sexuality, and identity.* Concord, MA: Paul and Company.

Weiler, K. (1988). *Women teaching for change: Gender, class, and power.* Massachusetts: Bergin and Garvey.

Weis, L. (1990). *Working class without work: High school students in a de-industrializing economy.* New York: Routledge.

West, C. (1991). Decentering Europe: A memorial lecture for James Snead. *Critical Quarterly 33*(1), 1–19.

Yang, J. (1991, October 5). Is Jesse Helms controlling the Senate? *Gay Community News 19*(11), 1, 6, 10.

Part III

Life in Classrooms: Teaching and Learning against the Grain

❖

9

FEMINIST ANTHROPOLOGY
AND CRITICAL PEDAGOGY:
THE ANTHROPOLOGY OF
CLASSROOMS' EXCLUDED VOICES

HOMA HOODFAR

Introduction

Critical pedagogy challenges the exclusionary practices of racism, sexism, ablism, and heterosexism in dominant society.[1] While the exponents of critical pedagogy, therefore, *theoretically* begin with a recognition that subject position matters, this attention to race, sex, gender, and sexuality has not carried over into how critical pedagogy is *practiced*. By "critical pedagogy" I am referring to the rejection of the traditional view that classroom instruction is a neutral and objective process removed from the crossroads of power, history, and social context, while attempting to encourage more critical teaching and learning methods. The techniques to be used to challenge the status quo are not themselves appreciated as gendered and racialized. Put simply, what works for a white female teacher may not work for a black female teacher, regardless of a shared commitment to be critical. It is the unveiling of some of these issues that I address in this chapter.

During the last two decades, teachers of different feminist perspectives have tried to adapt their critical approaches to conventional scholarship by addressing the way in which the dominant culture, through its universalistic views, creates and perpetuates social inequality. The goal is to encourage students to develop a critical and analytical approach to the social systems of which they are a part.

This currently evolving synthesis has been painfully difficult. If we begin with the early feminists' attempts to add women (read white middle class) to the universalist view of the dominant cultures of

North America and Western Europe, perhaps the most significant and painful breakthrough has been to overcome the blockade of "sisterhood is universal," which in effect had authorized the most privileged women to speak for all other women (hooks 1988; Mohanty 1991; Lazreg 1988; Spelman 1988). Thereafter, if slowly, feminist scholarship(s) moved on not only to recognize the social and cultural differences among women, but to hear and to recognize, though reluctantly, the other voices of feminism(s). This process has directed us to relate the oppression of women to other forms of oppression, thus making feminists' concerns and the agenda for social change broader than sexism alone.[2]

Critical/feminist pedagogy has been advocated essentially as teaching to influence and subvert the social system. However, the incorporation of critical pedagogy in the classroom has proved to be more problematic and challenging than simply including more diverse and critical material in the curriculum. There is a tacit agreement that a central objective of critical pedagogy is to encourage students to develop their ability to analyze and critically assess the social structure (Cannon 1990; de Danaan 1990; Weiler 1988; Nelson 1986; de Lauretis 1986). Students should be assisted to locate themselves, as well as others, within the social system so as to assess the way in which they and others have been shaped and in turn shape their social environments, albeit to various degrees and in different directions depending on their social positions (Razack 1993). One of the important roles of a teacher is, therefore, to facilitate the connection of the students' daily and life experiences to the critical literature, much of which is written in highly abstract language.

Giving voice to the life experiences of students and contextualizing these experiences within the social system have become the major strategy for encouraging a critical analysis of the socioeconomic environment (Frankenberg and Martens 1985). A first step, however, is for teachers to locate themselves within the structure of the society and the classroom. They can then initiate a discussion of difference. Taking advantage of the privileged position of a teacher in the classroom, they can facilitate the recognition that the students' interactions with one another and with their teachers are structured by the inequality of power between them.

Teachers, however, must sensitively guide this sharing of experiences and class discussion to prevent the process from becoming a matter of naming, blaming, or creating guilt feelings on the part of some. In some instances it may be helpful, as Cannon (1990) and Ellsworth (1989) have suggested, to lay some ground rules which could be recalled and discussed when needed. This process would empower students, particularly those less privileged, by providing boundaries within which critically to assess the classroom dynamics, the course materials, and the social structure. However, such explicit ground rules can promote a consciousness on the part of privileged members of how they, by virtue of their social position, may participate in the oppression of others (Frankenberg 1990).

Ellsworth (1989) has refined the debate further by pointing out that a peril of critical teaching lies in its underlying assumption that the experiences and knowledge of different social groups *can* be captured, defined, understood, and shared by others, thereby overlooking the gap between living an experience and learning about it. Based on her teaching experience, she argues that the way to influence social change is not only to recognize the presence of a multiplicity of knowledges in the classroom, resulting from the way in which difference has been used to structure social relations inside and outside of the classroom, but also to acknowledge that these subjectivities are contradictory, partial, and irreducible to a single master discourse, even that of critical pedagogy (321). The more constructive approach, therefore, would be to recognize differences and acknowledge that our experience of others will always be partial. Any alliances for change would have to be created on the understanding of working *across* differences.

Razack (1993) suggests a more complex mapping of differences along these lines. She points out that individuals have multiple identities, one or more of which may be played out at any one time in any one context. She suggests that we should pay more attention to and reflect critically on "how we hear, how we speak, to the choices we make about which voices to use, when and most important of all developing pedagogical practices that enable us to pose those questions and use the various answers to guide ethical choices we are constantly being called upon to make" (23).

She points out that focusing attention on oppression and discrimination has often meant that less attention gets paid to the meaning of privilege, particularly in relation to our various subject positions. Such a focus makes it possible to reflect not only on the way one is oppressed as a woman, black, native, minority, working class, middle class, and so on, but also on how we participate in the oppression of others. This contributes to the process of "unlearning privilege" and to developing the ability to listen and speak to other constituencies more effectively, which in turn would make working across differences more feasible.

Minority teachers illustrate the complexities of subject position in the classroom. Exponents of feminist pedagogy for some time have been concerned about the power and authority of teachers in the classroom (Briskin 1990; Delpit 1988; Bunch and Pollack 1983). However, the debates have been primarily framed from the point of view of white female teachers. A female teacher who is also a member of a visible minority cannot lay claim to the authority of the teacher in the same way that a white female might or that white males usually do. Moreover, what little discussion that has taken place on the issue of minority authority in the classroom has been on courses that explicitly deal with antiracist themes. Such courses may attract students already predisposed to critical thinking.[3]

However, the key to influencing social change lies in our ability to incorporate the critical/feminist pedagogy in more conventional courses. We must prepare to map the complex relationships within the triangle of subject matter, teacher, and student. To demonstrate the possibilities and challenges of developing such a mapping, in the following pages I explore some of my own experiences (both successes and failures) in the classroom. I will focus on the complexities arising from the conjunction of my minority status and femaleness with the discipline of anthropology and students who are predominantly white.

The Context of My Teaching

In keeping with anthropological traditions here I provide some information about myself (as the principal informant) and my teaching context. I am an Iranian social anthropologist educated in Iran and Britain and living and working in Montreal since 1989. In addition to my research I have been teaching several undergraduate courses both at McGill and at Concordia Universities since January 1989.

Both universities are cosmopolitan, serving students from diverse and often visible minority groups. A relatively large number of McGill applicants are graduates with high marks from colleges and schools from Quebec and other Canadian provinces. McGill undergraduates are full-time students, and many can rely totally or partially on their parents' financial support which means they have considerable time to study. McGill does not offer evening courses, and it is not enthusiastic about accepting part-time undergraduate students. In contrast, Concordia prides itself on offering educational opportunity to the working population, developing a reputation as a nonelitist university. It strives to offer flexible timetables, and almost all courses are offered both in the day and evening. On average the undergraduates at Concordia are older than those at McGill, many are registered part-time, and a large number of them have full-time jobs.

I taught the course Women in Socio-Political Movements in the Third World for two consecutive academic terms during 1989 as introductory Women's Studies courses at the Simone de Beauvoir Institute, Concordia (90 students). I also taught Femaleness, Maleness and Otherness in Cross-Cultural Perspective as a second-year Anthropology/Women's Studies course, (45 students). At McGill, I offered People and Cultures of the Middle East twice in fall 1989 and 1990 (43 students took the courses). I also taught two introductory anthropology courses, Cultures of the World and Comparative Cultures respectively in winter and fall 1990 at McGill (403 students). Presently, I am teaching Theories of Anthropology and Contemporary Issues (80 students) and Maleness, Femaleness and Otherness in Cross-Cultural Perspective (42 students), and I am testing some of the issues discussed in this chapter.

Historically, "participant observation" has been the major anthropological methodology. It entails that anthropologists learn the languages and live among the communities they study, and ideally they are to advance an understanding of the culture and world view from within that particular culture and community. Currently, anthropology as a discipline influenced by postmodernist theories is undergoing an appraisal from within (Marcus and Fischer 1986; Clifford and Marcus 1986; Wolf 1992). In particular there are debates around the failure of anthropologists to acknowledge the way in which their cultural values and intellectual interests have influenced the kind of data collected (Crapanzano 1986). Neither have they sufficiently paid attention to the differential power relation between them and their informants (Asad 1986; Rosaldo 1986). Methodologically, this chapter is an exercise in reflexive anthropology since it is but an anthropology of my own teaching with me as participant, observer, and reporter.

Teaching Anthropology

As an anthropologist, I am very aware of the way in which a discipline may influence, construct, or confirm social inequalities. Anthropology has grown out of the geopolitics of colonial domination, in particular British imperialism. The historical fascination with non-Western cultures was political in that it often sought to subordinate or devalue other societies and to justify the subhuman treatments meted out by the colonizer (Said 1978; Howard 1983; Asad 1973; Kabbani

1986). Simultaneously, the Western preoccupation with these societies resulted from a prior concern with understanding the origins of Western man. Therefore, in an uncritical way, Western cultures and world views formed a yardstick for assessing or, as is often claimed, translating non-European cultures for the European and the dominant North American cultures (Fabian 1983). Anthropologists attempted to reconstruct the distant past of Western Europe through an understanding of the so-called "primitive," preliterate cultures. That is to say, they viewed these societies as the living dead—a convenient perspective for the ideology and material practices of imperialism. The central question for Western anthropologists was neither how the other societies were organized nor whether everybody was "like us." Rather, the focus was on phenomenological differences which were perceived as subordinate even if at times exotic (Asad 1973; Said 1978).

Despite much criticism of anthropology from within (see for instance Gough 1968; Magubane 1971), very little serious effort has been directed at "decontaminating" the concepts and perspectives from the ideology of imperialism in the mainstream (read "respectable" and "scientific") anthropological writings.[4] It is the infiltration of postmodernism and reflexive anthropology which has opened up new possibilities (Marcus and Fischer 1986).[5]

The history of feminist anthropology during the last two decades provides a good example of the failure of anthropology to transform itself into a science which studies other societies "from within." Feminist anthropologists have had considerable success in reinstating women in anthropological perspectives by developing a critique of the male biases that had led to an exclusion and silencing of women.[6] However, they failed to extend their criticism to other forms of exclusion, largely due to a failure to examine their own privileged position as members of the Western societies (Lazreg 1988; Amos and Parmar 1984; Mohanty 1991). Anthropology still has to come to terms with the racism which has been inherent in its development as a discipline. Focusing on the much softer term ethnocentrism has blocked the development of analytical tools for the examination of power relations between anthropologists and their objects of study, the "other people."

Feminist anthropologists have criticized the way in which male biases have made women marginal despite their strong presence in the anthropological literature which historically evolved around the kinship systems as a form of social organization (Moore 1988). But in the eyes of the Third World, feminist anthropologists have been guilty of the same crime as conventional anthropologists. For example, in the sixties and seventies, feminist anthropologists typically studied and documented women's lives in the Third World in order to understand and to improve their own position in their own societies (see for instance the popular edited collections *Women, Culture and Society* [1974] and *Toward an Anthropology of Women* [1975]). Women of the Third World once again were the objects of study by the first world for its own ends (Mohanty 1991; Lazreg 1988). In striving for their own political objectives, Western feminist anthropologists frequently assumed that any apparent asymmetry in male-female roles in a society necessarily meant inequality (S. Rogers 1975; 1978; Dubisch 1986). They studied non-Western women as women and not as social agents in the context of their own societies. They contributed to a modernization of the stereotypes of women in primitive and uncivilized cultures by presenting them as the passive victims of barbaric males.[7]

Given its history, I had assumed that anthropology with its blatant shortcomings would provide an excellent example for students to see how the pervasive ideology of a society influences creation of "knowledge" which in turn reproduces the existing power relations.[8] However, my presence as a teacher of anthropology seemed to many students to contradict the criticisms directed at the discipline. They raised questions such as "If anthropology was a colonial discipline how would I [a Third world woman] explain my position within it?" or "Do you think that if Third World people were to conduct an anthropology of their own society they would do a better job of it?" I realized that they were not troubled by the substance of the criticisms of the discipline of anthropology as much as by me, a non-Western female, as their professor who ventured to raise such issues.[9]

However, some other students took the criticisms so seriously that they concluded that the task of decontaminating anthropology seemed impossible and the discipline therefore not worth studying. Both kinds of response are unsettling to me as an anthropology teacher. Because despite the criticisms, I foresee potentially great contributions from a reborn anthropology in the construction of a new and more inclusive world vision in both the Third and First worlds. There are at least two major trends that may result in the rebirth of anthropology. First, a considerable number of non-Western anthropologists, with their own national and cultural concerns, are joining the discipline. Their diverse outlooks will necessarily influence the reorientation and thereby lay the ground for the development of anthropology as a cross-cultural discipline (Gerholm and Hannerz 1982; Asad 1986; Marcus 1986). Second, recent debates among anthropologists have led to a much more thorough re-examination of all the theories, practices, and writings of anthropology, paving the way for the evolution of a new and more incorporative anthropology suitable for the emerging postmodern world (Marcus and Fischer 1986). However, in devising an appropriate set of strategies for a critical but constructive approach to my discipline, as a minority teacher I find little that is helpful, particularly for practical advice, when I look to the literature on critical pedagogy, despite its growing volume.

Teachers and Students

My experience in teaching does not support the implicit assumption in much current critical pedagogy literature that students are necessarily willing agents who welcome unconventional classroom interactions and a critical approach to the social structure. Developing such an approach demands more than commitment on the part of the students. It often entails an unlearning of the learning methodology they have relied on throughout their schooling. For instance, to learn to question material, particularly that written by famous and well-established academicians, is an unsettling perspective for many undergraduate students whose schooling has been oriented to texts as authoritative and to teachers as the repositories of knowledge. The situation is made more complicated by the fact that not all university instructors expect students to develop a new approach to studying. Students may even at times be reprimanded for such audacity.[10] One student once complained that he was discouraged because in my classes he always left with more questions than answers, and he claimed many other students felt the same way. Students who have to deal with uncertainty in many aspects of their personal life often resent classroom relations which are unsettling.

Another student objected to an assignment by asking how I could expect him to write a critique of Geertz's work (despite having discussed it in class) when he was only an undergraduate and Geertz was anthropology personified. He thought he was not in a position to question Geertz and would rather simply write a report on his work. After years of formal and informal education most students learn to accept and respect authority including that of well-established academicians, in spite of the conventional wisdom that freedom of thought is to be encouraged. Nonconformity is not always easy. Thus, one might wonder whether we have much ground to assume that students will be enthusiastic about courses which tend to question the answers they either have internalized or have left unexamined.

Studying in a critical manner demands more time. One of my mature students complained that I was demanding too much of students' free time, not because I had asked them to read more than other professors, but because they were required to question every paragraph, think of its implication for the wider society, draw parallels with other cultures, and more. This student said that he was just a student who, on top of his family responsibilities, wanted to graduate and perhaps find a better job and that he did not want to change society nor did he believe such efforts could change the world.

Similar exchanges with others confirmed at least some of the reasons for my experiencing more resistance from students at Concordia than at McGill. As indicated earlier, students at Concordia often are self-financed, and many have family responsibilities and thus have little time available for exploring alternative methods of learning regardless of their talent. In contrast, a bigger percentage of McGill students are young, full-time students, and are financially supported by their parents. Moreover, they also may have had a stronger preuniversity education which makes experimenting with different methods of learning less of a threat.

Teaching as a Position of Authority

Scholars of critical pedagogy have not questioned in their debates the position of minority teachers in terms of power and authority. Even feminists have tended to examine these issues mainly from the point of view of gender, omitting from consideration race, class, and sexuality. Such exclusion, in debates which have developed precisely to *challenge* exclusionary practices, is only one indicator of the difficulty and complexity of the battle that exponents of critical pedagogy have taken up.

Much of the literature is written as though all teachers engaging in critical pedagogy are middle-class whites, or occasionally from successful minorities within Western societies. As a "token" outgroup teacher, I am faced with reactions different from those encountered by most mainstream teachers.[11] The legitimacy of my occupying the powerful position of teacher in a classroom is, at best, shaky. As a rule, most minority teachers, particularly those in the early stages of their career, have to invest much energy in establishing themselves as bona fide teachers in the eyes of both their students and their colleagues (Bannerji 1991; Ng 1991).

The problems of a teacher who is visibly a member of a minority group can be highlighted with several of my own classroom experiences. On the first day of teaching an introductory women's studies course (Jan. 1989, at Concordia), Women in Sociopolitical Movements in the Third World, I introduced myself by giving some information about myself and my research areas. The first question I was asked was not on the course content or even Iranian politics but whether many Iranian women had doctorates. I answered by asking "Do a lot of Canadian women have doctorates?" Then, seizing the opportunity, I continued to discuss the fact that in many societies, whether Canadian, Iranian, or British, women have been discriminated against, and I drew their attention to some of their reading materials. I then turned their attention to the fact that Iranian women, like women in other societies, are not a single entity but constitute different classes, ethnic groups, and so on. I pointed out the perils of lumping women of other societies or social groups together and participating in stereotyping them. However, the next comments were, "But you could not have obtained your doctorate if you had remained in Iran," and "The West has given you that opportunity," which indicated that I had failed abysmally to communicate my points.

Many times, both in the classroom and outside it, students asked me to define myself more clearly. Once an organized group of my anthropology students at McGill asked me, "How could you in one single lecture say 'we in the West' as if you are a member of this society, then speak of 'we Muslims,' and later 'we in Iran' etc?" My answer was that I, like them, have several subject positions and identities which, naturally, I call upon as I see fit in order to communicate my point at any one time. I reminded them that this is not any different from the way they may refer to themselves at various times as a student, as men or women, as Canadian, as white, black, and so on. Their reply in turn, that "that's different" indicated that such an explanation was less than satisfactory, particularly for my white "mainstream" students. On the one hand, I feel I should congratulate myself on successfully bringing these issues to the attention of my first-year students to the extent that they want to discuss them. On the other hand, I cannot ignore that they have trouble coping with my multiple identities because to them these are contradictory while their own multiple roles are not; how could I be an Iranian woman and a professor at the same time?

Yet other groups of students frequently ask me why I insist on identifying myself as a visible minority, a Muslim woman, an Iranian, when clearly I could be simply a professor like others. These questions echo other comments from colleagues and friends who in different ways claim that "I can pass" or that "I am not so dark" or that "I am European looking." In other words, many would gladly accept me as mainstream, even forgive my foreign accent, as long as I do not insist on reminding them that I carry a cultural heritage and life experience which are different from their own. I often wonder whether here again, the crux of the matter for them is that my multiple identities, unlike theirs, seem to be incompatible and my calling on my other identities challenges their stereotypes of who should be an immigrant and who should occupy the position of teacher and colleague.[12]

My authority and knowledge are much more easily questioned, particularly if I deviate from conventional norms or if I criticize an anthropological or feminist approach to so-called Third World women. My acknowledging the inequalities in power relations between students and teachers is not seen as an attempt to point out institutionalized inequalities. Rather, it is viewed as my not being confident as a teacher, or as compensation for my lack of knowledge. In making room for dialogue, I am not taken as a liberal teacher experimenting with or advocating a different pedagogy, but as someone lacking experience in controlling a class, or worse yet as someone too lazy to deliver more conventional lectures. The risks of practicing critical pedagogy are clearly not the same for everyone.[13]

Dealing with students who are politicized and in courses which are more overtly political may cause even more serious problems for a visible minority teacher. I found it ironic that students of Women's Studies, a discipline which is founded on a critical approach to conventional scholarship, should be so resistant to raising questions about feminist scholarship.[14] For instance, in the course on Women in Sociopolitical Movements in the Third World, a discussion of why the notion of "sisterhood is universal" was rejected by "third World" as well as by marginalized women in the Western world and why it has been criticized as an imperialist idea, was interpreted by some of the women activists as an indication of *my* "incorrect" feminism. My criticism of the conventional feminist approach to Third World women, particularly Muslims, was openly challenged as being a cover-up for the injustices of Islam, though none had ever studied Islam or Muslim societies before taking my course. Not only did my being a Third World woman not help me in teaching the subject, but it invariably became a barrier to getting the students to focus on the debates. Clearly, a subtle but overt racism interfered with my authority as a teacher. One must ask, therefore, why it is that a discussion of these fundamental elements of critical/feminist pedagogy has been avoided.

The above reactions by the students occurred despite extensive lectures and class discussions about the necessity to contextualize each case and avoid broad generalizations about the popular but very gen-

eral category of "Muslim women" being no more useful in understanding women of a specific society than the category of "Christian
women." These reactions recurred despite my allocating an important
part of the course to exercises in deconstructing reading material and
data and placing both the writers and the objects of their writings in
their historical contexts. Furthermore, I had made it a rule for myself
always to mention, wherever applicable, the positive impact of the
West, even as colonial powers, on the economy and cultural change in
societies we studied. This was an attempt to distance myself from
those who have been trapped in total rejection of the West and what
the West has to offer other societies. Moreover, I calculated that this
strategy would pave the way for a healthy and constructive interaction
between the visible minority students and others. I had also hoped
that in this way I would enhance my credibility as an "impartial"
scholar in the eyes of my first world students. Nevertheless, the tension remained high, and many of the students' questions and class
interventions were designed to discredit me rather than to further an
analysis of the relationship between the oppression of First World
women and those of the Third World.

The resistance of my feminist activist students very closely
resembled the experience of a group of feminist professors at the University of Arizona, who, in order to encourage and facilitate inclusion
of a feminist framework in mainstream courses and scholarship, ran a
series of cross-disciplinary seminars and workshops for male members
of the faculty. They found that many male (mostly tenured and senior)
faculty members were very resistant to crediting feminist scholarship
or to seeing either women or themselves from a woman's perspective
(Aiken 1987). Resistance came in a variety of guises: often male faculty
were very selective about what they heard; feminist scholarship was
labeled as ideologically motivated; male faculty failed to explore the
ideological implications of traditional epistemology of the conventional discourse. In the same way, my white, committed feminist students were unable either to comprehend Third World women's perspectives or to see themselves critically.

I had speculated that this resistance was due to the fact that many
of the students in my class were activists and that some were also
engaged in or intended to engage in research on Third World women
and considered taking my course as a step towards their goal. In effect,
I had undermined their commitment to the notion of the universality
of the "sisterhood" and, in fact, had raised questions about their
motives. These discussions and the teaching of critical thinking did not
empower these students but questioning their commitment to the

women's struggle did augment their self-righteousness. I had forced them to see how their position as white women had given them the power to decide unilaterally *not just* to choose Third world women as the objects of their research and work but also to assume that their work would be a contribution to the lives of Third World women.

By the middle of the term, however, I realized that my understanding of the situation had been only partial at best. I invited a white female colleague of mine to give a guest lecture on women in Uganda.[15] In her talk she discussed some of the same issues and criticized the conventional feminists who, in dealing with women of the Third World, often fail to listen to them and, in a variety of ways, impose their own vision on the Third World. To my surprise, much tension in the class had evaporated by the following session. The few students who had tried to sabotage the class were isolated, and for the rest of the term we had very constructive discussions. Over the next few sessions many of the students drew parallels between the points I was making in my lectures and what my colleague had said in her talk to the class, as though to legitimize my points of view. I could not help but suspect strongly that the discussion by my colleague, who was a white woman with very acceptable scholarly credentials, had legitimized my position in the class. If this is a correct assessment (and I believe it is) it indicates that my being of a racial and cultural minority has compromised my authority in the classroom despite my occupying the position of a teacher.

On the positive side, I should acknowledge that I spend much less energy than many of my colleagues in devising special rules or methods for encouraging visible minority students to participate in class discussion. Some of these students have approached me to say that after so many years of being silent in school and in university they have, for the first time, participated in the classroom discussion and expressed their views. One veiled Muslim woman came to see me after class only to say that she and her friends, who had taken various courses with me, wanted me to know that it was refreshing and reassuring to them to see that I had managed to retain so much of my cultural identity without having to deny the influence of the West and Western scholarship on the construction of who I am. At times like that I feel rewarded and privileged. These comments remind me of the potential contribution that critical pedagogy can make in encouraging our society not just to tolerate differences as exceptions to the norm but to see them as equally valid and integral features of the collective. To minority students, however, I represent more than just potential change in the society: every time I assert my identity as a Muslim woman, an Iranian woman, an immigrant, I also communicate to them that the change is happening and is real, small though it may be. It is this communication that encourages them to break their silence. But I cannot ignore the fact that the majority of my students are white and middle class, and it is in reaching out to them that I can obtain the feeling of being a successful practitioner of critical pedagogy.

I sometimes wonder whether there would be greater engagement with the themes of imperialism, alternative feminisms, and other critical issues if I did not embody them. Some minority teachers have speculated that antiracist teaching may be more effective when whites teach whites.[16] I wonder whether I should, for the sake of more efficient teaching, seek affirmation through the direct and indirect intervention of my white colleagues. However, I ask myself how I can empower my less-privileged students if I, in the position of teacher with all the right credentials, were to fail to face up to the challenges of classroom interactions let alone of the society at large. How could I be expected to contribute to the development of critical pedagogy if the price I have to pay is the denial of my own identity? I wonder if my contribution to the development of critical pedagogy should be limited to my insistence on being recognized as who I am by incorporating my life experiences as a minority in the classroom interactions.

Ironically, in experimenting with different strategies I observed that students responded more positively to "critical thinking" when I distanced myself from them, even beyond providing "teaching leadership" (Briskin 1990; Shrewsbury 1987), to act as the more powerful and knowledgeable teacher delivering lectures and answering questions.[17] I incorporate minorities' life experiences and world views—including my own—in my lectures, not as subjects whose validity is open to question, but as a statement of a reality which they should know. By monopolizing the conventional language and authority of a teacher I implicitly make it difficult for the students to negate these experiences. Instead, I encourage them to ask questions to clarify the issues involved. What I have found to be useful was to provide them with questions and essay topics that would stimulate critical thinking. For instance in my anthropology classes, students routinely have to imagine they are anthropologists from the society we studied in the class and write an anthropological piece on an assigned topic concerning Canadian society from the point of view and for the consumption of the imagined society. Though some students resist, others enjoy the exercise in being ethnocentric from the point of view of an outsider. This then often gives me a chance to point out the pitfalls of the ethnocentrism, racism, and self-righteousness of one culture in facing others.

Despite my success in adopting this strategy, I wonder to what extent I can call this method of teaching "critical pedagogy," since my success seems to stem in part from my assertion of authority as a teacher. Turning to the critical or even feminist pedagogy literature offers little guidance for me. Clearly visible minority teachers are faced with questions and dilemmas which are fundamentally different from those faced by white teachers.

There are further issues that one should not overlook. To practice what I preach, I too, place myself objectively in the social structure of my environment. Thus I am conscious that I, like most other minority teachers at the early stages of their career, am even less secure than junior white male or female teachers. I should not talk too loudly about the problems I have in the classroom lest they be used against me; this is the warning that I frequently hear from my minority colleagues and friends whether they are accountants, economists, sociologists, linguists, or chemists. These warnings further confirm my feeling that what I am facing is more common than the literature indicates or what other minority teachers are prepared to admit in public.[18]

Visible minority teachers' choice of silence is the outcome of their lack of trust in the system and the support of their colleagues. I do not have any available statistics for universities, but a study in Toronto indicates that 50 percent of human rights complaints by nonwhites about whites in the workplace resulted in the nonwhites being disciplined (SPC, 1989). There is no reason as yet to assume that educational establishments are not generally quite prepared to view complaints from students as a sign of shortcomings on the part of minority teachers.

Moreover, as a token teacher I fail to be regarded as an individual either in my own or Other ethnic communities. I am but a representative of a variety of other social groups, and therefore my failure is viewed not just as mine but as theirs too. For instance, when I participate in Iranian community events often I am introduced to the younger generations as a person who should be their role model. Others express how proud they are that people like me will prove to "Canadians" that Iranian women are not all bundled up in the black veil at the mercy of their husbands. I can provide many more examples of the kind of pressure that I and my other minority colleagues face. By engaging in critical pedagogy, minority teachers confront a situation and take risks which are fundamentally different from those of mainstream teachers.

The success of teaching for change depends on our ability to develop a holistic and fluid pedagogy which can accommodate the dynamic interaction of a complex matrix of students, teachers, and subject matters, a matrix which has a built-in ability to allow the less central voices, whether they belong to the teachers or to the students, to be heard and incorporated in the collective without being forced to assimilate. Minority teachers cannot be expected to participate in developing feminist/critical pedagogy if their experiences are marginalized by the very movements that work to do away with the margins. For my part, I would like to see a much more pronounced recognition that not all teachers nor all students share the same relationships to the techniques traditionally associated with critical pedagogy. Lectures, for example, are more effective than relying on shared dialogue in some instances. They provide me the distance that I and my students seem to need in order to practice critical thinking, if not critical teaching.

Notes

1. Critical pedagogy is neither new nor a coherent body of theory. There are well-documented debates by the Workers Education Council of Britain and other European countries on the necessity of incorporating workers' world views and experiences in teaching materials and methods (Polanyi 1944; Johnson 1988; Mendell 1994). However, the more current debate is advanced by Henry Giroux, Roger Simon, Pamela Fishman and Peter McLaren to name a few.

2. In practice, as the theme of this chapter suggests, such a broadening of the feminist agenda has remained limited.

3. One important exception is the work of Patricia Williams (1991), who has written (as a black woman) on her experiences in teaching contract law to white students.

4. The continuing lack of credibility of the discipline in the Third World stems from this lack of effort (Howard 1983); perhaps the present crisis in anthropology and the fact that "the others" now talk back can lead to anthropology becoming a more international discipline (Rabinow 1986; Marcus, 1986).

5. However, the advocates of postmodern anthropology have yet to produce work that demonstrates a significant departure from the traditional anthropology.

6. For an overview of the development of feminist anthropology see Moore (1988) and Strathern (1987).

7. Guided by these findings many feminist anthropologists, along with others, unequivocally advocated the development of free market economic relations, Western style, in these societies claiming that such a change would necessarily lead to an improvement in women's position (Sivanandan 1982), thus disregarding work which documented that a market economy has worked to the disadvantage of women both in the West and in the Third World (Boserup 1970; Pinchbeck 1981; Friedl 1967; B. Rogers 1980). In the process of talking about women they talked for women. Ironically Third World women's rejection of Western feminists' political stands was dismissed as a sign of their backwardness.

8. For instance, I often review the role of anthropology in the development of social Darwinism and its sexist and racist implications (Gould 1981).

9. On a number of occasions I was asked if it was not hypocritical that I, who studied and earned my living from teaching and practicing anthropology should criticize it. Others asked whether if I participated in the discipline I would also have the right to be critical of it? I reminded them that at least part of their reading material Gough (1968), Asad (1973), and Howard (1983) was also written by anthropologists both from the First and the Third Worlds and that such criticisms are intended to improve the discipline, not negate it. But often they were not convinced. It is like an immigrant not having the right to criticize the "host" society.

10. In fact some students have confided in me their complaints about instructors who had criticized their work with comments such as "Studying is more than talking about women, how about some real work?" or "When you become a prof., you can teach what you like, but now you have to study what I teach."

11. I have used the term *token* to refer to those included in small numbers to confirm the "tolerance" of the mainstream without being so numerous so as to threaten the mainstream group's group dominance (hooks 1981; de la Luz Reyes and Halcon 1988).

12. For a discussion of forms of everyday racism see Essed (1991, 1990).

13. The comments in this paragraph are based on my course evaluations. Many students praise my personality as friendly, approachable, and informal. They enjoyed the lively classes and yet in the same breath they wished I could "control the class so that students could learn more rather than listening to one another."

14. Although I have taught mainly introductory Women's Studies courses, a considerable number of students were beyond their first

year of university. This was due in part to the pattern in which women's studies courses are offered and in part to the fact that my course was the only course that the Simone de Beauvoir Institute offered on Third World women.

15. Rosalind Boyd, Centre for Developing Areas, McGill University had just returned from Uganda and gave a talk on Ugandan women's political activities in recent years. Part of her talk was subsequently published (1989).

16. Dr. Sherene Razack (personal communication, May 1991).

17. I have continued to experiment with different strategies. Although I have not received all the course evaluations for this period yet, I have felt that I am more effective in teaching critical thinking when I assume the role of a conventional teacher and distance myself from my students.

18. This is not unlike the experience of women and particularly feminist teachers. The major difference is that even the feminist pedagogy literature deals mostly with sexism in the classroom but remains silent on the question of racism and problems of minority teachers.

References

Aiken, S. (1987). Trying transformations: Curriculum integration and the problem of resistance. *Signs, 12*(2), 255–275.

Amos, V., and Parmar, P. (1984). Challenging imperialist feminism. *Feminist Review, 17,* 3–19.

Asad, T. (1986). The concept of cultural transition in British social anthropology. In James Clifford & George E. Marcus (Eds.), *Writing culture: The poetics and politics of ethnography* (pp. 141–164). Berkeley and Los Angeles: University of California Press.

————. (Ed). (1973). *Anthropology and the colonial encounter*. New York: Humanities Press.

Bannerji, H. (1991). But who speaks for us? Experience and agency in conventional feminist paradigms. In Himani Bannerji, Linda Carty, Kari Dehli, Susan Heald, and Kate McKenna, *Unsettling relations: The university as a site of feminist struggles* (pp. 67–108). Toronto: Women's Press.

Boserup, E. (1970). *Women's role in economic development*. New York: St. Martin's Press.

Boyd, R. (1989). Empowering of women in contemporary Uganda: Real or symbolic. *Labour, Capital and Society, 22*(1), 19–40.

Briskin, L. (1990). Feminist pedagogy: Teaching and learning liberation. *Feminist Perspectives Feministes.* Ottawa: CRIAW/ICREF.

Bunch, C., and Pollack, S. (Eds.). (1983). *Learning our way.* New York: The Crossing Press.

Cannon, L. (1990). Fostering positive race, class, and gender dynamics in the classroom. *Women's Studies Quarterly, 1–2,* 126–134.

Clifford, J., and Marcus, G. (Eds.). (1986). *Writing culture: The poetics and politics of ethnography.* Berkeley and Los Angeles: University of California Press.

Crapanzano, V. (1986). Hermes' dilemma: The masking of subversion in ethnographic description. In James Clifford & George E. Marcus (Eds.), *Writing culture: The poetics and politics of ethnography* (pp. 51–76). Berkeley and Los Angeles: University of California Press.

de Danaan, L. (1990). Center to margin: Dynamics in a global classroom. *Feminist Studies Quarterly, 1–2,* 135–144.

de Lauretis, T. (Ed). (1986). *Feminist studies/Critical studies.* Bloomington: Indiana University Press.

Delpit, L. (1988). The silenced dialogue: Power and pedagogy in educating other people's children. *Harvard Educational Review, 58*(3), 280–298.

Dubisch, J. (1986). *Gender and power in rural Greece.* Princeton NJ: Princeton University Press.

Ellsworth, E. (1989). Why doesn't this feel empowering? Working through the repressive myth of critical pedagogy. *Harvard Educational Review, 59*(3), 297–327.

Essed, P. (1990). *Everyday racism: Reports from women of two cultures.* (Cynthia Jaffe, trans.) CA: Hunter House.

――――― . (1991) *Understanding everyday racism: An interdisciplinary theory.* New York: Sage Publications.

Fabian, J. (1983). *Time and other: How anthropology makes its object.* New York: Columbia Press.

Frankenberg, R. (1990). White women, racism and anti-racism: A women's studies course exploring racism and privilege. *Women's Studies Quarterly 1 & 2,* 145–153.

Frankenberg, R., and Martens, J. (1985). Racism: More than a moral issue. *Trouble and Strife, 5,* 17–22.

Friedl, E. (1967). The position of women: Appearance and reality. *Anthropology Quarterly, 40*(3), 97–108.

Gerholm, T. and Hannerz, U. (Eds.). (1982). The shaping of national anthropologies. *Ethnos* Special Issue, Ethografiska Museet, Stockholm.

Gough, K. (1968). New proposals for anthropologists. *Current Anthropology, 9,* 403–407.

Gould, S. J. (1981). *The mismeasure of man.* New York: W. W. Norton.

hooks, b. (1981). *Ain't I a woman?* Boston: South End Press.

———. (1988). Toward a feminist pedagogy. In *Talking back.* Toronto: Between the Lines.

Howard, M. (1983). *Anthropology: A brief critical history.* South Pacific Forum, Working Paper No. 1.

Johnson, R. (1988). Really useful knowledge 1790–1850: Memories for education in 1988. In Tom Loveett (Ed.), *Radical approaches to adult education: A reader* (pp. 3–34). London and New York: Routledge.

Kabbani, R. (1986). *Europe's myths of Orient.* Bloomington: Indiana University Press.

Lazreg, M. (1988). Feminism and difference: The perils of writing as a woman on women in Algeria. *Feminist Studies, 14*(1), 81–107.

Magubane, B. (1971). A critical look at the indices used in the study of social change in colonial Africa. *Current Anthropology, 12,* 419–430.

Marcus, G. (1986). Contemporary problems of ethnography in the modern world system. In George E. Marcus and Michael M. J. Fischer (Eds.), *Anthropology as cultural critique: An experimental moment in the human sciences* (pp. 165–193). Chicago: University of Chicago Press.

Marcus, G., and Fischer, M. M. (Eds.) (1986). *Anthropology as cultural critique: An experimental moment in the human sciences.* Chicago: University of Chicago Press.

Mendell, M. (1994). Karl Polyani on Socialism and Education. In Kenneth McRobbie (Ed.), *Humanity, Society and Government.* Montreal: Black Rose Press.

Mohanty, C. (1991). Under Western eyes: Feminist scholarship and colonial discourses. In Chandra Talpade Mohanty, Ann Russo, and Lourdes Torres (Eds.), *Third world women and the politics of feminism* (pp. 51–80). Bloomington and Indianapolis: Indiana University Press.

Moore, H. (1988). *Feminism and anthropology.* Oxford: Polity Press.

Nelson, G. (1986). *Theory in the classroom.* Urabana: University of Illinois Press.

Ng, R. (1991). Teaching against the grain: Contradictions for minority teachers. In Jane Gaskell and Arlene McLaren (Eds.), *Women and education: A Canadian perspective* (second edition). Calgary: Detselig Enterprises.

Pinchbeck, I. (1981). *Women workers and the industrial revolution 1750–1850.* London: Virago (Originally published 1930).

Polanyi, K. (1944). *The great transformation: The political and economic transformations of our times.* New York: Reinhart and Co.

Rabinow, P. (1986). Representations are social facts: Modernity and postmodernity in anthropology. In James Clifford and George E. Marcus (Eds.), *Writing culture: The poetics and politics of ethnography* (pp. 234–261). Berkeley and Los Angeles: University of California Press.

Razack, S. (1993). Story telling for social change. *Gender and Education, 5*(1), 55–70.

Reyes, de la Luz, M., and Halcon, J. (1988). Racism in academia: The old wolf revisited. *Harvard Educational Review, 58,* 299–314.

Rogers, B. (1980). *The domestication of women: Discrimination in developing societies.* London: Tavistock.

Rogers, S. (1975). Female forms of power and the myth of male dominance: A Model of female/male interactions in peasant society. *American Ethnologist, 2,* 727–757.

———. (1978). Women's place: A critical review of anthropological theory. *Comparative Studies in Society and History, 20,* 123–162.

Rosaldo, R. (1986). From the door of his tent: The fieldworker and the inquisitor. In James Clifford and George E. Marcus (Eds.), *Writing culture: The poetics and politics of ethnography* (pp. 77–97). Berkeley and Los Angeles: University of California Press.

Said, E. (1978). *Orientalism.* London: Routledge & Kegan Paul.

Shrewsbury, C. (1987). What is feminist pedagogy? *Women's Studies Quarterly, 15,* 3–4.

Sivanandan, A. (1982). Capitalism, highest stage of imperialism: Warren and the Third World. *Race and Class, 24.*

Social Planning Council of Metropolitan Toronto, The. (1989). *A time for change: Moving beyond discrimination in employment.* Toronto: Urban Alliance on Race Relations.

Spelman, E. (1988). *Inessential woman: Problems of exclusion in feminist thought.* Boston: Beacon Press.

Strathern, M. (1987). An awkward relationship: The case of feminism and anthropology. *Signs, 12*(2), 276–292.

Weiler, K. (1988). *Women teaching for change: Gender, class and power.* Critical Studies in Educational Series. New York: Bergin & Garvey.

Williams, P. (1991). *The alchemy of race and rights.* Cambridge, Mass: Harvard University Press.

Wolf, M. (1992). *A thrice-told tale: Feminism, postmodernism, and ethnographic responsibility.* Stanford, CA: Stanford University Press.

10

COMPULSORY HETEROSEXUALITY
IN A UNIVERSITY CLASSROOM

LINDA EYRE

School health education in Canada supports a primarily conservative agenda. Health education is typically grounded in Western, patriarchal, abled, middle-class, heterosexist assumptions. In school health curricula the experiences of women, native peoples, people of color, people with disabilities, lesbians, and gay men are usually either ignored or distorted and thereby constructed as other.

Feminist and critical theorists call for liberatory education. This does not mean "adding on" the experiences of so-called minority groups to a predominantly white, male, middle-class, heterosexist curriculum. As Ursula Kelly (1990) points out, "It is necessary to critique those forms of subjection informing our human subjectivities" (36). She writes of the pain and struggles as well as the joys of such difficult work—a way of being as a teacher fraught with tensions and inevitable contradictions. She describes the focus of her own work as follows:

> Teaching to and for social change is only possible as and when we teach for subject change . . . [necessitating] that each of us critiques the place of our own practices as teachers . . . [while setting up] a terrain of sharing through tension, difference, and critique, a terrain on which are acted out the moments of race, class, gender, sexual, regional and abled constitution which are our subjective and social selves. (37)

I was reminded of my own contradictory positioning in Celia Haig- Brown's (Bryson, de Castell, and Haig-Brown 1993) account of a nine-day "gender equity" course we team taught in the summer of

1991. She wrote about our efforts as white, heterosexual women to
address anti-essentialism by inviting to class resource people from so-
called minority groups:

> We exploit our friends. We call [on] them to be what Suzanne [de
> Castell] calls performing parrots. "Step right up: a real live Les-
> bian. She walks and talks and you can ask her anything you
> want." We expose our friends to ignorance and abuse: "Black
> woman, First Nations woman, Woman of Asian origins, Lesbian.
> Come to my class and enlighten us." When is a token not a
> token? How many differences, how much diversity to really
> address this theoretical position called anti-essentialism? How
> many lives? How much pain? (48)

In personal communication, Suzanne de Castell described her
talk to our "gender equity" class (de Castell 1991) as "personally
awful." Impressed with her eloquence and humor, I was unaware of
her pain. Our "real live Lesbian" powerfully affected my understanding of feminism: I was shocked to hear her describe how lesbians were
not women as far as feminism was concerned. I learned from her that
it was up to me to critique my own heterosexism and to incorporate
this critique into my own practice.

While recognizing that forms of oppression intertwine in complex and mutually determining ways (de Lauretis 1990), liberatory
pedagogues are beginning to describe their concrete struggles with
heterosexism. Joseph Neisen (1990) describes heterosexism as:

> a form of oppression incorporating a belief in the inherent supe-
> riority of one form of loving over all others. The belief then is
> used to justify dominating those who do not subscribe to the
> privileged practice . . . [it] is the continual promotion by major
> social institutions of heterosexuality and the simultaneous sub-
> ordination of all other lifestyles (that is gay, lesbian and bisex-
> ual). . . . When our institutions knowingly or unknowingly per-
> petuate these prejudices and intentionally or unintentionally act
> on them, heterosexism is at work. (36)

In her widely cited work about the power of compulsory heterosexuality, Adrienne Rich (1980) writes: "This assumption of female heterosexuality seems to me in itself remarkable: It is an enormous
assumption to have glided so silently into the foundations of our
thought" (9). She says that failure to examine heterosexuality as an

institution would be akin to failing to admit the variety of forces that maintain the economic system of capitalism and the caste system of racism.

Activists have challenged schools to confront heterosexism and homophobic acts of individual and institutional violence against lesbian and gay students and teachers (Khayatt 1990; Rofes 1989; Trenchard 1992; Wicks 1991; Martindale this volume). They argue that curricula continue to reflect heterosexist assumptions, homophobic slurs are commonplace, and the school system has failed to support lesbian and gay students and teachers. Fearing reprisals, many lesbian and gay students and teachers continue to hide their sexuality, often with disastrous personal consequences. Meanwhile, activists call upon gay, lesbian, and heterosexual teachers and administrators to work actively on behalf of lesbian and gay youth and teachers.

But efforts to deal with heterosexism in schooling come face to face with opposition from communities entrenched in heterosexism and accepting of homophobic violence. Social institutions such as schools, the nuclear family, the church, the medical and legal systems, and the media reinforce what Helen Lenskyj (1991b) describes as "heterosexual hegemony" (62)—a form of hegemony kept in place through intimidation and violence. Not surprisingly, James Sears (1992a) found prospective teachers unwilling to become proactive on behalf of lesbian and gay students and teachers.

Health education researchers have drawn attention to the social construction of heterosexism in school health curricula and classroom practice (Fine 1988; Lenskyj 1991a, 1991b; Patton 1990; Sears 1992b; Whatley 1988, 1992). Generally, these researchers have raised questions about the invisibility of bisexual, gay, and lesbian sexuality, and the stereotypical portrayal of lesbians and gay men in school health curricula and resources; they support a vision of school health education that celebrates diversity of human sexuality, counters heterosexism and homophobia, politicizes lesbian and gay issues, and legitimizes the experiences of lesbian and gay students and teachers.

Feminist academics who deal with the politics of difference in their classrooms have documented their experiences (Ellsworth 1989; Lather 1991; Lewis 1990; Orner 1992). Each searches in her own way to understand student response to liberatory curriculum. Collectively, their work shows how efforts toward emancipatory education can still reinforce relations of dominance. Others have focused specifically on how the topic of sexual identity is taught in women's studies courses (Crumpacker and Vander Haegen 1990; Fonow and Marty 1992). But little attention has been given to classroom experiences of educators attempting to challenge heterosexism in mainstream or health education classrooms.

This chapter is about my attempts to incorporate critique of heterosexism and heterosexual privilege into an undergraduate course in teacher education at a maritime university, about what happened when I took a step toward challenging compulsory heterosexuality in a university classroom with prospective health education teachers. I have chosen to represent this aspect of the course because for me it illustrates the difficulties I faced attempting to do critical pedagogy in a social climate that is at best conservative and at worst sexually repressive (Williams 1990).

The course I teach is intended to prepare B.Ed. students to teach health education. It is compulsory for physical education majors, but other students take it as well. I structure the course around student presentations and assigned readings intended primarily to raise critical questions about health education, including the ideologies inherent in traditional approaches to health education. I expose contradictions in curriculum materials that explicitly intend to educate students about their bodies, yet are silent on the relationship between the body and lived experiences of oppression. I point in particular to silences related to gender, ethnicity, disability, socioeconomic status, and gay and lesbian existence, showing how health education contributes to systemic racism, sexism, heterosexism, and prejudice against persons with disabilities and has a synergetic effect.

I have selected four critical episodes in my teaching of heterosexism as a curriculum issue. These experiences occurred the first time I taught the course, and at the beginning of my first full-time position in a faculty of education. The ten women in the course were elementary, home economics, and physical education majors. The nine men were all physical education majors. All students but one had entered the B.Ed. program directly from high school, and all were in either their third or final year of a four-year program.

Critical Episode 1

I first introduced the topic of heterosexism in an introductory talk about the politics of curriculum. To illustrate a point, I asked students to evaluate any health education book for sexism, ethnocentrism, ageism, ableism, and heterosexism and to present their findings to the group. The students selected books ranging from stories for preschool children to university-level textbooks. The students' presentations were well done, evincing critical thought; the students seemed to have a good grasp of this level of political criticism.

Whereas most students could show how health education texts promote heterosexism by ignoring, marginalizing, or distorting gay, lesbian, and bisexual existence, classroom discussion revealed that some students viewed this as acceptable given the reactionary climate of the province. Although not all students participated in the discussion, those who did framed their argument as follows. They said that an antiheterosexist pedagogy would be seen as promoting homosexuality; many people believe homosexuality is morally wrong; and teachers who attend to heterosexism in the curriculum are at risk because of objections from parents and school boards. Thus, although students could name heterosexism some students believed an antiheterosexist pedagogy was inappropriate.

Critical Episode 2

A second critical episode occurred in response to selected readings about social relationships in classrooms. I asked students to respond in writing to an article about homophobia in schooling published by the British Columbia Teachers' Federation (Wicks 1991). In the article, Michael Wicks writes about his experiences as a gay student and teacher in a homophobic school environment and calls for an end to the conspiracy of silence surrounding homosexuality and to the destructive expression of homophobia in schools.

The students' written responses varied according to gender. Most men and a few women questioned Wicks' statistics on the number of people who define themselves as lesbian or gay. Some men said Wicks exaggerated the extent of homophobia in schools, a response I read as a rejection of lesbian and gay existence and a denial of homophobia.

In contrast, most women and a few men supported Wicks' argument. They wrote with a tone of care and concern and an openness about the issues presented. Women students were also more willing to critique their own practice. One woman thought lesbians and gay men should be accepted, but said she did not know whether she approved of them showing affection in public. She noted that this was a contradiction she would have to resolve.

Almost all the women and men said that prejudice against gay men and lesbians was wrong and that lesbian and gay students and teachers should not be discriminated against. But these views often were presented with the caveat that they held "as long as homosexuals do not force their 'lifestyle' on others." This response suggests that students supported the heterosexist stereotype that lesbians and gay men relentlessly attempt to recruit "heterosexuals," and that students accepted heterosexuality as given rather than as a political institution.

Whereas some students said homophobia should be discussed in the classroom, most of these students said it would be best dealt with either in a social studies classroom under the topic of "human rights," or by a public health nurse. This response suggests the students believed that dealing with heterosexism and homophobia in the classroom was a matter of choice, that it could be taught as an isolated topic, and that it was something that should be dealt with by someone else. As well, most students reasserted the arguments presented earlier: to do something about heterosexism and homophobia in school curricula would be seen as promoting homosexuality, and teachers' jobs would be in jeopardy.

Critical Episode 3

A third critical episode occurred when I dealt with approaches to teaching "Human Growth and Development," Department of Education discourse for sexuality education. We discussed how the curriculum promoted sexism and heterosexism by ignoring lesbian sexuality and dealing with gay sexuality only in the context of AIDS. During the discussions, vocal students reasserted their opinions and concerns about teaching about gay and lesbian existence.

A junior high school teacher, whom I invited to speak to the group about her approach to sexuality education, confirmed the students' opinions. She said it would not be safe for teachers to talk about lesbian and gay sexuality in the classroom, that local communities were "very conservative," and she advised the students not to deal with such "controversial topics" in the classroom. Thus, rather than challenging the students' assumptions, the teacher reinforced heterosexist ideology. This experience further isolated me from the students.

Critical Episode 4

While teaching about sexuality education I received a notice from a university-based lesbian and gay men's speakers' bureau offering to provide speakers for faculty who wished to include gay and lesbian content in their classrooms. I grasped the opportunity—though Suzanne de Castell's comment about the "performing parrot" rang in my ears—still believing that it would be helpful for my students to hear about experiences of being lesbian or gay from those directly involved. I thought the presentation would raise the students' awareness about the necessity of dealing with homophobia and heterosexism in schooling.

The presenters, Anne and Jim (not their real names), talked about their developing awareness of being lesbian or gay, their experiences coming out, and their present lives. Anne described how she came to terms with her unhappiness in a heterosexual relationship and how her experience of being lesbian interconnected with her experience as a black woman. Jim said he internalized homophobia and repressed his sexuality for twenty years. He said that he regretted not having had the opportunity to learn acceptance of his sexuality when he was in school.

The presentation was one of the most moving I have experienced. The students listened intently, but asked few questions. The three women and two men who did speak asked relevant and thought-provoking questions. I resisted filling in the silence, allowing the students space to participate in their own time. I assumed the silence meant students were overwhelmed, as I was, by the power of the presentation. I felt sure that the presentation had helped clarify any hesitancy among the students about the importance of antiheterosexist practice. I left the class exhilarated, though exhausted, from the intensity of the session.

The next day I asked for feedback about the session with Anne and Jim. I was totally unprepared for the students' responses. A male student began by saying that the students had been talking together after class. He said something like, "We think that the presentation promoted homosexuality . . . and we think it is wrong." I remember the "we" clearly. Another male student said that he could not see what the presentation had to do with teaching, and another student said that he could not relate to Jim's description of his having no sexual relations for twenty years. This prompted laughter. I asked the students if anyone else had any other opinion. No one answered. The attack continued for almost thirty minutes. I do not remember anyone expressing a positive reponse. I have never been so aware of my body—my heart pounded as I listened to the angry words.

At the end of the session I told the students I needed time to think about their comments. I asked them to put their thoughts in writing so that I could think further about what they had to say.

Reflecting on the experience, with the help of a woman colleague, I realized that only a small group of students had dominated the conversation. Most were men. I remembered that a woman had tried to interrupt, but a man had stopped her by shouting, "Well that's not what you said before!" As the same student had become more angry and contradicted himself, I had heard another woman ask, "What is it that you are saying?" I had not picked up on the women's comments. I had not questioned the man student's use of "we." I had assumed that all the students agreed with those who spoke.

Many written responses to the presentation were contradictory and confusing. Most students either began or concluded by saying that prejudice and discrimination against lesbians and gay men is wrong. But buried in the texts of some of the men's responses were comments such as "The presentation turned my stomach," and "It doesn't interest me to hear about love lives that aren't normal." Some students also said that all their friends agreed with them, that they knew someone who had been "hit on" by gay men, or that they had been taught by lesbian and gay teachers and considered them to be their "best" teachers. It seemed to me that these students were trying to justify or deny their homophobic responses to the presentation.

I was particularly interested in the written responses of the students who did not speak during the classroom discussion. Although these students did not openly disagree with the negative responses of the vocal students, their responses were more positive. Typical comments were: "I was uptight at the beginning, but I became more comfortable during the talk"; "I felt self-conscious and afraid to say anything"; "I learned a lot from the presentation"; "I lost my fear of homosexuals." A few of these students used the written response to analyze their own homophobia. A woman student wrote:

> My reaction at the beginning of the talk was both ignorant and immature. I was surprised at my reaction because I have studied about homosexuality before. Sometimes I feel open-minded about this concept but other times I feel so closed off. It is difficult to change the way one has been socialized, and topics such as this raise confusing moral questions about what one considers is right and wrong.

> It was interesting to see how our behavior changed with these guest speakers [as compared] with others. . . . It was evident [that there was] homophobia in the classroom as very few people spoke or asked questions.

A man said:

> I thought that I was going to spend the entire class listening to two people tell us how wonderful homosexuality is for everyone.

I soon lost that idiotic attitude. During the entire presentation they did not try to promote or impose homosexuality. They were clearly there for our benefit and tried to give us a better understanding of what it is like to be a homosexual. I felt ashamed that I had prejudged the speakers. I did not realize the severe [added later] pain.

Clearly the discussion after the presentation would have been quite different had these students found the classroom a safe place in which to speak.

In my written responses I asked these students to tell me why they did not speak during that classroom discussion. One woman wrote: "I felt intimidated to speak up against the strong opinions raised by some. It is still hard for many of us to speak freely about homosexuality—our silence did not mean we agreed with the negative responses, we are still a little uncomfortable." A man wrote: "I felt my opinions were best left untold. Many times they deviated from the class majority. Thus I felt it better to remain silent." Another woman was more explicit: "I didn't ask many questions because I had an irrational feeling that if I did people in the class might wonder if I was gay. That sounds crazy but I feel that this might be the reason why others didn't speak."

Both women and men reasserted their fears about talking about anything to do with gay or lesbian experience in the classroom. They spoke about the threat of repercussions from parents. A woman student wrote:

I do not think that students should be taught about homosexuality in schools because I do not feel that society is ready to accept it. We are still at the point where parents or guardians must sign permission slips before their children can take basic sex education. And in [this province] can teachers honestly teach that homosexuality is acceptable when many people in these communities refer to homosexuals as "queers" and "fags" and in many cases assault them for this reason only?

Although this is only one of a possible twenty versions of what had happened in the classroom, it raises questions about the possibility of liberatory pedagogy. My work is shaped and limited by my experience as a heterosexual woman. Although teaching about heterosexism poses some threat to my being in the world, particularly in the untenured world of academe, as a heterosexual woman I speak from a safe place relative to women who define themselves as lesbian (Doe 1991; "Miss Is a Lesbian" 1989).

My heterosexual privilege was clearly revealed in Suzanne de Castell's response to an earlier draft of this chapter. I wrote "I have a feeling that my lesbian sisters will have lots to say about how I approached the study of heterosexism," and I asked "How might a professor who is lesbian or gay have dealt with heterosexism in the classroom?" She suggested that I talk not about how my lesbian sisters might do it differently, "but how they wouldn't do it at all, and if they did, and failed (as they would) they couldn't tell the story of that failure. It's just not a matter of difference here but of existence at all." Of course—so obvious now—how much more is there to unearth?

So, limited by my own heterosexist myopia, I am in a contradictory position of benefitting from heterosexism while attempting to challenge heterosexist practice. My experience fits Elizabeth Ellsworth's (1989) statement that classroom practice is "always partial, interested, and potentially oppressive to others" (324). This leaves me wondering, Where to from here? How can I do my work differently?

Solutions do not lie simply in teaching strategies or more careful use of language. Joseph Neison (1990) argues that use of the language of "heterosexism" rather than "homophobia" "avoids the trap of continual dialogue on the 'pros' and 'cons' of homosexuality and concentrates on the real problem—discrimination and prejudice against gay men and lesbians" (37). But in this instance using "heterosexism" as a starting point did not put the problem of heterosexism in the lap of heterosexuals. Although the discussion began at the level of heterosexism, it was reduced to an argument about the appropriateness of gay or lesbian experience as a "lifestyle"—ending in an "us" versus "them" argument. Powerful groups redefine problems in their own interests.

Nevertheless, any antiheterosexist practice threatens patriarchy. The response papers, textbook analysis, and guest speakers did provide different levels of threat to heterosexual privilege. And the response papers did allow some students a place to "speak" in support of an antiheterosexist pedagogy. Providing such opportunity would seem to me particularly important when attempting liberatory pedagogy. Textbook analysis is less threatening to the social order than listening to the live voices of those engaged in consciousness raising. Clearly, the objections of those most threatened grew louder as the critique grew stronger. As Magda Lewis (1990) says, consciousness raising is threatening because it *is* successful. If such critique were incorporated into examination of heterosexism, students might be better prepared to understand and deal with their own reactions and those of others.

Simplistic solutions to improving student-student and student-teacher interaction in the classroom also are problematic. Despite my understanding of feminism, I neglected to recognize the role silence plays in coeducational classrooms. In the heat of the moment I assumed that silence meant affirmation of the dominant voices. I neglected to consider alternative understandings of student silence (Orner 1992), and, as Magda Lewis (1990) says, "the threat to women's survival and livelihood that a critique of patriarchy in its various manifestations confronts" (473). These words took on new meaning for me when I read the response of the student who said that she did not speak out in the classroom because other students might think she was "gay." What could be more damaging to patriarchy and consequently more threatening to a young woman's survival than defining herself as lesbian?

Similarly, no doubt hegemonic masculinity played a role in the men's responses. Robert Connell (1987) argues that an important condition of hegemonic masculinity is that it is heterosexual. Connell says that "contempt for homosexuality and homosexual men . . . is part of the ideological package of hegemonic masculinity" (186). Given that hegemonic masculinity requires subordination of homosexuality, this might account for the anger some men expressed and the silence of those who responded positively to the presentation. Such critique must be incorporated into teaching about heterosexism.

As well, the fact that all the men were physical education majors may have played a role in expressions of homophobia in the classroom. Helen Lenskyj (1991a) writes:

> Unfortunately, the male physical education teachers who are responsible for boys' sex education in most high schools are unlikely to present the most progressive views on homosexuality. After all, male team sport constitutes the classic training ground in machismo, and the acceptance of different sexual orientations is not compatible with the rigid sex role conformity required in the male "jock" sub-culture. (291)

The paradox is that the many lesbians and gay men who are in sports and physical education and who might challenge the status quo are forced to hide their sexuality for fear of losing their jobs (Lenskyj, 1991b).

Job security is, understandably, uppermost in the minds of many prospective teachers, and this was no doubt reflected in the students' concerns about community opposition to liberatory pedagogy. For me to acknowledge that parental opposition is a problem is not enough. Students' concerns raise questions about the extent to which B.Ed. programs provide prospective teachers with opportunities to develop the knowledge and skills required for working with parents and community groups as well as administrators and school board members.

Regrettably, I did not pursue further why many of the prospective teachers were reluctant to deal with homophobia and heterosexism in their own classrooms. If, as Helen Lenskyj (1991a) says, "any teacher, homosexual or heterosexual, who confronts homophobia will almost certainly be suspected of being homosexual" (291), the students may have felt threatened. This feeling, coupled with "the myth that lesbians and gay men frequently recruit and proselytize from the ranks of the young . . . despite the overwhelming evidence that the major perpetrators of child sexual abuse are heterosexually oriented men whose targets are young girls" (Lenskyj 1991b, 62–63), could intimidate prospective teachers and prevent them from taking a proactive stance against heterosexism and homophobia in schooling. Teacher education programs should, therefore, provide opportunities for students to examine their own homophobia and heterosexist assumptions and to expose the myths, stereotypes, and distortions that keep heterosexual hegemony in place.

Clearly, prospective teachers bring their beliefs, prejudices, and fears to the classroom. This raises the question of whether the cry of parental opposition to liberatory pedagogy is a red flag or a red herring, a question that must be taken up in the health education literature and with prospective and practicing teachers.

Is liberatory pedagogy possible? What can one learn in an unsafe space? There are always gems that provide hope, and some are embedded in this article. But there is no room for complacency. On the last day of class I received a note from three women students. They said, "You've done an excellent job at opening our eyes to issues of gender, equality, and sexuality," and they added, "(perhaps an overemphasis on homosexuality)." The jury is out!

References

Bryson, M., de Castell, S., and Haig-Brown, C. (1993). Gender equity/gender treachery: Three voices. *Border/Lines, 28,* 46–54.

Connell, R. W. (1987). *Gender and power.* Sydney: Allen and Unwin.

Crumpacker, L., and Vander Haegen, E. M. (1990). Valuing diversity: Teaching about sexual preference in a radical/conserving curriculum. In J. Antler & S. K. Biklen (Eds.), *Changing education: Women as radicals and conservators* (pp. 201–215). Albany: State University of New York Press.

de Castell, S. (1991, August). Presentation to Education 372 (Gender Equity Issues in Education), Simon Fraser University, Burnaby, British Columbia.

de Lauretis, T. (1990). Eccentric subjects: Feminist theory and historical consciousness. *Feminist Studies, 16*(1), 115–151.

Doe, J. (1991). Teaching on thin ice. *Our Schools/Our Selves, 3*(2), 74–79.

Ellsworth, E. (1989). Why doesn't this feel empowering? Working through the repressive myths of critical pedagogy. *Harvard Educational Review, 59*, 297–324.

Fine, M. (1988). Sexuality, schooling, and adolescent females: The missing discourse of desire. *Harvard Educational Review, 58*, 29–53.

Fonow, M. M., and Marty, D. (1992). Teaching college students about sexual identity from feminist perspectives. In J. Sears (Ed.), *Sexuality and the curriculum: The politics and practices of sexuality education* (pp. 157–170). New York: Teachers College Press.

Kelly, U. A. (1990). "On the edge of the eastern ocean": Teaching, marginality and voice. In D. Henley & J. Young (Eds.), *Canadian perspectives on critical pedagogy* (pp. 35–42). Winnipeg: Canadian Critical Pedagogy Network with Social Education Researchers in Canada.

Khayatt, M. D. (1990). Lesbian teachers: An invisible presence. In F. Forman, M. O'Brien, J. Haddad, D. Hallman, & P. Masters (Eds.), *Feminism and education: A Canadian perspective* (pp. 191–218). Toronto: Ontario Institute for Studies in Education.

Lather, P. (1991). *Getting Smart: Feminist research and pedagogy with/in the postmodern.* New York: Routledge.

Lenskyj, H. (1991a). Beyond plumbing and prevention: Feminist approaches to sex education. In J. S. Gaskell & A. T. McLaren (Eds.), *Women and education* (2nd ed.) (pp. 283–298). Calgary: Detselig.

———— . (1991b). Combating homophobia in sport and physical education. *Sociology of Sport Journal, 8*, 61–69.

Lewis, M. (1990). Interrupting patriarchy: Politics, resistance, and transformation in the feminist classroom. *Harvard Educational Review, 60*, 467–488.

Miss is a lesbian (1989). In H. DeLyon and F. W. Migniuolo (Eds.), *Women teachers: Issues and experiences* (pp. 154–165). Milton Keynes: Open University Press.

Neisen, J. H. (1990). Heterosexism or homophobia? The power of language we use. *Outlook* (Fall): 36–37.

Orner, M. (1992). Interrupting the calls for student voice in "liberatory" education: A feminist poststructuralist perspective. In C. Luke & J. Gore (Eds.), *Feminisms and critical pedagogy* (pp. 74–89). New York: Routledge.

Patton, C. (1990). *Inventing AIDS.* New York: Routledge.

Rich, A. (1980). *Compulsory heterosexuality and lesbian existence.* Denver, CO: Antelope.

Rofes, E. (1989). Opening up the classroom closet: Responding to the educational needs of gay and lesbian youth. *Harvard Educational Review, 59,* 444–453.

Sears, J. T. (1992a). Educators, homosexuality, and homosexual students: Are personal feelings related to professional beliefs? In K. M. Harbeck (Ed.), *Coming out of the classroom closet: Gay and lesbian students, teachers and curricula* (pp. 29–80). New York: Harrington Park Press.

———. (Ed.) (1992b). *Sexuality and the curriculum: The politics and practices of sexuality education.* New York: Teachers College Press.

Trenchard, L. (1992). Young lesbians at school. In D. Spender & E. Sarah (Eds.), *Learning to lose: Sexism and education* (pp. 193–200). London: The Women's Press.

Whatley, M. H. (1988). Raging hormones and powerful cars: The construction of men's sexuality in school sex education and popular adolescent films. *Journal of Education, 170*(3), 100–121.

———. (1992). Images of gays and lesbians in sexuality and health textbooks. In K. M. Harbeck (Ed.), *Coming out of the classroom closet: Gay and lesbian students, teachers and curricula* (pp. 197–212). New York: Harrington Park Press.

Wicks, M. (1991). A day without homophobia. *Teacher: News Magazine of the B.C. Teachers' Federation, 3*(7), 7.

Williams, R. (1990). Growing up in a man's world: Reflections on sexism and sexual politics in the Maritimes. *Our Schools/Our Selves, 2*(2), 131–139.

11

ANY MORE COLORFUL
WE'D HAVE TO CENSOR IT

CHARMAINE PERKINS

Introduction

A recent advertising campaign for Life-brand film, found at various bus shelters across the city, declares, "Any more colourful we'd have to censor it," promoting the capacity of this film to compete with other name-brand products, noted for capturing all those "colorful" and memorable moments in life. Here, the play is on "color," the term *colorful* referring not only to that which is full of color but to its other connotations of being interesting and full of life, racy and risqué even. In this sense, this product is almost too colorful, or "too hot too handle," that it risks censorship. The ad succeeds in its ability to evoke our knowledge of the related meanings of these terms and how they function, in this case of sexual innuendo, to refer to the (almost) "off-color" and offensive nature of this product itself—and by extension, what it can be used to capture—hence its appeal and excitement. This campaign counts on us knowing which meanings are the *right* ones, as opposed to meanings which convey colored in the sense of "having a distorted or false" knowledge of events, and of "knowingly" misrepresenting and falsifying information. What is also relevant is the references to race where *colored*, a descriptive and often derogatory term, refers to anyone who is not white and who, therefore, has color.

On thinking of race with its now decontextualized substitution with the term *color*, in many ways a far more innocuous euphemism, I found this ad helpful in laying the foundations for my discussion of race and its popular articulations. By the term *popular*, I intend to convey the various meanings of generally accepted assumptions, what usually passes for common sense, a kind of homogenized public knowledge, as well as the way in which information/knowledge is encoded and transmitted via mass media to form and inform popular opinion, and indeed, shapes consciousness. Hence, my inclusion of newspaper articles. Also important are the intersections between the popular (usually associated with "low" culture) and the "high" academic spaces and how race is articulated and mediated by subjects, students, and faculty, that inhabit these and other spaces—since as students, we enter into academic spaces already knowing and already constituted in various ways, as opposed to merely being empty vessels waiting to absorb knowledge. Moreover, our professors are not merely disinterested subjects; they construct, disseminate, and legitimate—both actively and passively—what students come to accept as knowledge. In this way, there is always the potential for conflict if and when students contest the authority of *the* professor, where challenges are now being interpreted as the obstruction of academic freedom, in other words, a form of censorship, and even rebellion, given the hierarchical power structure of the university. The outcome for students, in spite of the adoption of various antiharassment policies by universities to address the power differential between professors and students, is often the trivialization and denial of their very concerns, and in the case of students of color, our very subjectivities and presence are doubly jeopardized; our "colorful" presence is one that must be negotiated with great care.

> These examples point to the unsettling facts that classrooms are not hermetically sealed worlds; that teachers and students bring to the construction of school knowledge contradictory and conflictive criteria by which knowledge and identity are deemed relevant and irrelevant; that the larger social conditions of racism, sexism, hetero-sexism, and class domination fashion the borders of interpretation and meaning; and that the interruption of practices that are "normal"places the speaker—as well as her knowledge—"at risk." (Britzman et al. 1993, 190)

Section One: Popular Con/texts

> So now they want underdog status, too, and the moral clout that comes with victimhood?
>
> —David Gates, *White Male Paranoia*

> That the once proud white male would proclaim himself a victim was inevitable—even if the jujitsu-like maneuver has left members of officially victimized groups agape.
>
> —Ellis Close, *To the Victors, Few Spoils*

The discourses, both popular and scholarly, of civil rights and feminism, emerging as they did out of historical conditions of group oppression and struggle, are no longer exclusive to those experiences of oppression or to the groups which experienced it. In fact, within the current conservative climate, U.S. courts are dismantling many of the programs that were designed to address blatant inequities within society. This new reconstruction regards categories of race as irrelevant and racist, in that these categories perpetuate notions of racial entitlement and privilege, the underlying justifications for racial superiority and the oppression of "other" races. In this "revisionist" exercise, prompted by the more privileged members of dominant society, the discourse of individual sovereign rights,[1] particularly in light of charges of reverse discrimination, has taken precedence over, and is threatening to obliterate, earlier recognition of systemic and institutionalized racism (against certain groups) within society. Moreover, any attempts toward implementing antiracist legislation and other forms of redress to ensure that the rights of disadvantaged groups are maintained, in turn, are being "read" as racist and discriminatory, particularly if they infringe on the rights of the individual, usually white and male.

In this "market of cultural differences and relative freedoms,"[2] to quote Himani Bannerji, equity becomes a negotiable commodity, where individuals can conveniently and strategically "dress up" and disguise themselves in terms heavily coded with someone else's experience and someone else's meaning. The alibi used for this theft is the pretense that we are all equally endowed with the same rights, privileges, and means of access. Robert Fulford, a white Canadian writer, responded to the policy of the Writing Thru Race Conference—to have closed sessions that would allow writers of color and First Nations writers the opportunity for discussion amongst themselves—by stating indignantly that this was a clear case of "apartheid."[3] According to his account, he, an established writer, is experiencing the dehumanizing conditions of oppression and segregation forced upon him by a racist regime of people of color, who were the dominating decision-making processes not only of the Writer's Union but of Canadian social policies. Words such as *apartheid, slavery, colonization,* and *rape* have now become metaphors with slippery referents that do not always refer to material and historical realities.

Similarly, there is also the case of Tony McAleer, the well-known white supremacist in British Columbia, who heads the Canadian Liberty Net, an organization with established links to other supremacist organizations such as WAR (White Aryan Resistance). McAleer, "twice convicted of spreading hatred against minorities and homosexuals,"[4] has filed a complaint with British Columbia's Council of Human Rights. He claims that he has been discriminated against "by the staff of a provincial review of human-rights legislation," which "has singled him out for rude and hostile treatment because he represented a white-rights group." McAleer concedes that although "he's no fan of human rights legislation, it's there and it's going to be used against me or against our types of groups, let's at least have a level playing field." McAleer inhabits that privileged space from which he can secure not only his basic human rights to absolute freedom of speech and expression, guaranteed by the Charter of Rights, but he can also access the very organizations designed to protect people from the hate groups he promotes to advance his newly "justified" feelings of being a victim.[5] In this dangerous inversion, McAleer has become the oppressed whose civil "white" rights are being threatened and even undermined by what can be seen as the privileging of the rights of people of color over his own. He even goes so far as to compare his experience of feeling limited in advancing "white rights" to the oppression of black people who were denied their civil rights in a racist society. Disingenuously, McAleer explains, "It's like saying in the South in the 60's, 'Sure, black people can ride the bus. They just have to sit at the back.'" What next? White fear of state-sanctioned, colored lynch mobs? Furthermore, McAleer contends that "white people—especially white males—are 'brutally' discriminated against by employment-equity programs."

Rey Chow (1993), in her introduction to *Writing Diaspora: Tactics of Intervention in Contemporary Cultural Studies*, articulates clearly this phenomenon of nouveau victimhood whereby certain persons/groups engage in processes of identification with the "disdained other" (13). In fact, this way of thinking has produced "a way of talking in which notions of lack, subalternity, victimization, and so forth are drawn upon indiscriminately, often with the intention of spotlighting the speaker's own sense of alterity and political righteousness" (13). Chow focuses on the way academics in particular are complicit in the appropriation of specific discourses such that a kind of "representational violence" occurs. By extension, many other privileged and powerful groups within society now "identify with powerlessness to displace their own power" (14). This threat from the other to overthrow and displace the power of the dominant society, whether imagined or indicative of a perceived fear of what could and will happen, has led to the sudden "collective social amnesia"[6] and erasure of cultural, historical, political, economic, racial, sexual, and gendered specificities:

Whether sincere or delusional, such cases of self-dramatization all take the route of self-subalternization, which has increasingly become the assured means to authority and power. What these intellectuals are doing is robbing the terms of oppression of their critical and oppositional import, and thus depriving the oppressed of even the vocabulary of protest and rightful demand. The oppressed whose voices we seldom hear, are robbed twice—the first time of their economic chances, the second time of their language, which is now no longer distinguishable from those of us who have had our consciousnesses "raised." (13)

In an attempt to maintain their positions of authority, certain privileged groups are imposing and claiming strategic victim identities/positions as a means of neutralizing challenges being brought forward by oppressed peoples, while strategically obliterating the way in which they have historically contributed—and continue to contribute—to the very oppression of, as they—we—are often called, "special-interest" groups.

This appropriation of the discourses born out of oppression and struggle, by those who, in fact, possess power, is the strategy of choice for the traditionally privileged to assuage their own feelings of guilt and or complicity—achieved through active and passive participation in racist structures—by *identifying* with the oppressed. In fact, as is usually quickly pointed out, they are *equally* oppressed in many ways. So although many such individuals feel genuine concern, very few, it seems, are prepared to do anything about it, least of all to give up any of the perks that come within traditional power structures:

"The system is screwing me so why not screw the system?"

Mark, 22, a political science student at the university of Windsor, who cheats on exams because he fears women and minorities have an edge on white men like himself. (*The Vancouver Sun*, May 1, 1993)

The general conception that racism is practiced often unknowingly by those who are ignorant overlooks the ineffectiveness of education in and of itself to eliminate racism and other practices of discrimination. The assumption is that racism is not itself an effect of certain ways of "knowing" and ordering the world, an organizing principle as it were, and that the enlightened individual will reject and even be able to identify racist practices that are not immediately apparent or overt. As Rosemary Brown (1991) emphasizes in "Overcoming Sexism and Racism—How": "For many years, I believed that discrimination of all types could be routed by a knowledge of 'the true facts.' Indeed I was taught that people who held prejudices did so because they were unenlightened and ignorant" (170).

Brown's naiveté (and my own) is based on the myth of transcendence and enlightenment on which the very premises of Christianity and liberal humanism were founded: these universalizing ideologies contain and manage differences, while maintaining hierarchical structure intact.[7] These ideologies, let us not forget, actively supported and justified the worst forms of exploitation, including slavery and apartheid and the residential school system. Thus, as Brown (1991) argues, institutions such as education are deeply rooted in ideological practices of structural inequity:

> But I have learned a lesson from years of witnessing discrimination by and in academic institutions, in their conduct and in the content of what they teach, and from further analytic exploration. This experience has revealed to me the role which education as an institution plays in maintaining the status quo. Though education may modify the practice of discrimination, by itself it cannot terminate it. (171)

Moreover, racism itself often is so normalized and rendered invisible, it functions as a kind of common sense, and a way of being that is rarely challenged even by those individuals who have had their consciousness raised. As such, it informs our daily practices and the very ways in which we see and organize the world.[8] In *Thinking through Essays on Feminism, Marxism, and Anti-Racism*, Himani Bannerji (1995) describes the pervasive nature of racism that is embedded in European/Western societies: "Racism is not simply a set of attitudes and practices that they level towards us, their socially constructed 'other,' but it is the very principle of self-definition of European/Western societies. It could be said that what is otherwise known as European civilization—as manifested in the realm of art and ideas and in daily life—is a sublimated, formalized, or simply a practiced version of racism" (46). As such, critiques that focus solely on "differences" and identity/subjectivity positions fail to take into account how they are positioned in a world that is "historically and socially" constituted in certain ways and how they intend to "reconstruct" those relations (48). Generally speaking, however, there is a complacency and a tentativeness in discussions about race and racism, especially in classrooms. It is often seen as an inappropriate subject of inquiry, unsettling both for white professors and for their students, who do see it or "know" it to be a problem, especially here in Canada. The myth that is perpetuated is that racism is an "American" problem and that furthermore multiculturalism offsets "those" kinds of problems.

It is crucial therefore to examine the ways in which race is articulated and practiced in more "popular" forums outside the university, an arena where the most violent forms of racism are prone to occur. The kinds of explanations that are typically given for individuals who engage in racist activities (hate crimes) are that they are dysfunctional, uneducated outcasts of society, "freaks," and that these occurrences are not the norm. However, as Marke Andrews (1994) affirms in his review of Warren Kinsella's *Web of Hate: Inside Canada's Far Right Network*: "Contrary to popular thought, members of the far-right movement—neo-Nazis, skinheads, anti-Semites, white-power-heads—are a sophisticated, educated group."[9]

Andrews continues,

> When Kinsella set out to write about these groups and individuals, he expected the 'redneck, mouth-breather' stereotype. But a survey in Germany showed that of those arrested in 2,000 hate crimes, 75 per cent of the perpetrators had some form of post-secondary education. Most of the white power leaders in Canada, he says, are bright and articulate. Furthermore, many leaders and members of hate groups are *employed* in Canada's education system. These people recognize that the system is a tremendous opportunity for them to promulgate their views to new people.

What Kinsella is pointing to is the resurgence in hate crimes against First Nations peoples, Jews, gays, lesbians, and many other immigrant and nonimmigrant people of color—with established communities in Canada—who have become convenient targets of hate and discrimination. Clearly, these white power groups feel that their absolute and sovereign rights are not being secured, while too many others are demanding that they be treated fairly and equally. The Canada emerging through Andrews' review is one with an educated, racist *zeitgeist*: "Conditions are ripe for recruitment. Memories of the Holocaust are fading, economic prospects are bleak for young people (who may look to a minority group to be a scapegoat) and the times are becoming increasingly violent."

In an earlier article, "Hate on the Rise," William Boei (1993) also examines the way in which conservative, right-wing governments, along with extreme right factions, have used harsh economic climates as an alibi to legitimate their racial concerns about nonwhites. From the lack and the loss of jobs to violent crime in society, nonwhite ethnic groups have become the source of the problem: "White people believe that they (and their culture) are under attack."[10] Despite the proliferation of mass-media discussions, this strategic backlash against nonwhites and other targeted groups has not, for the most part, been met with very much *public* resistance and outrage. If editorials and letters to the editor are any indication, many people are not afraid to name and blame immigrants, minorities, First Nations peoples, homosexuals, or single mothers for society's problems. This form of racism has, in some ways, become acceptable and even reputable, if not, ironically, politically correct. In the face of racism, the Charter of Rights and other antiharassment policies can guarantee only symbolically certain others their rights, providing their rights do not conflict with the greater "good" and "freedoms" of society. High-profile proponents of the right to free speech include Rush Limbaugh, various professors, and Canadian cabinet ministers, including various reform MPs who claim to be representing the popular concerns of the average "Canadian." Who else is responsible for an unmanageable deficit, unemployment, and unaffordable housing if not these newcomers and "special-interest" groups? Ian Kagedan, the national director of government affairs for B'nai Brith, offers a valuable perspective on this situation:

> We have to look at ourselves and our history. We have to look at our society in its essence, and recognize that racism has been part of the package and in many respects has been institutionalized. And we've never really attended to that. So when things get rough, all of a sudden it starts bubbling to the surface. Well it didn't come from nowhere. Good people don't turn racist overnight. The racism has been there. (Boei 1993)

For all the paranoia of a racial take-over, people of color and other disenfranchised groups have not, in reality, greatly succeeded in displacing the ruling class. David Gates (1994) in "White Male Paranoia" concedes that "for blacks, employment has gotten worse relative to whites," and that the so-called attack on white men is largely "ideological and attitudinal" (52–53). Indeed, disparities between blacks and whites in the United States may have worsened since the Kerner Commission's findings in 1968.[11] More recent reports emphasize that although some levels of integration have been successful and that a "strong, black middle class has emerged, . . . the situation for the majority of blacks has worsened." Other findings reveal that the life expectancy for blacks has declined; infant mortality has increased; and unemployment, as compared to whites, is twice as high, with black males earning less than three-quarters of the money earned by whites, and the median income of black families being 57 percent of white family earnings. In addition, the poverty rate is three times as great for blacks as it is for whites. Whites may feel threatened, but the one must question how real this perceived threat is.

In Canadian terms, several studies have indicated that affirmative action and other equity programs have largely failed the very groups that they were attended to assist: First Nations people, peoples with different abilities, and visible minorities. For the most part, white women are the only group who have benefited (and statistics have not been released which define *which* white women in particular, since class interests play a significant and perhaps central role in relation to this population).[12] A recent survey which focused on British Columbia's civil service "confirmed that white men have had an edge when it comes to working for the B.C. government," proving that for all the consciousness-raising programs and alleged job training for employers, things have not changed significantly. Yet for all these reported findings, there have been many disgruntled white people who feel that unqualified others are stealing jobs and are invoking the inadequate term *reverse discrimination*: "Politicians are so afraid of discriminating against able-bodied white men that they shy away from ending discrimination against the disabled and other under-represented groups."[13] Other studies also indicate that most of the money in these programs is spent on raising awareness within the departments themselves, leaving little for the actual recruitment of individuals from the target groups. Another conclusion drawn from these reports indicates that equity policies exacerbate tensions and resentment already present in the workplace, resulting in further discrimination, not less. Systematically very few changes have been made to dismantle structural barriers; in fact, many of these artificial attempts are now being eliminated in Ontario by the conservative government and by the U.S. Supreme court, where affirmative action was deemed "unconstitutional."

In the midst of all this resentment, "Canadians" also feel that more should be done to protect their rights, instead of sharing these rights with others who are not like them. A recent poll found that "one in four Canadians [sic] believes that non-white minorities are threatening the fabric of the country."[14] Fifty seven percent of Canadians believe that minority groups should assimilate more and be like other Canadians, while 42 percent believe that recent immigrants to Canada should not have "as much say as people who were born and raised here." These non-Canadians seem to be threatening the notion of a fixed, homogenous, white identity, an identity that continues to render invisible Canada's First peoples and all of us who have a history of contributing to this country without any official recognition. One of the crucial educational problems we continue to face is the inability—and disinclination—of some Canadians to remember and locate themselves in relation to certain historical practices. This failure to name and remember, in which actual differences are erased, is accompanied by the sentiment that the slate of history has been "wiped clean." I continue to hear from innocent, sincere, and well-intentioned white people that they "didn't practice genocide on Natives because we haven't been here for more than three generations," and "Why should I be responsible for the sins of my grandparents; I am not a racist." Many people use their ignorance as a vehicle for their "innocence" since they feel that they are being asked to be responsible for problems that they did not create or even participate in. Unfortunately, it does not work in the same way for those of us who continue to be told "not to hold on to past wrongs." To add to these and other injustices, we are now being told that there is no longer a problem: the playing field has been leveled. Now, more than ever, white men especially feel that the playing field has tilted, to their dismay, and they become the new victims, the disempowered, the "disdained other": "Generations of white males judged women and minorities not for what they did but by who they were. Turn about is fair play. White men are now beginning to say: only fair play is fair play It figures that they'd think of that now" (Gates 1994, 53).

Section Two: Academic Con/texts

Some of the most radical criticism coming out of the West today is the result of an interested desire to conserve the subject of the West, or the West as Subject. The theory of pluralized "subject-effects" gives an illusion of undermining subjective sovereignty while often providing a cover for this subject of knowledge. Although the history of Europe as subject is narrativized by the law, political economy, and ideology of the West, this concealed subject pretends it has "no geo-political determinations." This much-publicized critique of the sovereign subject thus actually inaugurates a subject.

—Spivak, "Can the Subaltern Speak?"

In an attempt to conceptualize perhaps one of the central dilemmas surrounding subjectivity, I turn to Gayatri Spivak's essay "Can the Subaltern Speak?" Here, I am thinking first of the way in which the subject in Western discourses functions as an authoritative, fixed, unitary, and all-knowing body, who is constituted by multiple intersecting ideological and other determining systems.

Second, I am also thinking of *disciplinary* "subjects" of study, who form the epistemological ground of this all-knowing "subject." The idea then that we all exist in some sphere as equal subjects with room and access for everything and everyone is a seductive ruse, one embraced by intellectuals and nonintellectuals alike. The perception that there exists a playing field of equally matched individuals, playing on the same team and certainly for the same stakes, suggests that the systemic barriers of oppression have already been dismantled. We therefore have the freedom or luxury, some of us anyway, to snip the cords of memory and history. The kind of disremembering or "social amnesia" serves as a camouflage for the actual relations of "powered differences" that remain very much in place. It is therefore not unusual within "popular" and academic circles to see how individual "differences" are played out, often to conceal and cancel out counter-claims of racism and privilege.

One of the newer anxieties that has emerged stems from the term *people of color*. Many white people feel that they are somehow excluded by this term and that this exclusion is tantamount to discrimination of some sort. This kind of discrimination focuses solely on individual feelings of exclusion and on *color*, the new euphemism and less discomforting substitution for race. In a witty essay, Stacey D'Erasmo (1994)[15] focuses on the desire, in the context of fashion, to re(dis)cover whiteness, to redeem it in some sense as just another color. While there is a limit as to how far one can "read" into fashion as a vehicle for maintaining social relations, D'Erasmo makes some interesting suggestions: "The new rage for white might have something to do with the recent renaissance of cultures of a different colour. This is the snaky kind of thing white people do when they feel pushed to the wall. We're different too!" (23). While this piece pokes fun at white anxiety and largely looks at what's "in," it also captures the tendency to base racial differences solely on dermatology and biological taxonomies of "visible" differences. A classic example of this tendency is Benetton's catalogue published a few years ago that depicted the races in all their naked "different-but-same" splendor. Resulting from this universalizing tendency is the depoliticizing and devaluing of terms such as *people of color*. This term can no longer be a political marker, but rather a sort of optional identity. This kind of superficial pluralism can only have meaning in a (cosmetic) marketplace of imagined (and imaginary) relativist (and therefore falsely equal) subject/group realities. This racial blurring is a highly desirable strategy which eliminates difference and privilege by asserting that white is a color like all other colors.

What D'Erasmo highlights as well is not just the "sudden" emergence of white as a color, as opposed to its former status as a noncolor (read as not "colored" and therefore transparent), but the claim that whiteness has become just another racial/ethnic subculture in this palette of colors and cultures:

> A cynical observer might speculate that, feeling the chill wind of demographic and political social change, the white race is scrambling to get its freckled self into a Benetton ad, fast, so it can pass as just another subculture. Which it is, but this new willingness to be objectified, commodified, particularized has suspicious timing. (23)

While I agree with D'Erasmo that whiteness is trying to give itself a "face-lift," I fail to see the "subculture" status of white society, unless D'Erasmo is speaking perhaps of shifting demographics and the anxieties, and even feelings of guilt, that some white people have about their privilege.

By focusing on the individual, as opposed to multiple intersecting sociocultural systems, the illusion is fostered that "improvement" can occur *developmentally*. The model here is a psychological one: self-knowledge has replaced the need for any systemic restructuring (although for women and other minorities we have only "improved" our condition to be included as subjects in recent history). As Chandra Mohanty (1990) explains in "On Race and Voice: Challenges for the Liberal Education in the 1990's," "This process of individualization of histories of dominance is characteristic of educational institutions and processes in general, where the experiences of different constituencies are defined according to the logic of cultural pluralism" (190). She further illustrates how all the individual has to do is to become more "sensitive"; thus difference can be "managed" and known through *interpersonal* interactions. Since no political action or change is required, a new class of educational professionals can emerge, experts capable of instructing us about difference, and by this, I mean racial and gendered differences, that are understood in exclusively textual terms, in terms that have nothing to do with concrete, material, or embodied action. As *objects* of knowledge, people of color, and especially women of color, are there to be known and consumed, to provide the thrill of the different and the exotic, without threatening to discomfort its consumers. Commodified and divorced from the actual, people of color are no longer subjects but subjects of study, safe, contained in an academic tradition, and homogenous.

The fact that discomforts remain for those of us who are other within the institutions of learning presents no problem. In his critique of policies that aim to eliminate harassment and discrimination on university campuses, Robert Fulford highlights what he feels is being overlooked in this need not to offend anyone, a kind of legislated civility: "In its zeal to offend no one," Fulford says, "the province overlooks the fact that 'being offended' is part of learning how to think" (*The Vancouver Sun*, March 26, 1994). But who decides what kinds of offenses are inappropriate, and is the ensuing discomfort only worthy of consideration when it is experienced by professors who have already learned how to think? These and other questions are especially relevant given that the loudest hue and cry about "nouveau-victimhood" come so often from the beleaguered white male professor regarding academic freedom and "open debate." Fulford claims that this antiharassment policy "poses a perilous threat to freedom of speech" and furthermore, "Our society has recently entered a period of grim, humourless, rigid intolerance." At the fore of this fight for civil libertarian values are the intellectual elite, who can be heard decrying the dark days of our society, falsely equating it to fascist regimes. Those of us who oppose harassment and discrimination, asking for more responsible speech and treatment, are now not only "humourless," but "rigidly intolerant." In fact, as students, and as women of color, our rights and freedoms must be sacrificed and limited at the expense of gaining knowledge. We are often told that we are "too sensitive" and we cannot "take a joke." So goes the debate on campuses across the continent: white male professors are being demonized as brutally intolerant student-oppressors.

And so, those of us opposed to the "discomforts" of the intellectual process, where this term becomes a handy euphemism for harassment, are deemed "politically correct," the "thought police." We have become guilty of suppressing the academic right of professors to teach and do research according to their interests, free from political and other interferences, according to the precepts of the "liberal" university. No wonder students are often called "militant," "subversive," or "radical" when they call for their rights, an act which supposedly openly questions the intellectual expertise of the individual professor within the sanctions of the university. He (for it almost always is "he")

can be the only expert in the class. Where the proponents of academic
freedom focus on the "freedom" to speak (and teach) in the way they
see fit, regardless of other subjectivities—since any form of prohibition
is tantamount to censorship—they often neglect to concern themselves
with their own power in the university, and, concomitantly, with any
commitment to principles, let alone practices, of responsibility and
accountability. Since professors are not accountable to students, who
do not have the same rights, then to whom *are* they accountable?
Within the university, are there policies truly informed enough, or
administrative bodies knowledgeable enough, to "fairly" judge one of
their peers while also being "fair" to students? Upon this playing field,
where there is such an imbalance of power between professor and student, the student must suffer the invariable "discomfort."

Section Three: Discord in the Classroom
(Where the Popular Meets the Academic)

As a black intellectual, I am both intrigued and horrified by the contradictory nature of the black presence in North American universities. We
are, as students, as teachers, as cultural producers, simultaneously present in, and starkly absent from, university life.

—Hazel Carby, "The Multicultural Wars"

Given that certain curricular inclusions, however modest, have
occurred over the last ten to twenty years, issues of race and literature
by people of color are available for study in some universities. One of
the contradictions that emerges for me, as a student of color, is that this
inclusion has acted as a substitute for any real political and social
changes within the institution, reaffirming the continuing absence of
any genuine commitment to making such changes. Indeed, liberal,
pluralist ideology has been remarkably conducive to the adoption of
ideas/interests without any concomitant interest in systemic changes
and responsibilities. What is hidden in this agenda (to teach texts by,
for example, women of color) is the fact that the professor/authority
effectively suspends and eradicates momentarily his own subjectivity,
replacing it with the voices of the women whose texts he teaches. This
form of appropriation—a ventriloquist act of mind-numbing proportions—eliminates any need for actual women of color to be present,
representing their own subjectivity. Because this appropriation is so
complete, and so completely acceptable within the university, individual professors can make up the rules of this intellectual playing field,
without our consent and without presence, positioning themselves

always at the center of this knowledge which has become, absurdly, "their own." In her essay, "Multicultural Wars," Hazel Carby (1992) critiques this superficial kind of abhorrent inclusion:

> We need to ask why black women, or other women who are non-white, are needed as cultural and political icons by the white middle class at this moment? What cultural and political need is being expressed, and what role is the black female subject being reduced to play? I would agree that it is necessary to recognize the contradictions between elevating the black subject to the status of a major text within multiculturalism and failing to lead students toward an integrated society, between making the black female a subject in the classroom and failing to integrate university student and faculty bodies on a national scale. Instead of recognizing these contradictions, the black female subject is frequently the means by which many middle-class white students and faculty cleanse their souls and rid themselves of the guilt of living in a society that is rigidly segregated. Black cultural texts have become the fictional substitutes for the lack of any sustained social or political relationships with black people in a society that has retained many of its historical practices of apartheid in housing and schooling. (192)

The white professor can erase his power while identifying and representing otherwise powerless and repressed voices and subjectivities. It is therefore not surprising that in a course about race, in which literature by women of color was being taught, the professor, when challenged to explain what he meant by "of color," since he had included texts by white writers, would protest his innocence, or his own whiteness, too much. The professor in question began apologizing for being white, which was never under scrutiny—given the relative absence of nonwhite professors in any university department that I have ever attended—explaining that he was being "sensitive" and only "trying to do his best." In his identification with these fictional texts, and by extension fictional women, he could identify with being "of color" since he reinterpreted the term to include himself, a white man. He was more interested in color as it pertained to colorations and the literally outdated metaphor of light and darkness: he wanted to look at how light *revealed* color. Darkness then would only signify the absence of light. He felt that this perspective should be free from critique, for he intended it to be a "scientific," and not a racial, metaphor.

However, as the course progressed, it became clearer that he had intended to discuss race, but he now felt uncomfortable by our presence, several students of color, in the classroom. The meaning of the term *of color* was then opened up to include anyone who is sensitive to issues of race and ethnicity, since we are all "colored": we all have pigmentation. Accordingly, the expert, this professor, included white female writers on the course as "women of color," and thereby robbed the term of its specificity. Being of color is usually acknowledged as a strategy of alliance between groups of *racialized* peoples who experienced discrimination, a term of empowerment that makes explicit its potential for political struggle; in this classroom, the term was emptied of its significance. Within this new reconfiguration, the professor contains and "manages" any differences between himself and women of color. Instead of extending his simplistic notion of race to include relations of power, race for him was irrelevant and merely a new literary metaphor. Toni Morrison (1992) clearly articulates the proliferation of a complex and contradictory presence of "race" in various texts, and I would add, contexts:

> Race has become metaphorical—a way of referring to and disguising forces, events, classes, and expressions of social decay and economic division far more threatening to the body politic than "biological" race ever was . . . [and it] has assumed a metaphorical life so completely embedded in daily discourse that is perhaps more necessary and more on display than ever. (63)

Predictably, as the course, and the material, became "unmanageable," the professor made counter-claims of feeling "silenced" and "harassed" by the students of color within in his classroom. Ironically, the presence of women of color, in a course about representations and texts by women of color, became highly problematic: how were we to *speak out* of this kind of institutional "violence" and *speak as* "disinterested" subjects? Within this kind of racializing environment, we were both highly visible and, paradoxically, rendered invisible. Ultimately, the course dissolved when the professor accused the students of color of disrupting the class and impeding the transmission of his knowledge; one of us had put forth a reading of a story that was different than his. He did not want to teach the course if students of color were still enrolled in it. When we spoke out against the harassment that occurred, we were accused of imposing our political agendas on a course that was intended to address literary matters, not political ones. This professor, with the support of various administrative bodies, later accused students of color of harassing him on the grounds of his race, gender, and even his religion(?!?), making it impossible for him to pursue his "interest" and to teach without interference. What happens then, when the professor's absolute power and knowledge are questioned and there are "knowledgeable" students of color present in his classroom? From what position do we speak within already racialized identities?

In fact, students of color are *further* marginalized, where they are so racialized that they become, within their bodies, the *source* of the problem. For in their need to "know" and consume us, white academics do *not* require our presence, nor our participation—except as passive and grateful supplicants who will bear witness to our "victimhood" in sad stories, tearful testimonies, and candid confessionals—hence our colorful appeal. As active, present, intervening, intellectual subjects, to exist in these classrooms we have two choices: we must either be mute or complicit, or if we speak out and demonstrate our knowledge and assert our subjectivities, we must expect negative consequences. Knowing we can only add to our further harassment, characterized as "trouble-makers" and "hostile" types with "problems," we risk the very careers that we are there to pursue. We have yet to be included or welcomed as intellectual in these institutions. In this way, we continue to be anomalies and exceptions, especially in graduate studies, and if American statistics are indeed accurate, increasing numbers of us are abandoning the rocky road of education: "The percentage of black students in college populations has steadily decreased throughout the last decade, as has the number of B.A.s awarded to black students, even though the absolute number of bachelor's degrees has been increasing nationally. . . . Clearly, if the black student population continues to decline at the undergraduate and graduate levels, the current black intellectual presence in academia, small as it is, will not be reproduced" (Carby 1992, 189).

Because the classroom remains a contestory site of unresolved tensions, students who insist on their right to certain subjectivities, their right to learn and to engage with various materials in ways that are more relevant to them, in light of their lived realities, will continue to be positioned on the academic fringes, another "special-interest group." For all the "chilly climate" reports, "zero-tolerance" policies, and other forms of antiharassment measures, there still exists the denial of actual problems within academic institutions with their superficial notions of equality. Furthermore, many of these policies do not recognize or include racism, except in its most overt demonstrations.

During the 1995 through 1996 academic year, for example, the University of British Columbia's Political Science Department found itself firmly planted in the glare of the media spotlight, following the widely disseminated findings of an external investigator, lawyer Joan McEwen. The Canadian media spent much time and newsprint publishing the critiques of several professors who used this incident to speak of a putatively horrendous state of professorial censorship and the misguided, albeit vindictive, allegations made by the students involved. One University of British Columbia professor publicly claimed that the "allegations" "had less to do with sexual and racial discrimination than with *normal* tensions in the relationship between professors and graduate students" (my emphasis). But as investigator Joan McEwen explained, "This is not about pedagogy, or academic freedom of professors; it is about promulgating pervasive and oppressive structures; it is about ensuring an equitable environment in terms of students' academic abilities and performance" (*The Vancouver Sun* 1995). Moreover, McEwen invoked the responsibility and leadership role of the university to ensure an equitable environment for *all* students. As a result, justifications that racism and sexism are just a "part of life and students had better get used to it" are inadequate. Given the normalizing and rational justifications that were employed to trivialize and quash the students' claims of harassment and discrimination, and the relative lack of support in these spaces, the classroom, and the very institution, remains a site of discord.

Notes

1. Throughout this chapter, I emphasize the way in which legal discourses, for example, the Canadian Constitution and the Charter of Rights and Freedoms, construct and celebrate individualism and the "rights" of the individual to pursue, without obstruction, certain basic "human," and in the related Christian framework, "God-given rights." The focus is on individual, as opposed to collective, rights. Moreover, the term *the rights* often assumes that individual/agents are already equally positioned, so that structural and other inequities become invisible and irrelevant.

2. This quote is taken from the introduction of *Returning the Gaze: Essays on Racism, Feminism and Politics*, (1993, xxix). Bannerji argues that liberal discourses, for all their attention to "difference" and "diversity," remain largely ineffective in radically changing the political and economic structures that maintain inequitable practices; freedoms, rights, and differences are, for the most part, discursive, language effects.

3. See an article in the *Vancouver Sun*, "Bid to end harassment 'threat to free speech,'" by Mary-Jane Egan: March 26, 1994. All references to statements made by Robert Fulford are taken from this article.

4. This article, "Supremacist seeks civil rights help," appeared in the *Vancouver Sun* July 12, 1994. All subsequent quotes are taken from this article.

5. In his article "Things fall apart; the centre cannot hold," John Forrest (1994) presents an insightful critque of the racist right in Canada. He makes an interesting point regarding the "constitutional evasion for white supremacists" in the way in which they invoke their "legal right to "freedom of expression" (25), many of them, like Ernst Zundel, successful.

6. In *Frontiers*, Marlene Nourbese Philip discusses the collective amnesia of societies like Canada that would have us forget its imperialistic and colonialist past and its exploitation of various peoples. As a result, she addresses the significance of memory and its potentially "subversive" role toward political action, for people of color, since, to forget would be "to collude in our own erasure, our own obliteration" (19–24).

7. Universalizing Christian ideologies were closely connected historically to other imperialist and colonialist imperatives. Also, for an insightful critique of pluralist and liberal conceptions of difference and their consequences (as and end product and not as an ongoing mediated process), see Himani Bannerji's (1991) essay, "But Who Speaks for Us? Experience and Agency in Conventional Feminist Paradigms," in *Unsettling relations: The University as a site of feminist struggle.* Himani Banneji's (1993) introduction in *Returning the gaze: Essays on Racism, Feminism and Politics* was also helpful in its articulation of "powered differences" and the limitations of "neo-pluralist and marketist" notions of difference and diversity.

8. "Slips That Show and Tell: Fashioning Multiculture as a Problem of Representation" (Britzman et al. 1993) highlights the problems of investing in ways of thinking, where students are seen as ignorant, possessing a kind of "false" knowledge, which can be remade into a better and more socially responsible individual. This enlightenment metaphor does not, therefore, take into account the effects of the knowledge that students possess prior to their entrance into classrooms and the way in which individuals are acted upon by various political and social forces. Moreover, the authors point out that students are seldom eager to have their consciounesses raised, that the "interruption of these practices that are 'normal' places the speaker—as well as her knowledge—'at risk'" (190).

9. All quotes by Marke Andrews are taken from his review, "Most neo-nazis more brains than brawn," in the *Vancouver Sun's Saturday Review*, April 9, 1994.

10. William Boei's article, "Hate on the rise," appeared in the *Vancouver Sun*, June 5, 1993.

11. These statistics were found in the *Vancouver Sun*, March 1, 1993, in "U.S. black/white divide widens, study shows." All quotes refer to the findings of this study.

12. Although Chandra Talpade Mohanty's (1990) essay in *Cultural Critique*, "On Race and Voice: Challenges for Liberal Education in the 1990's," is a critique of various American individual attempts at inclusion, her analysis of certain failures to produce actual change applies to a Canadian context.

13. Here I am relying on the findings presented in "Minorities losing out in jobs, study says," by Justine Hunter in the *Vancouver Sun*, July 27, 1994. The following are, more specifically, some of the details in the report: "While aboriginal people make up 5.3% of the population of B.C., they have only 1.6% of the jobs in the civil service. Visible minorities constitute 14.2% of the population, but hold 5.1% of the government jobs. For people with disabilities, the ratio is 8% of the population to 6.3% of the workforce. Furthermore, the number of aboriginal people working in the cabinet ministries is so low that the numbers were suppressed in the data released to prevent identification of the survey respondents." In addition, the report concluded that several governmental departments like the ministries of energy, mines and petroleums, forests, aboriginal affairs and agriculture, fisheries and food have some of the worst records for employment equity.

14. "Twenty-five per cent see threat in non-whites, poll finds," (*Vancouver Sun*, April 12, 1993). Yet another article, "Notion of cultural diversity rejected by most Canadians," by Allyson Jeffs in the *Vancouver Sun* (December 14, 1993), notes that "three of every four Canadians reject the notion of cultural diversity and think that ethnic minorities should try harder to fit into mainstream society," according to a Decima Research survey. See also "Opposition to newcomers on the rise, analysts say," by Dianne Rinchart in the *Vancouver Sun*, January 14, 1994.

15. The *Village Voice* literary supplement (1994) dedicated an issue to "Whiteness," featuring articles such as "White Noise," "White Lies," and Judith Levine's "The Heart of Whiteness: Dismantling the Master's House," an essay that reviewed new texts that revisit and historicize "whiteness." In D'Erasmo's article, she highlights the nostalgic return to whiteness, albeit through fashion, and the yearning for a white of old in all its blue-veined, fragile beauty, innocence, and purity. This return is, however, haunted by history, and its vulnerability for imperialistic tales of glory; herein lies the contradiction. As whiteness seeks to rid itself of memory, it holds on reluctantly to those guilty pleasures of conquest and empire.

References

Andrews, M. (1994, April 9). Most neo-nazis more brains than brawn. *The Vancouver Sun's Saturday Review*.

Bannerji, H. (1995). *Thinking through: Essays on feminism, Marxism, and anti-racism*. Toronto: Women's Press.

————. (Ed.) (1993). *Returning the gaze: Essays on racism, feminism and politics.* Toronto: Sister Vision Press.

Bannerji, H., Carty, L., Dehli, K., Heald S., and McKenna, K. (Eds.) (1991). *Unsettling relations: The university as a site of feminist struggle.* Toronto: Women's Press.

Boei, W. (1993, June 5). Hate on the Rise. *The Vancouver Sun.*

————. (1994, July 12). Supremacist seeks civil rights help. *The Vancouver Sun.*

Britzman, D., Santiago-Valles, K., Jiminez-Munoz, G., and Lamash, L. (1993). Slips that show and tell: Fashioning multiculture as a problem of representation. In Cameron McCarthy and Warren Crichlow (Eds.), *Race, identity and representation in education* (pp. 188–200). New York: Routledge.

Brown, R. (1991). Overcoming sexism and racism: How? In O. McKague, (Ed.), *Racism in Canada* (pp. 163–178). Saskatoon: Fifth House Publishers.

Carby, H. (1992). The multicultural wars. In Gina Dent, (Ed.), *Black popular culture. A project by Michele Wallace.* Seattle: Bay Press.

Close, E. (1994, March 29). To the victors, few spoils. Why the supposed conquerors aren't celebrating yet? *Newsweek.*

Chow, R. (1993). *Writing Diaspora: Tactics of Intervention in Contemporary Cultural Studies.* Bloomington and Indianapolis: Indiana University Press.

Egan, M.-J. (1994, March 26). Bid to end harassment "threat to free speech." *Vancouver Sun.*

D'Erasmo, S. (1994). Flavour of the month. *Village Voice Literary Supplement* on "Whiteness," 128.

Forrest, J. (1994). Things fall apart; the centre cannot hold. Prospects for the Racist Right in Canada. *Fuse, 18.*

Gates, D. (1994, March 29). White male paranoia. Are they the newest victims—or just bad sports? *Newsweek.*

Gram, K. (1995, June 22). Report blasts UBC for discrimination. *The Vancouver Sun.*

Hunter, J. (1994, July 27). Minorities losing out in jobs, study says. *The Vancouver Sun.*

Jeffs, A. (1993, Dec. 14). Notion of cultural diversity rejected by most Canadians. *The Vancouver Sun.*

Mohanty, C. (1990). On race and voice: Challenges for liberal education in the 1990s. *Cultural Critque, 18*(14), 179–208.

Morrison, T. (1992). *Playing in the dark: Whiteness and the literary imagination.* Cambridge: Harvard University Press.

Parton, N. (1995, June 28). UBC report "fails" to prove claims. *The Vancouver Sun.*

Philip, M. (1992). *Frontiers essays and writings on racism and culture.* Stratford: The Mercury Press.

Rinehart, D. (1994, Jan. 14). Opposition to newcomers on the rise. *The Vancouver Sun.*

Southam News. (1993, April 12). 25 per cent see threat in non-whites, poll finds (reprinted in *The Vancouver Sun*, no author indicated).

Spivak, Gayatri Chakravorty. (1988). Can the subaltern speak? In Cary Nelson and Larry Grossberg (Eds), *Marxism and the Interpretation of Culture* (pp. 271–313). Urbana: University of Illinois Press.

The Independent (1993). U.S. black/white divide widens, study shows (reprinted in *The Vancouver Sun*, no author indicated). March 1.

12

Queer Pedagogy?!: Praxis Makes Im/Perfect[1]

Mary Bryson and Suzanne de Castell

> After all, she is this Inappropriate/d Other who moves about with always at least two/four gestures: that of affirming "I am like you" while pointing insistently to the difference; and that of reminding "I am different" while unsettling every definition of otherness arrived at.
>
> —Trinh, *She, Inappropriate/d Other*

This article examines tensions between poststructuralist theories of subjectivity and the political/pragmatic necessity of essentialist constructions of identity, not from the standpoint of their *theoretical* resolution—which is, at least in principle possible (see, for example, Fuss 1989)—but from the standpoint of their insistent irresolvability in the context of pedagogical practice.

We resisted writing this chapter for a long time, knowing from past experience that to speak publicly about the possibilities and the dangers created by being "out" as "queer"[2] educators is a speech act either of unconscionable arrogance or of profound masochism! Invariably, *speaking as* a lesbian, one is the discursive outsider—firmly entrenched in a marginal essentialized identity that, ironically, we have to participate in by naming our difference—this is rather like having to dig one's own ontological grave. Lesbianism—how might it matter that this is a "difference that dares to speak its name"? Who are we to suggest that the "subaltern" might speak after all (Spivak 1988)? Talking about the *being* of *being queer* is fraught with dangers—risks particularized as a function of location, both cultural and geopolitical.

For a highly privileged few, these risks are primarily aesthetic, rather than corporeal or economic, in nature. Recent intellectual fashions in North American scholarship, for example, dictate an emphasis on the performative function of sexual affinities (see Butler 1990; Escoffier 1990). Carnival, transgression, and parody are in, and essentialist appeals to an unproblematized or coherent identity are out. From these sites, the greatest danger one faces as a speaker consists in a charge of essentialism, or perhaps of race- or class-ism.[3]

In the various fields of education, however—whether discursive or embodied—heterosexism and homophobia are rife (Friend 1993; Khayatt 1992; Sedgwick 1991). And this despite the fact that, in Canada, to cite but one example, (a) sexual orientation is a named ground for human rights protection federally, and in many cases, provincially, (b) many school boards have endorsed policies opposing discrimination on the basis of sexual orientation, and (c) many locals have specifically included sexual orientation in the employment equity clauses of teachers' contracts.

Consider, for example, letters published in the news magazine of the British Columbia Teachers' Federation (BCTF), *Teacher*, after the publication of two articles (one written by the Gay and Lesbian Educators of B.C. and another written by a gay teacher) addressing homophobia and the specific needs of lesbian/gay students and teachers (see *Teacher*, 1991, 3[7] and 4[1 and 4]). Authors of five of the seven letters angrily criticized at length the BCTF's editorial judgement in publishing what are construed as "articles which condone homosexuality." In these letters, teachers write, for instance: "How can one say that the fear of gays and lesbians is irrational when it is common knowledge that the AIDS epidemic we all must guard against was introduced to society by homosexuals?"; "Homophobia is defined as an unnatural fear of homosexuality. In reality, there is nothing more natural than to oppose unnatural and harmful practices"; "I reject and am appalled by a group such as this trying to legitimize their lifestyle to our young people, a lifestyle a majority of society rejects as unnatural. I am also upset that the BCTF sees fit to give them this platform." The two supportive letters were very short, one written by a retired teacher and one by an anonymous contributor. Not one supportive letter was published that had been written by a working teacher with a name. The only editorial comments accompanying these letters suggested the importance of including "varied perspectives on this topic." What was extraordinary and disheartening was that the majority of these letters contained statements directly contravening the BCTF's own explicit policy commitments on sexual orientation as an explicit basis both for human rights protection and for proactive interventions at every level of the public school system. Good theory, good policy. (Shame about the practice!)

In the university faculties of education where we work, talk about being queer is a gross violation—a discursive im/possibility which we have elsewhere (Bryson and de Castell 1993b) referred to as constituting (paraphrasing Brossard 1988) an "unten<ur>able discursive posture," duly punished by daily acts of heterosexism, long-term social exclusion, personal and professional marginalization, and constant "reminders" (read threats) about upcoming tenure and performance reviews and the need to do "work" (i.e., getting published in academic journals) that is "relevant" (i.e., to white, middle-class heterosexuals). In the classrooms where we teach future educators, coming out in response to direct student questioning has prompted reactions of anger, verbal abuse, and distinctly punitive student evaluations of competence. In our neighbourhoods, being identified as queer has resulted in abuses ranging from verbal assault to bashing of such ferocity as to result in long-term physical disability. The list goes on . . .

What difference does it make—*being queer* in the classroom? What would that mean, anyway—*being* queer? How does it matter—with whom, or how, we re/construct sexual and affectional relations? How could it have come to pass that, paradoxically, while current liberal/critical speaking about pedagogical matters (e.g., Aronowitz and Giroux 1991; Burbules and Rice 1991; Weiler 1988) echoes loudly the intertextualized words of queers—Foucault (1980b, 1982), Butler (1990), Fuss (1989), Lorde (1984), Barthes (1977), Rubin (1975, 1981, 1984), Rich (1979), de Lauretis (1987), Moraga and Anzaldua (1983), Wittig (1980), and others—a heavy cloak of willful silence continues to shroud sexualities as important sites for the production and reification of *difference* both in the textually constructed subjects of educational discourses and in the actual embodied subjects who in/habit the contexts of institutional schooling? Many influential and widely cited authors in postcritical pedagogical discourses today are queer—yet few are coming out as queer, are speaking *as* one, and almost no one is talking about the impact of sexual difference on pedagogical processes in relation to *their own* sexual identity. Is this not a difference that makes a difference? It is, then, with a large measure of reluctance and hesitation that we directly address, *speaking as one*, the thorny issues of queer identity politics and pedagogical practices. The sheer invisibility, in practice, of flesh and blood speaking/acting lesbian or gay subjects, coupled with the extraordinary acts of textual objectification and appropriation that hit us squarely between the I/eye/s every time we encounter what passes as postmodern pedagogy have made it impossible, finally, not to speak "out."

This article, then, addresses the issue of problematized sexual identities and liberatory pedagogy from within the specific context of an undergraduate "lesbian studies" course (WMST 666)[4] we co-taught in 1991 at a major urban Canadian university. We envision this course as an instance of something here referred to as "queer pedagogy"—a teaching against-the-grain, or, in this particular case, an amalgam of "performative acts"(Butler 1990) enfleshing a radical form of what we envisioned to be potentially liberatory enactments of "gender treachery" (Bryson, de Castell, and Haig-Brown 1993) with/in the always already (Derrida 1978) heterosexually coded spaces of academic women's studies programs.

In a period in which uncertainty and ambivalence are the order of the day concerning the ostensibly liberatory projects of modernism's critical white knights (perhaps most notably, Jurgen Habermas), we envision praxis—typically conceptualized as reflexive, reconstitutive action—as a necessary corrective to the often overly abstract, aesthetically self-indulgent, politically ambivalent, and obtusely textualized forms of postmodern theorizing (see Lazarus 1991). Reflexive oppositional action undertaken within key sites for the production of oppression does not seem optional so long as anti-Semitism, racism, homophobia, sexism, classism, and the other forms of hegemonic violence continue to proliferate within educational (and other) contexts. In this article, we focus on our own attempts to design and co-teach a lesbian studies course; to forge a kind of queer praxis. This kind of transformative work represents an embodied application of *feminist poststructural* theories of subjectivity (Ellsworth 1990; Luke 1992) within which we attempt to engage simultaneously with issues of sexuality, identity, difference, agency, voice, and pedagogy.[5]

Queer Pedagogy In/Deed . . .

Our reflections on subjectivity and pedagogy were brought to a head by our contradictory and sometimes agonizing and disorienting experiences in co-teaching WMST 666—a special topics course[6] entitled Lesbian Subjects Matter: Feminism/s from the Margins. The theoretical tensions between postmodern discourses of deconstruction and postcolonial, postfeminist discourses of agency created the conceptual terrain within which we situated WMST 666. The potentially contradictory subject positioning these tensions engender is neatly summed up by Rosi Braidotti (1987), who points out: "In order to announce the death of the subject one must first have gained the right to speak as one" (237). Guided by Braidotti's articulation of the paradoxical consequences of a postmodern identity politics, we chose to focus on two major questions in constructing the course.

First, we asked whether the claiming of cultural representation and voice necessarily entails the inevitability of essentialism. Deliberate representations of sexual difference—for instance, lesbian sexuality—play a key and effective role in an oppressed group's struggles for voice, visibility, and empowerment. Yet, this culture-building strategy often creates a semblance of coherent subject/matter where there actually exist multiple subjectivities, contradictions, and dislocations, and a fragmentation both of identities and of knowledges.

Second, we questioned whether a politics of identity—especially an identity constructed on the margins—could be a viable strategy, either theoretically or politically. Specifically in relation to mainstream feminist theorizing, the relationship between lesbian and feminist theory/praxis is unclear and often represents a stormy and unsatisfactory union for both parties. While it seems fair to say that during the eighties the greatest impetus for transformative growth in feminist theorizing has been work at the margins—by women of colour in particular—occupying a place at the margins has been as much a site for entrenching boundaries and limiting possibilities as a site for contesting these positionings (Chung, Kim, and Lemeshewsky 1987; Culley and Portuges 1985; hooks 1984; Omosupe 1991).

Since we intended to interrogate not only the contents but also the forms by means of which to represent identity, we deliberately made use of (invited to our classes and/or arranged for equipment and instruction in the uses of) a wide range of resources in WMST 666 (both products and producers in radio, video, photography, desk-top publishing, and so on), hoping thereby to expand and to reconstruct the typically limited opportunities both for access to and for production of radical representations of lesbian identities and cultures. By "radical" we mean to imply that a primary aim of the course was to enter eyes and arms open into the perilous arena constituted by various projects of queer identity politics (see Escoffier 1985a, 1985b; Fuss 1989; Omosupe 1991; Phelan 1989).

Pedagogically speaking, we structured WMST 666 as follows. The course was constructed around a series of texts and presentations by lesbian subjects: people actively engaged in community-based lesbian-identified cultural constructions—lesbians doing photography, theatre, law, AIDS work, music and video production, and so on. We chose a wide range of presenters and readings, so as to engage students with the ways in which the sliding signifier "lesbian" would be differently constructed as a function of age, ethnicity, race, class, body size, and other key axes that could/do function as sites for systems of domination, as bell hooks (1990) describes the interlocking forces of oppression. Having been provided with access to, and instruction in video production, photography, desk-top publishing, and the like, students were asked to do a project during WMST 666—either individually or collaboratively—exploring some aspect of lesbian identity/representation and making use of any appropriate technology.

Three lesbian artists—known as the Kiss and Tell Collective—for example, came and performed a reading of/about their widely distributed photo montage entitled "Drawing the Line" (Kiss and Tell Collective 1991). In this interactive exhibit, viewers are invited to move around a room where photographs of "lesbian sex" are affixed to write-on surfaces. Under the viewer's gaze, the montage of photographs becomes a surface to be textured with a melange of lines and comments depicting reactions, perceived limits exceeded or unattained, likes, dislikes, and so on. Only female viewers are permitted access to the walls as write-on texts; male viewers' comments and demarcations are confined to a book placed on a table nearby. To date this exhibit has toured Canada, the United States, and Australia, and has invariably generated heated debate about representation, race, sexualities, and identity. In WMST 666, the artists read a piece, written in three parts, describing their work and the contradictions therein: "What makes a photograph 'lesbian'?" "Why aren't there any lesbians of color in these photographs?" "What about lesbians who like to have sexual relations with men?" "What about the sexual activities depicted? These are models—are we/they *really* having sex?"

As a strategy for engaging students with the theoretical perspectives provided by a postmodern, deconstructionist perspective on lesbian-identified cultures and histories, we created an activity that came to be referred to as "The Dating Game," an intentional parody of the "Lesbians through the Ages" approach typifying introductory women's studies curricula. During the first week, students picked out of a hat slips of paper on which were printed two names of "historically noteworthy (for some) North American (mostly) lesbians"—for instance, "Jane Rule and Pat Califia," "Lee Lynch and Gertrude Stein," "Gloria Anzaldua and Cherrie Moraga," "Bessie Smith and Ma Rainey," "Sappho and Artemis Oakgrove." Students then created a presentation focusing on a transhistorical "date" between the two persons. This activity had a dual purpose: first, it required participants to seek out standardly overlooked information about our own histories as a group, the purpose being to learn something about people of whose names we knew, but little else. Second, in thinking about what the two would discuss, fight about, be attracted to, or enjoy doing together, students had the opportunity to consider all the many socially and historically contingent details that go into the construction of an identity, enabling them to explore "identity" not as an *individual* accomplishment, but as a function of community and relation.

Similarly, to materialize the constructed and artifactual nature of lesbian culture, history, and identity itself as discursively produced, we created Lesbian Jeopardy, a pseudo-positivistic, overtly ironic game of "Facts We Know about Lesbians." Students created Jeopardy questions throughout the course, which were amalgamated to make the first version of Lesbian Jeopardy—played against an outside team of "experts" from Vancouver's lesbian community during the final class—our parodic alternative to a final exam.

We decided, as instructors, not intentionally to define the term "lesbian" or "sexual orientation" or to consider material presented as "lesbian" in opposition to heterosexually identified material. We talked a lot, in the first weeks of class, about the ways in which difference functions in the construction of identities, and about the need to theorize difference, particularly in relation to agency or political projects. We said that, in the class, there could be "no consumers and no voyeurs," and therefore, in articulating possibilities for dialogue, each of us would have to develop a clear "ethics of consumption" and a "reflexive gaze." We talked about the importance of our articulated and unexamined purposes for participating in the course, particularly in relation to self-identification. That is, we explained, heterosexually identified students would have to consider aspects of privilege and authority, as they would function and circulate differently in a lesbian-identified space.

White participants, similarly, would have to deal with the often unnamed assumption of compulsory whiteness in articulations of purportedly universal themes of lesbian history, culture, and praxis. We encouraged students to do their class projects collaboratively, and in that process to focus on the functioning of differences in their ability, or lack thereof, to work together productively and equitably.

Dis/Covering Out/Comes

Students in WMST 666 included thirteen white women and two women of color. Students identified a range of class backgrounds and, initially, chose either to remain silent about their sexual identification or to present themselves as "out lesbians." We quickly found that only the students whose lives were constructed within oppression, with or without the added contradiction of privilege afforded by, say, white skin—that is, a straight-identified woman of color, and the bisexually and lesbian-identified women, both of color and white—could effectively engage in the work we had prescribed for our course. The white heterosexually identified students (many of whom were majors in women's studies) came to visit us, as instructors, during office hours, to talk about their difficulties participating effectively in class, but did not voice their frustrations during class time. We found that white students who identified as heterosexual made, for example, lifeless presentations *about* lesbians that bore painful testimony to their inability to imagine an encounter between, say, Audre Lorde and Mary Daly, or between k.d. lang and Ferron. In their journals, white, straight-identified women did not make use of textual or in-class discussions of identity to reflect on the constructedness of their *own* identities, but chose, rather, to consume or reject the material on the basis of abstract arguments and "critical" rationality. *Lesbians* and *lesbianism*, in this form, became commodified texts or artifacts to be recklessly appropriated for purposes entirely "academic"; these students thus disregarded our earlier appeals for an *ethic* of consumption. Students with no direct experience of heterosexism as violence, either material or symbolic, asked questions of or made requests to the class that betrayed their privilege and that failed to meet the needs of lesbians in the class in relation to issues of safety or rights to privacy. With dismay we gradually realized that, somehow, in selectively focusing on lesbianism as a site for the construction of difference/s, we had created an us/them structure that effectively made working together across difference/s a seemingly unreachable goal, although this had been our explicit original intention.

After a grueling first month of classes during which a large group of mostly silent students "passed" as lesbian, students who considered themselves to be "out lesbians," and we instructors—feeling that a great deal of deception was taking place at the expense of the safety of the lesbian students—suggested that students who identified as "heterosexual" would probably be better able to contribute to the discussions/collaborative projects if they positioned their in-class comments/work by referring to their own experiences and dealing explicitly with their privilege and power-over. Needless to say, the next month was spent negotiating the tricky terrain of authority and experience, but the result was that two heterosexually identified women began to take responsibility for their speaking in the class; the bisexually identified women formed a tight affinity group and organized a series of pot-luck suppers and contacts outside of class; and the lesbian-identified women created a powerful affinity group that met regularly, outside WMST 666, for discussions, planning, strategizing, and a lot of dancing. There was a fairly strong coalition between the bisexually identified and lesbian-identified students—especially in dealing with issues of racism and anti-Semitism.

By the end of the course, all but one of the heterosexually identified students chose to complete standard essays, created individually and produced on word processors in print form. These students dealt with the topics of identity and difference by means of a critique of the heterosexism of institutional knowledges, such as other women's studies courses. The one heterosexually identified student—a woman of color—who did not choose the traditional "final essay" form, dealt explicitly with issues of her own sexual orientation/identity in the construction of, and commentary about, a collage (replete with hundreds of same-yet-different paper-doll cut-outs) depicting representations of "self-improvement" for women portrayed in popular culture—particularly magazine advertisements and television images. This student conducted extensive and thoughtful dialogues with students in the class whose identities differed from her own in one or more respects. Two white bisexually identified students created an extraordinary video about a couple of bisexual room/mates doing the dishes and chatting—in the nude. The dish-washing episodes served as a kind of contradictory representation of an ostensibly simple process which can become ridiculously complicated and rulebound if engaged in by following a set of externally defined rules. The women's conversations dealt with many of the ambiguities, ironies, and impossibilities of a so-called bisexual lifestyle. A lesbian of color worked with other lesbians—both white and of color—to create a series of photographs dealing with representation, racism, and essentialism in the construction of lesbian identity. She also created a lesbian safe-sex poster using a desk-top publishing program. The poster invoked a simulation of a regular box of latex gloves, except that, among uses for the gloves, one finds gardening, first aid, and fisting. In the photograph for the gloves advertisement, we see two women, one white and one of color, locked in an embrace that appears to blur the boundaries between them. A white working-class lesbian created a sophisticated forty-five-minute video dealing ironically with the topics of sexual identity, racism, classism, and lesbian theorizing. She worked collaboratively with others inside and outside WMST 666—lesbians and gay men, both white and of color.

For many participants in WMST 666, then, access to alternative media of representation provided the means for (a) reconstructing the division of labor in classroom tasks traditionally assigned to, and completed by, individual students; (b) restructuring power relations between participants in educational contexts, who typically occupy very unevenly positioned discursive roles in relation to power; and (c) transforming received knowledges, texts, and images through ironic acts of mis/representation, mimicry, collage, montage, and re/degendering.

What we saw in much of the work were examples of the kinds of "politically articulate" uses of technologies of cultural production characteristic of postmodernism—specifically, postmodernist practices of "recycling," which salvage icons, images, and artifacts resurrected from within their original socio-historical context and re-inserted into another context, within which this "detritus" takes on a new, significantly greater cultural value. It is postmodernism's characteristic montage of previously unconnected events, its unprecedented and often unlikely juxtapositions of what, in its original context, might conversely have been at best commonplace, ordinary, seemingly without value, which we see instantiated in these pedagogic tactics. In this postmodern "transvaluation of values," videos, photographs, posters, and paper dolls became capable of articulating sophisticated and complex theory, while formal essays and conventional book reviews were relegated to the margins . . . Inversion indeed!

It is of course interesting to observe that students usually given the space, voice, and liberty to speak and to be heard ended up in this course reverting to tepid, formulaic, disengaged essays, while students "of difference" took permission to play with form, genre, substance, and personal/political purposes and produced what was undeniably outstanding, innovative, and, above all, engaged work. These outcomes bear out the familiar pedagogic wisdom about acceptance of student identities and abilities being conducive to achievement; at the same time, and most uncomfortably for us, given our original intents, the outcomes seemed also to bear out the heterosexual women's "reverse discrimination" arguments.

But a good deal more interesting to us was the question of what lay behind this surface appearance, which was that from the time of the initial "discovery" of what we then saw as "deception"—the heterosexual "cross-dressing" attempted in the course, every ounce of our emotional, intellectual, and social energies was consumed by the problem of accommodating the white heterosexual women's discomfort (a problem perhaps familiar to women's studies instructors who have had straight male students in their classes). And this happened, it must be noted, despite our repeated insistence that this was not something we wanted to do, that this was not something we *would* do, and despite lesbian students' protestations that, as one put it when the term was half through, "straight women have had all of their lives to deal with their homophobia and their privilege. I now have just six weeks left to learn everything about my life" (Rhenby 1992).

By the end of the term, there was in fact really only one student who steadfastly refused to engage at all with these questions, and it seems to us most important to stress this. As a white, middle-class heterosexual woman fully invested in the naturalness and unquestionability of heterosexism, this student's refusal throughout the course was principally, we would now argue, a refusal *of identity*. In an almost—to us—surreal act of externalization, she offered as her principal impediment to success in this course nothing at all to do with conflicts or confusions about the constructedness of identity, whether theoretical or embodied. In explaining late and incomplete work, she said nothing about the problematics of "inwardness" (although she criticized us as instructors for a "lack of trust" and "safety" in the class, for a "power imbalance," and for "unwanted and unfounded suspicion and judgement"). Instead, our resisting student subordinated all of these difficulties to the (indissolubly *physical)* impediment of a sore, swollen, and discolored toe—far, indeed, from the ontology, ethics, and politics of identity. This, it seems to us in retrospect, was because "identity" is so often not something freely chosen or "naturally" emergent, but created in reaction, in defense, by difference, and by opposition (hooks 1990).

This student also showed us the disproportionate power of one. For as long as even just *one* student "held the line" in the representation of hegemonic (non)identity, all our discourses, all our actions, were inescapably interpolated, were threaded through, with the continuous and inescapable subtext of white heterosexual dominance, the backdrop against which everything else in these institutions happens. (And how *un*like this is the "invisibility" of one lesbian or gay man in these same settings, and, correlatively, the scarcely imaginable anxiety and hostility unleashed when "*more* than one are gathered together.") What this taught us is that lesbianism, although it could of course be any other subordinated identity, is *always marginal*, even in a lesbian studies course, and that lesbian identity is *always fixed* and stable, even in a course that explicitly critiques, challenges, deconstructs "lesbian identity."

Just When You Thought It Might Be Safe to
Come Out in the Classroom: Queer Praxis Makes Im/Perfect . . .

It was useful, in conceptualizing this de/constructive work on gender, sexual identities, and pedagogy, to return to one of the origi-

nal sites for the production of a distinction between sex and gender—
a distinction both of historical and of political import that circulated,
for a time, within feminist writings and conversations as a source of
optimism, with its refusal of biological determinism and, hence, its
affirmation of the plausibility of agency by means of direct cultural
intervention within sites of cultural re/production. According to
Donna Haraway (1987), the first textual use of the signifying construct
"sex/gender system" was by Gayle Rubin (1975), in a landmark paper
entitled "The Traffic in Women: Notes on the Political Economy of
Sex." In relation to issues of pedagogical practice, this distinction typically has been used to justify arguments about both (a) the liberatory
aspects of lesbian sexuality for women in general, and (b) more specifically, the equation of women's studies with lesbian studies. Early
models of lesbian studies and related practices (e.g., Cruickshank
1982) tended, for example, overwhelmingly to situate lesbianism
with/in feminism, and, to argue, for example, that the ethical axioms
of feminism ought, necessarily, to inform the practices of lesbian sexuality (as in the ubiquitous "Feminism Is the Theory and Lesbianism the
Practice"). The conceptual and practical slippages between gender and
sexuality proved greater than could be accommodated by these early
attempts to theorize lesbianism within feminism. Critiques, particularly by women of color (hooks 1984; Moraga and Anzaldua 1983) and
by lesbian practitioners of sadomasochism (see review in Phelan 1989),
created a significant rupture in the giddy post-Stonewall days of lesbian community. And so the question of how to theorize, say, a truly
queer pedagogy became, once more, entirely problematic.

In more recent work, a further distinction has been made that has
proven to be of enormous significance to the development, in the fields
of lesbian and gay studies, of theoretical models capable of more adequately informing the conceptualization and implementation of radical practices—a distinction between sex/gender and sexuality (e.g.,
Rubin 1984; Sedgwick 1990). As Sedgwick (1990) argued: "The study
of sexuality is not coextensive with the study of gender; correspond-
ingly, antihomophobic inquiry is not coextensive with feminist
inquiry" (27).

Rubin's (1975; 1984) sex/gender/sexuality distinctions were
made within a historically, materially, and socially contingent context
characterized by a kind of radical, oppositional theorizing (see Sawicki
1991). Gayle Rubin is, among other things, a self-proclaimed lesbian
sadomasochist (Rubin 1981; 1984; 1991) and the author of several now-
classic essays on the topic of "radical sex practices" and their significance for theories and politics of sexual difference. In Rubin's words:

"In addition to sexual hierarchies of class, race, gender, and ethnicity, there is a hierarchy based on sexual behavior. . . . It is time that radicals and progressives, feminists and leftists, recognize this hierarchy for the oppressive structure that it is instead of reproducing it within their own ideologies" (1984, 226).

In creating and implementing WMST 666, we attempted to reflect on what it might mean to take Rubin's challenge seriously in rethinking, or *queer<y>ing*, normatively sanctioned pedagogies so as to insist on the right to "speak as one," to make pedagogical spaces where the hitherto unsayable could be uttered, where so-called deviant images could be represented, and where conscious efforts could be made to rethink forms of subjectivity and relations within the oppressive confines of the always-already heterosexualized classroom. How to accomplish some of this while concurrently resisting the incredible pressures to instantiate and reify essentialized representations of queer sexuality—marginal subject positions that function like fixed locations on the outer perimeter of normalcy, ironically, as Foucault (1978, 1980a) and others (Butler 1990; hooks 1984) have argued, without thereby fortifying and stabilizing dominant subjectivities and knowledges?

We have argued elsewhere (Bryson and de Castell 1994) that it is principally within postmodernist accounts of pedagogy (see, for example, Britzman 1991; Ellsworth 1989; Hoodfar 1992; Lather 1991; Leach 1992; Weiler 1988) that one encounters talk of opportunities for agency among the oppressed, located in ironic, *"enfant terrible,"* or *"*bad attitude" models for the reconsideration of received notions of identity. In these accounts, being any gender is a drag, and carnival and a dis/continuous shifting among and between identities is the order of the day. The problem is construed as the need to dissolve the impasse created by conceptual dualisms, such as male/female gender models, natural/artificial ontological systems, and essentialist/constructionist intellectual frameworks for thinking about sexual identity (see especially Fuss 1989; Phelan 1989; Sedgwick 1990). The goal is to discover how to conceptualize/materialize new and "politically articulate" (Penley and Ross 1991) relations with/in classroom discourses and practices, by reflecting critically on, and making fundamental changes in, conceptualizations about both the discursive categories of, for example, "gender," "lesbian," and "difference," and actual lived practices and social relations circulating in pedagogical practices, and relations between and within subjects.

Postmodernist discourses (see Barthes 1977; Baudrillard 1983; Bordo 1990; Derrida 1978; Fraser 1989) displace the fixed subjects both of modernist and of critical theorizing; that is, both the notions of (a) the individual (e.g., "lesbian") as constituting a unified subject whose true or essential "nature" can be determined under the penetrating gaze of science and of (b) bodies of knowledge, such as "lesbian studies," as constituting coherent subject matters, with clear epistemological boundaries, appropriate methodologies, truth conditions, and so forth. One of postmodernism's main contributions to theories of "difference" has been the deconstruction of the kinds of essentialist theorizing about sites of oppression in traditional and critical theorizing, such as in essentialist accounts of sexual identity in terms of, say, "lesbian-feminism" or "lesbian sexuality," as fundamentally raced, classed, and probably politically unproductive in an ongoing struggle for equity, voice, and empowerment (Escoffier 1985a; 1985b; Fuss 1989).

In educational discourses, postmodernist theorizing (Lather 1990) has cast doubt on latter-day critical theorists' monolithic claims of being able to identify the ideological underpinnings of oppressive pedagogies and, from a safe distance, therefore, to restructure educational environments so as to realize the goals of their "liberatory" or "emancipatory" projects. Ellsworth (1989) paints a complex portrait of her practices as a white middle-class woman and professor engaged with a diverse group of students developing an antiracist course. She describes her experience of the contradictions inherent in actively engaging with liberatory pedagogy as follows:

> Our classroom was the site of dispersing, shifting, and contradictory contexts of knowing that coalesced differently in different moments of student/professor speech, action, and emotion. This situation meant that individuals and affinity groups constantly had to change strategies and priorities of resistance against oppressive ways of knowing and being known. The antagonist became power itself as it was deployed within our classroom—oppressive ways of knowing and oppressive knowledges. (322)

We have attempted in this chapter to determine the relevance of postmodernist theorizing about difference and pedagogy, such as the terrain of contradictions traversed by Ellsworth, for revisioning and reforming praxis in a lesbian studies classroom. In this project of queer identity, our (that is, we instructors') embodied existences within a set of overlapping, yet incoherent, communities created a set of material conditions and practices that informed our interlocking experiences of discrimination, privilege, sexuality, and gender, in very particular ways. We found that we could not, however, represent ourselves "as lesbian" within institutional contexts (such as our respective faculties of education) without instantiating profoundly unproductive essentialist notions of fixed, stable, and marginal "lesbian identities."

Lesbian Identity? Memory/Counter-Memory

Some days, the only aspect of my so-called "lesbian identity" that seems even remotely interesting is that I am prepared to die for the way I like to fuck. Now that's a cause! The other day, my partner and I were walking from the supermarket to the video store. A man approached us, pointed, and shouted "Dykes!" in a voice that was incredibly angry and hostile. So strange, to be framed like that; poured into an identity that is, at one and the same time, self-identical and also sufficient cause for verbal abuse, intimidation, bashing, and much, much, worse. I wanted to shout out, "No! I am not that. I am not your 'dyke'! I am not that name." Identity as ascribed, rather than assumed, or chosen. Is it ever any different? Ontological straightjacket or revolutionary battle cry? "Dyke" certainly seems preferable to the terribly prim "lesbian" or the clinical "homosexual." My c.v. states that I do lesbian studies, but I do not envision myself "as a lesbian." I remember practicing the word over and over again in the mirror, trying to say it with pride and confidence during my obligatory "coming out" phase. During this brief period, I truly thought I had "found myself," that I had discovered, at long last, a "place called home" within an unproblematically assumed community loosely based on "lesbian-feminist" identity politics. Needless to say, there were many aspects of this new "identity" to which I could not simply conform, particularly, injunctions to downplay sexual pleasure and to embrace the ideals of egalitarian sisterhood. Similarly, highly charged relationships with women of color have confronted me over and over again with "the unbearable whiteness of (my) lesbian being" and an acute sense of my own complicity in re/producing racism through an unproblematized taking-up of a so-called "lesbian" identity. Yet, can we afford to say, "I am not that name"? How to problematize heterosexuality without invoking an other? Sometimes, this is (and has proven to be) a question of life and death.

So how can we talk about issues that may be specifically of concern to lesbians without claiming "the" authoritative voice of experience—without claiming a unique capacity to speak as lesbians? Our own capacity to speak is entirely a set of effects of contradictory and overlapping discursive/material positions—white-skin privilege, middle-class roots, able-bodyness, faculty positions, and so on.

Students are likewise placed in contradictory speaking positions in relation to experience and oppression. Students, however, probably have even more dire need than white faculty for opportunities both to speak as lesbians and to passionately engage with lesbian content within the profoundly heterosexist, homophobic, racist, and sexist context that is enacted in the everyday relations and practices of the academy, whether at our own universities or elsewhere.

From "Queer Theory" to "Queer Pedagogy":
Locating the Unspeakable in a Pedagogy of the Repressed

Clearly, the distance from queer theory to queer pedagogy is great. It is interesting to note that in the first lesbian and gay studies reader published to date (Abelove, Barale, and Halperin 1993), there is, among 666 pages and 42 chapters spanning a wide range of intellectual domains, *not a single entry* that deals explicitly with the educational implications or applications of these new discourses. And so the question remains—What could be made "queer" about pedagogy? Queer pedagogy could refer here to education as carried out *by* lesbian and gay educators, to curricula and environments designed *for* gay and lesbian students, to education for everyone *about* queers, or to something altogether different. Queer pedagogy could refer to *the deliberate production of queer relations and to the production of subjectivities as deviant performance*—that is to say, to a kind of postmodern carnivalesque pedagogy of the underworld, as agitation *implemented deliberately to interfere with, to intervene in the production of so-called normalcy in schooled subjects.* Reading the *Concise Oxford English Dictionary* one discovers: "*Queer: adjective—sexual deviate, homosexual. Pedagogy: from pedagogue, paid—boy and ago—lead, orig.: the slave who escorted children to school.*" And hence one version of a *queer* pedagogy—the stereotypical image of the pederast fondling boys on the way to school, or the gay teacher, fired for "indecent exposure" or "inappropriate touching." But what of another reading? What of the active form of the word *queer*—its agentive form? Reading a little further, the same dictionary includes: "*Queer: verb—to spoil, put out of order, to put into an embarrassing or disadvantageous situation.*"

It seems that a worthwhile avenue for the elucidation of a queer praxis might be to consider the value of an actively *queerying* pedagogy—of queering its technics and scribbling graffiti over its texts, of coloring outside of the lines so as to deliberately take the wrong route on the way to school—going in an altogether different direction than that specified by a monologic destination. This seems a promising approach indeed for refashioning pedagogy in the face of the myriad institutionally sanctioned "diversity management" (Mohanty 1990) programs that, today, threaten to crowd out and silence most opportunities for radical emancipatory praxis (de Castell and Bryson 1992).

As we learned in WMST 666, praxis makes im/perfect; that is to say, an eclectic mélange of the wonderful, the awful, and the in-between. And perhaps, in pedagogical matters, im/perfect outcomes are necessarily the norm. Just as "safe sex" has been discredited, there may, in/deed, as Ellsworth (1990), Hoodfar (1992), Razak (1993), and others have argued, be no such thing as a "safe pedagogy." But what about the notion of a "safer" pedagogy? It seems imperative to explore and to articulate a set of pedagogical practices that might offer greater opportunities than those currently available both to students and to teachers "of difference" for the construction of, and participation in, democratic, engaging, pleasurable, interesting, generative, and non-violent learning environments. This gargantuan task is nothing less than intimidating. After all, determining where to begin keeps many of us from ever getting started.

After teaching WMST 666, it seemed clear to us that one of the most invariably accessible, urgent, and relatively unexamined areas of so-called progressive classroom practice lies in the function, risk, and purpose of "dialogue across differences," and hence of encouraging students of difference to exercise their "voices" (see especially Burbules and Rice 1991; and the critique by Leach 1992). At this juncture, it appears to us that little or no educational value lies in getting minority students to recount their experiences of difference/s, to listen to their fellow students' or instructors' "unassimilated difference" (Ellsworth 1990), or to engage in verbal arm wrestling about issues of authenticity or authority. The difficulties and perils, for example, of "speaking as" are, as Linda Alcoff (1991) cogently argued, no less significant than the challenges posed by "speaking for," "to," or "about." As Gayatri Chakravorty Spivak (1990) reminds us:

> The question "Who should speak?" is less crucial than "Who will listen?" . . . When the card carrying listeners, the hegemonic people, the dominant people, talk about listening to someone "speaking as" . . . when they want to hear an Indian, a Third World woman speaking as a Third World woman, they cover over the fact of the ignorance that they are allowed to possess. (59–60)

And so one might do well to consider the possibilities for re-tooling pedagogical practices offered by the notion of an "ethics of consumption and of production" in relation to one's engagements with classroom discourses. Questions about who ought to speak, and about what/to whom, or as what category of speaker, do not seem, finally, as significant as questions about to what end and, most critically, at what cost. In WMST 666, women who identified unproblematically as white heterosexuals seemed completely stymied, and, indeed, mightily offended when asked, both by instructors and by other students, for the basis of their participation in a lesbian studies course. Their responses, about being "interested in the topic," or wanting to "know more about lesbians," seemed symptomatic of a sense of automatic entitlement, of an identity that is constructed in a parasitic relation of unquestioned privilege vis à vis Others—others' lives, stories, words, and traces represented thus as objects of consumption assimilated for purposes of self-advancement and little more. This kind of "border crossing" seems to have much more in common with a colonizing kind of "intellectual tourism" and its attendant strategies of massive cultural appropriation and devastation than with any kind of reflexive and tentative journey into the unknown and unexamined "differences and oppressors within" (Anzaldua 1987; Lugones 1987; Pratt 1984).

One might be forgiven for not knowing this, given the current proliferation of discourses about difference/s, whether sexual or otherwise, discourses which make it seem as if at long last we might be permitted to begin *seriously* to grapple with "what difference it makes" to our theorizing within and outside of feminism, about identity, about epistemology and ethics, about politics and praxis. So it might seem given the growing popularity and increasing availability of courses dedicated to black studies, to chicana/o studies, postcolonialism, and, not least, gay/lesbian studies (Escoffier 1990; Mohr 1989; Saslow 1991) all currently flourishing in the academy. It might seem as if we could at last accommodate both our urgent desires and our demands for a "home" in these institutions (Bryson and de Castell 1993a) without having to abandon our desires and demands as students, as scholars determined that we should not have *always* to subordinate our intellectual inquiries to our political and emotional needs just to be here and to speak with a chance of being heard, with the hopes of someday even being listened to. Or so, as we said, it might seem.

But here, we find, is how it is: although lesbians now occasionally are permitted to speak in the academy, we can only speak *about* but we cannot speak *as* lesbians, except insofar as we are prepared, in such speaking, to make of ourselves not lesbian subjects, but lesbian objects, objects of study, of interrogation, of confession, of consumption. Nor can we speak *to* lesbians, except as we are prepared to place them in jeopardy, to open and dissect a subjectivity created for and by the dominant other. Queer pedagogy it is indeed, that, after all, in trying to make a difference we seem only able to entrench essentialist boundaries which continue both to define and to divide us.

Postscript

The most common educational prescription for dealing with the problems we have taken up here is, typically, some kind of pluralistic exhortation for "dialogue across differences" (e.g., Aronowitz and Giroux 1991; Burbules and Rice 1991; Kaplan 1992). The expected discursive move for us in concluding this piece, then, would be to affirm dialogue and boundary crossing, affinity and coalition, and the like. But this, we find, despite the obligation to prescribe solutions, to outline a "better way," to say what we learned and how to do it better "next time," we cannot in honesty do. For it is by now our strong conviction that such discourses are at worst motivated by careerism, vacuous and disingenuous, and at best premature. All that remains available to us, then, by way of conclusion, is to issue a challenge: let those who still believe "queer pedagogy" to be possible tell it like it is, or, at least, how it might be. We leave the last words to an inspired creator of undoubtedly im/perfect queer praxis, the late Michel Foucault (1980b):

I have a dream of an intellectual who destroys evidences and universalities, who locates and points out the inertias and constraints of the present, the weak points, the openings, the lines of stress, who constantly displaces himself [sic] not knowing exactly where he'll be or what he'll think tomorrow because he is too attentive to the present; who in the places he passes through contributes to the posing of the question of whether the revolution is worth the trouble, and which (I mean which revolution and which trouble), it being understood that only those who are prepared to risk their lives to reply can do so. (14)

Notes

1. Authors' names are listed alphabetically. An abbreviated version of this chapter was presented at a meeting of the American Educational Research Association, in San Francisco, April 1991. We are indebted to the two reviewers of this chapter for their helpful criticisms and suggestions.

2. We invoke the adjective/noun *queer* in the particularizing sense in which it has been used to signify noncanonical, polyphonic, transgressive, contradictory, and problematic codings (de Lauretis 1991)—not in its totalizing sense, as in "Queer Nation." In Case's (1991) words:

> The queer, unlike the rather polite categories of *gay* and *lesbian* [italics added], revels in the discourse of the loathsome, the outcast, the idiomatically-proscribed position of same-sex desire. Unlike petitions for civil rights, queer revels constitute a kind of activism that attacks the dominant notion of the natural. The queer is the taboo-breaker, the monstrous, the uncanny. Like the Phantom of the Opera, the queer dwells underground, below the operatic overtones of the dominant; frightening to look at, desiring, as it plays its own organ, producing its own music. (3)

3. We are not implying here that charges of racism or classism are innocuous, but that in *academic* discourses, these critiques are, so often, formulaic and rarely result in (or even intend) significant transformations to subsequent work.

4. We use a fictitious course number to protect students' right to confidentiality.

5. It is important to acknowledge from the outset the particular limitations framing this account. First and foremost, we make no claim to present an inclusive, valid, or comprehensive "story" about teaching WMST 666. A priori, we had no intention of writing about this course, and had specifically decided ahead of time *not* to transform our "students" into our "subjects" by presenting ourselves as some kind of Janus-like teacher-ethnographers eager to peek voyeuristically into their journals for juicy anecdotes, to furiously scribble down in-class dialogues for future publication purposes, and the like. And so we did not interview students concerning their experiences in this course. Nor did we keep a running set of comprehensive field notes. Rather, we have chosen after the fact to write about our experience attempting to construct and to implement a queer pedagogy because, finally, we could not *not* do so, and, relatedly, because we had found no one else who had (see Mohr 1989).

6. Special topics course: the locution of choice for papering over, or burying, queer content in university/women's studies programs, transcripts, and syllabi.

References

Abelove, H., Barale, M., & Halperin, D. (Eds.) (1993). *The lesbian and gay studies reader.* New York: Routledge.

Alcoff, L. (1991). The problem of speaking for others. *Cultural Critique, 92,* 5–32.

Anzaldua, G. (1987). *Borderlands/La frontera.* San Francisco, CA: Aunt Lute Foundation Books.

Aronowitz, S., & Giroux, H. (1991). *Postmodern education: Politics, culture, and social criticism.* Minneapolis: University of Minnesota Press.

Barthes, R. (1977). *Roland Barthes by Roland Barthes* (R. Howard, Trans.). New York: Hill & Wang.

Baudrillard, J. (1983). *Simulations* (P. Foss, P. Patton, & P. Beitchman, Trans.). New York: Semiotext/e.

Bordo, S. (1990). Feminism, postmodernism, and gender-skepticism. In L. Nicholson (Ed.), *Feminism/Postmodernism* (pp. 133–156). New York: Routledge.

Braidotti, R. (1987). Envy: or, With my brains and your looks. In A. Jardine & P. Smith (Eds.), *Men in feminism* (pp. 233–241). New York: Routledge, Chapman, and Hall.

Britzman, D. (1991). *Practice makes practice.* Albany: State University of New York Press.

Brossard, N. (1988). *The aerial letter* (M. Wildeman, Trans.). Toronto: The Women's Press.

Bryson, M., & de Castell, S. (1993a). En/Gendering equity: On some paradoxical consequences of institutionalized programs of emancipation. *Educational Theory, 43,* 341–355.

Bryson, M., & de Castell, S. (1993b, April). *Queer pedagogy: An unten<ur>able discursive posture?* Paper presented at a meeting of Queer Sites, Toronto.

Bryson, M., & de Castell, S. (1994). So we've got a chip on our shoulder? Sexing the texts of educational technology. In J. Gaskell & J. Willinsky (Eds.), *Gender in/forms curriculum: From enrichment to transformation.* New York: Teachers College Press.

Bryson, M., de Castell, S., & Haig-Brown, S. (1993). Gender equity/Gender treachery: Three voices. *Border/Lines, 28,* 46–54.

Burbules, N., & Rice, S. (1991). Dialogue across differences: Continuing the conversation. *Harvard Educational Review, 61,* 400–423.

Butler, J. (1990). *Gender trouble: Feminism and the subversion of identity.* New York: Routledge, Chapman and Hall.

Case, S. (1991). Tracking the vampire. *differences: A Journal of Feminist Cultural Studies, 3*(2), 2–20.

Chung, C., Kim, A., & Lemeshewsky, A. (Eds.) (1987). *Between the lines: An anthology by Pacific/Asian lesbians.* Santa Cruz, CA: Dancing Bird.

Cruickshank, M. (1982). *Lesbian studies.* New York: The Feminist Press.

Culley, M, & Portuges, C. (1985). Introduction. In M. Culley & C. Portuges (Eds.), *Gendered subjects* (pp. 41–76). Boston, MA: Routledge.

de Castell, S., & Bryson, M. (1992). En/Gendering equity: Emancipatory discourses or repressive regimes of truth? *Proceedings of Philosophy of Education Society, 48,* 357–371.

de Lauretis, T. (1987). *Technologies of gender: Essays on theory, fiction and film.* Bloomington: Indiana University Press.

de Lauretis, T. (1991). Queer theory: Lesbian and gay sexualities. *differences: A Journal of Feminist Cultural Studies, 3,* iii–xviii.

Derrida, J. (1978). *Writing and difference* (Alan Bass, Trans.). Chicago: University of Chicago Press.

Ellsworth, E. (1989). Why doesn't this feel empowering? Working through the repressive myths of critical pedagogy. *Harvard Educational Review, 59,* 297–324.

Ellsworth, E. (1990). The question remains: How will you hold to the limits of your knowledge? *Harvard Educational Review, 60,* 397–405.

Escoffier, J. (1985a). Sexual revolution and the politics of gay identity: Part 1. *Socialist Review, 15*(4), 126–196.

Escoffier, J. (1985b). Sexual revolution and the politics of gay identity: Part 2. *Socialist Review, 15*(5), 133–142.

Escoffier, J. (1990). Inside the ivory closet. *OUT/LOOK, 3,* 40–50.

Foucault, M. (1978). *The history of sexuality: Vol. 1. An introduction* (R. Hurley, Trans.). New York: Random House.

Foucault, M. (1980a). Afterword. In H. Dreyfus & P. Rabinow (Eds.), *Michel Foucault: Beyond structuralism and hermeneutics* (2nd ed.; pp. 217–227). Chicago: University of Chicago Press.

Foucault, M. (1980b). The history of sexuality. *Oxford Literary Review, 4,* 14.

Foucault, M. (1982). The subject and power. *Critical Inquiry, 8,* 785.

Fraser, N. (1989). *Unruly practices.* Minneapolis: University of Minnesota Press

Friend, R. (1993). Choices, not closets: Heterosexism and homophobia in schools. In L. Weis & M. Fine (Eds.), *Beyond silenced voices* (pp. 52–71). Albany: State University of New York Press.

Fuss, D. (1989). *Essentially speaking: Feminism, nature and difference.* New York: Routledge.

Haraway, D. J. (1987). Geschelt, gender, genre: Sexualpolitik eines wortes. In K. Hauser (Ed.), *Viele Orte: Uberall? Feminismus in bewegung. Festschrift for Frigga Haug* (pp. 22–41). Berlin: Argument-Verlag.

Hoodfar, H. (1992). Feminist anthropology and critical pedagogy: The anthropology of classrooms' excluded voices. *Canadian Journal of Education, 17*, 303–320.

hooks, b. (1984). *Feminist theory: From margin to center.* Boston, MA: South End Press.

hooks, b. (1990). *Yearning: Race, gender, and cultural politics.* Boston, MA: South End Press.

Khayatt, M. (1992). *Lesbian teachers: An invisible presence.* Albany: State University of New York Press.

Kiss & Tell Collective. (1991). *Drawing the line: Lesbian sexual politics on the wall.* Vancouver, BC: Press Gang Publishers.

Lather, P. (1990). Postmodernism and the human sciences. *Humanistic Psychologist, 18*, 64–84.

Lather, P. (1991). *Getting smart: Feminist research and pedagogy with/in the postmodern.* New York: Routledge, Chapman and Hall.

Lazarus, N. (1991). Doubting the new world order: Marxism, realism, and the claims of postmodernist social theory. *differences: A Journal of Feminist Cultural Studies, 3*, 94–138.

Leach, M. (1992). Can we talk? A response to Burbules and Rice. *Harvard Educational Review, 62*, 257–263.

Lorde, A. (1984). *Sister outsider: Essays and speeches.* Trumansburg, NY: Crossing Press.

Lugones, M. (1987). Playfulness, "world" travelling, and loving perception. *Hypatia, 2*, 160–179.

Luke, C. (1992). Feminist politics in radical pedagogy. In C. Luke & J. Gore (Eds.), *Feminisms and critical pedagogy* (pp. 25–53). New York: Routledge.

Lyotard, J. (1984). *The postmodern condition: A report on knowledge* (G. Bennington & B. Massumi, Trans.). Minneapolis: University of Minnesota Press.

Mohanty, C. (1990). On race and voice: Challenges for liberal education in the 1990s. *Cultural Critique, 18* (14), 179–208.

Mohr, R. (1989). Gay 101: On teaching gay studies. *Christopher Street, 89*, 49–57.

Moraga, C., & Anzaldua, G. (Eds.) (1983). *This bridge called my back: Writings by radical women of color.* New York: Kitchen Table Press.

Omosupe, E. (1991). Black/Lesbian/Bulldagger. *differences: A Journal of Feminist Cultural Studies, 3,* 101–111.

Penley, C., & Ross, A. (1991). Introduction. In C. Penley & A. Ross (Eds.), *Technoculture* (pp. viii–xvii). Minneapolis: University of Minnesota Press.

Phelan, S. (1989). *Identity politics: Lesbian feminism and the limits of community.* Philadelphia, PA: Temple University Press.

Pratt, M. B. (1984). Identity: Skin blood heart. In E. Bulkin, M. B. Pratt, & B. Smith (Eds.), *Yours in struggle* (pp. 9–64). Brooklyn, NY: Long Hand Press.

Razak, S. (1993). Storytelling for social change. In H. Bannerji (Ed.), *Returning the gaze: Essays on racism, feminism, and politics* (pp. 83–100). Toronto: Sister Vision Press.

Rich, A. (1979). *On lies, secrets, and silence.* New York: Norton.

Rhenby, Nadine. (1992). "An open letter to my classmates."

Rubin, G. (1975). The traffic in women: Notes on the political economy of sex. In R. Rapp Reiter (Ed.), *Toward an anthropology of women* (pp. 157–210). New York: Monthly Review.

Rubin, G. (1981). The leather menace: Comments on politics and S/M. In SAMOIS (Ed.), *Coming to power: Writings and graphics on lesbian S/M* (pp. 194–229). Boston: Alyson.

Rubin, G. (1984). Thinking sex: Notes for a radical theory of the politics of sexuality. In C. Vance (Ed.), *Pleasure and danger* (pp. 267–319). London: Routledge & Kegan Paul.

Rubin, G. (1991). The catacombs: A temple of the butthole. In M. Thompson (Ed.), *Leatherfolk: Radical sex, people, politics, and practice* (pp. 119–141). Boston, MA: Alyson.

Saslow, J. (1991, September 24). Lavendar academia debates its role. *The Advocate*, pp. 66–69.

Sawicki, J. (1991). *Disciplining Foucault.* New York: Routledge.

Sedgwick, E. (1990). *Epistemology of the closet.* Berkeley: University of California Press.

Sedgwick, E. (1991). How to bring your kids up gay. *Social Text, 29,* 18–27.

Spivak, G. (1988). Can the subaltern speak? In C. Nelson & L. Grossberg (Eds.), *Marxism and the interpretation of culture* (pp. 271–313). Urbana: University of Illinois Press.

Spivak, G. C. (1990). *The post-colonial critic* (S. Harasym, Ed.). New York: Rout-
    ledge.

British Columbia Teachers' Federation. (1991) *Teacher,* 3(7), 2–3.

British Columbia Teachers' Federation. (1991) *Teacher,* 4(1), 2.

British Columbia Teachers' Federation. (1991) *Teacher,* 4(4), 3.

Trinh, M.-h. T. (1986). She, inappropriate/d other [Special issue]. *Discourse, 8.*

Weiler, K. (1988). *Women teaching for change.* New York: Bergin & Garvey.

Wittig, M. (1980). The straight mind. *Feminist Issues* (Summer), 103–111.

CONTRIBUTORS

Deborah P. Britzman teaches in the Faculty of Education, York University.

Mary Bryson teaches in the Faculty of Education at the University of British Columbia.

Suzanne de Castell teaches in the Faculty of Education, Simon Fraser University.

Linda Eyre teaches in the Faculty of Education at the University of New Brunswick.

Maxine Greene teaches at Teachers College, Columbia University.

Annette Henry teaches in the Faculty of Education at the University of Illinois, Chicago.

Homa Hoodfar teaches in the Sociology Department, Concordia University.

Francisco Ibanez is a doctoral student at Simon Fraser University.

Kathleen Martindale, at the time this chapter was written, taught in the English Department at York University.

Roxana Ng teaches in the Graduate Faculty of Education at the University of Toronto.

Charmaine Perkins is a doctoral student at Simon Fraser University.

María de la Luz Reyes teaches in the Faculty of Education at the University of California, Monterey Bay.

Sheila Te Hennepe teaches in the Faculty of Education at the University of British Columbia.

INDEX